FISHING GUIDE

—— 12th Edition ——

FISHING GUIDE

12th Edition

Published by Gregory's Publishing Company.
(A division of Universal Press Pty Ltd)
64 Talavera Rd., Macquarie Park, New South Wales, 2113 Australia,
Telephone: (02) 888 1877

First Edition published 1946
Twelfth Edition 1991
Copyright maps Universal Press Pty Ltd (Publisher)
Copyright text and photography individual authors
Marketed and Distributed by Universal Press Pty. Ltd.
Adelaide: 21 Wright St. Adelaide 5000 Phone (08) 231 9944
Brisbane: Cnr Manning & Boundary Sts., South Brisbane 4101 Phone (07) 844 1051
Melbourne: 228 St Kilda Rd., St. Kilda 3182 Phone (03) 534 0684
Perth: 38a Walters Dr., Osborne Park 6017 Phone (09) 244 2488

Colour Separations by International Lithographic Co. Ltd., Unit 2215 Hong Man Industrial Centre,
2 Hong Man Street, Chai Wan, Hong Kong
Printed by Colourwork Press Pte. Ltd., 21 Mandai Estate Singapore 2572

ISBN: 0 7319 0391 9

Display Photographs

Front Cover: A fine example of a mangrove jack
Title Page: Fly fishing saltwater flats
Pages 8 & 9: Snapper fishermen, South Coast NSW
Pages 18 & 19: Sweetlip – Rib Reef Townsville
Pages 60 & 61: Maribou poppers
Pages 112 & 113: Tropical sport fishing action – Northern Territory barramundi
Pages 174 & 175: Saltwater barramundi

Acknowledgements

The preparation and production of any book such as this depends to an immense degree on the contribution of many talented and able people. This entirely revised 12th Edition of Gregory's Fishing Guide is no exception to that rule. Many people, each expert in at least one field (and sometimes in several) have done a great deal to ensure that the information in this edition is accurate, relevant and up to date.

For their willingness, talent, co-operation and occasional forebearance, the publishers extend their sincere thanks and appreciation.

Tackle Bait and Marine Equipment Loaned for Photography:

The vast bulk of the gear for the chapter on Fishing Tackle was supplied by courtesy of Tim Simpson, manager of The Compleat Angler's two Sydney stores. The Compleat Angler stores are listed below.

Compleat Angler Head Office - 19 McKillop St Melbourne VIC 3000 Phone: (03) 670 2518
Sydney City Store - 3rd Floor, Dymocks Building 424 George St Sydney NSW 2000
Phone: (02) 241 2080
Villawood Store - 938 Woodville Rd. Villawood NSW 2163 Phone: (02) 724 7474
Dandenong Store - 132 Walker Street Dandenong VIC 3175 Phone: (03) 794 9367
Box Hill Store - 702 Station St Box Hill VIC 3128 Phone (03) 890 7439
Ringwood Store - 92 Maroondah Highway Ringwood VIC 3134 Phone: (03) 870 7792
Moorabbin Store - 915 Nepean Highway Moorabbin VIC 3189 Phone: (03) 557 8011
Hobart Store - Bridges Brothers 142 Elizabeth St Hobart TAS 7000 Phone: (002) 34 3791

Other specialist flyfishing equipment and clothing was loaned by:

Andrew Brzoz of: The Australian Fly Fisherman - 143 Bayswater Road Rushcutters Bay NSW 2011 Phone: (02) 360 2830
Brian Hale of Silstar kindly loaned the flyrod for photography on pages 62 and 63.

The bait used in the section on choosing and rigging baits was supplied by:

Laurie Pukallas of Mac's Bait Bar - 428 Princes Highway Blakehurst NSW 2221
Phone: (02) 546 1341

All boat chandlery was supplied by:

Pat Drury of Penrith Marine - Lot 40 Coreen Avenue Penrith NSW 2750
Phone: (047) 31 5205

Articles, photographs and illustrations for this 12th Edition were supplied by:

Bill Classon	Vic McCristal
Gene Dundon	Lawrie McEnally
Greg Finney	Shane Mensforth
Ashley Hallam	David Roche
Rod Harrison	Steve Starling
Hal Harvey	Warren Steptoe
Peter Horrobin	Roger Swainston
Alex Julius	Barry Wilson
Ron McBain	Geoff Wilson

All cartography was supplied by:

The staff of Universal Press

Managing Editor: Peter Horrobin
Artwork and Design: Julie Baran
Cover Design: Above the Line
Cover Photograph: Warren Steptoe

contents

contents

KEYS TO BETTER FISHING

Better Fishing

Fishing is one of Australia's most popular outdoor recreations. Almost everyone wets a line now and again, but at the same time, most people would admit they'd like to be able to catch more fish than they generally do.

The good news is, you can improve your fishing results, and get more enjoyment from your fishing while you're at it.

Many casual anglers have the suspicion that successful fishing relies on luck. Accomplished fishermen know that success depends on many things.

Fishing skills such as casting are important, as is the ability to tie good knots and to set up appropriate rigs. It's also important to have the right gear and concentrate your efforts in places where fish can be found, especially when they're in a feeding mood.

Much as it surprises some people, you can get pretty good at predicting where fish will be, as well as when they'll be biting. All you need to begin with is the willingness to learn, and to develop your skills of observation. With experience, you'll be able to relate what you see to known patterns of fish behaviour, and that will help you work out techniques that produce fish.

The reason fishing strategies can work is because fish behaviour is reliably influenced by interlocking natural systems. The first step toward fishing success therefore, is to discover what those systems are.

Discovering Natural Systems

Fish behaviour is determined by their basic physical needs and by recognisable and recurring situations. Fish need enough water to swim in, they need shelter, and they need food. The rule beyond these basics is that fish always seek out the best water quality and food supply they can find, and preferably within easy reach of shelter.

'Shelter' can be any underwater structure that breaks the force of a local flow, enabling fish to hold position where the current can bring food to them. Shelter can also be shade, or some respite from bright or direct light, such as water depth or the camouflaging effect of broken water. Feeding shelter can be different to danger shelter, but the best kinds offer good feeding opportunities with a clear path of escape to the protection of a deep hole, a weedbed, a gutter or cave, or a tangled snag.

Few places offer all these benefits together, but those which combine as many

Snags provide shelter & ambush points

Fish are found where conditions allow easy feeding

as possible are prime locations to concentrate angling effort. If there are a number of such places in an area, bear in mind that the largest, most aggressive fish will be found in the very best spot.

Because the fish's environment is constantly changing, the exact location of such optimum conditions can shift. Accordingly, fish tend to move around too and if their movements are restricted, they often modify their behaviour to suit the altered circumstances. This is why at different stages of a tide, or times of day, fish behaviour can change from hunger to territorial aggression, or to hiding, or simply resting.

In saltwater systems, tides are a pivotal daily factor. They create significant changes in water depth, the speed and direction of currents, and consequently, in the activity of fish and their food supplies.

Every month there are roughly four phases of the moon, loosely called 'quarters', two of which are called 'neaps'. During these, the gravitational pull of the sun and moon work against each other, resulting in periods of reduced tidal movement. During 'spring' tides, when the sun and moon's pull is synchronised, the tidal fluctuations are much larger. The

term 'spring' here does not refer to the season, but to the relative volume of water being moved. These varying volumes and extents of water movement have enormous bearing on where fish will be and how successfully they can function. For this reason it is important to take the phase of the moon into account when planning a saltwater fishing trip.

Some influences on fish location are annual, such as seasonal patterns of fish movement. These are often spawning runs, but sometimes relate to changing regional water temperatures and food cycles. Marlin for example, are more plentiful off Sydney in the summer than they are in the colder months, yet the recognised time for big yellowfin tuna in the same place, is from autumn through winter. Tailor migrate up the east coast in late winter and early spring, and there's a similar northward run of blackfish every Easter.

Seasonal movements of freshwater fish are typified by the downstream spawning run of bass to the brackish estuaries from April through to July. At about the same time, trout run upstream to the gravelly headwaters of the highlands. The breeding cycles of many inland native fish depend on summer floods to create the right conditions of turbidity and warm, shallow water.

Beyond those regular and predictable cycles, there are other phenomena like floods, storms, droughts, changes in global ocean currents and not least of all, man-made interventions like pollution, or damming, or changing the path of water courses. All these can change fish location and behaviour, some temporarily, others more permanently.

In freshwater, the impact of the lunar cycle is a matter of debate, but daily movements of fish relate to barometric pressure, humidity, and air and water temperatures. Other factors are light intensity, and wind strength and direction. Some fish movements relative to rainfall and turbidity are self evident at the time.

Sudden changes in the availability or abundance of food can trigger feeding sprees among both fresh and saltwater fish. Bream fishing can be brilliant on a rising tide as water covers the shallows and provides access to food-rich sandflats. Flathead often bite at the start of a run out tide however, because that's when baitfish and prawns are swept off the shallows and into the deep channels.

A massed 'hatch' of insects can have a dynamic effect on previously dormant trout, and offshore, a passive group of kingfish can suddenly switch into feeding mode at the arrival of a school of travelling baitfish.

Floods stimulate spawning of fish and can also drastically alter habitat

It's not always the arrival of prey that triggers a bite though. Sometimes the big fish aren't specifically located, but out on the prowl. In these cases, the bite starts when they cross paths with a suitable concentration of food.

Whether you start with the fish, or the bait, or just the location, the better your fishing skills, the more advantage you'll be able to take of any bite that starts.

Developing Fishing Skills

Think Like a Fish

One of the most basic fishing skills you can acquire is to think like a fish, that is, to see things from the fish's point of view. For example, many casual anglers restrict their fishing to days when conditions are bright and sunny and windless. Similarly, the sad tale of no fish is told chiefly by those who like to sleep in, rather than be up in time to greet the sunrise on the water. Conversely, late bites on bright days do occur.

For saltwater fish particularly, rough days with overcast skies and a wind ruffled surface are better times to be out and about. The subdued light encourages them to feed actively and the broken surface makes it harder for predators to spot them from below. Major predators such as marlin and tuna often move up to hunt in the surface layers during these conditions. This is good news for fishermen because it brings these fish within range of readily practised surface techniques like trolling or berleying with shallow set baits.

The principle of fishing during periods of changing light works in the early morning for forage species like bream and drummer, as well as mobile predators like tailor, salmon, kingfish and tuna. Late afternoons are productive for the same reasons and these two periods of low light are also prime times for many freshwater species.

The Importance of Fishing Knots

It's impossible to over-rate the skill of being able to tie good knots. The only

*This kingfish took a live bait during
an early morning tide change*

for each kind of fishing style, and don't be afraid to practise your casting.

You can improve your short range accuracy by setting up a target like a plastic bucket in your back yard and trying to land a sinker or lure in it every time. A tip on distance casting is to concentrate on form and timing more than power. Just like developing a golf swing, mastering correct technique will provide the distance. Without it, applying more power just accentuates your mistakes.

Getting Organised

Organising your gear so everything necessary is within easy reach is something everyone has to learn. Initially, you'll take everything but the kitchen sink with you and discover you've never got quite what you need. Over time, you'll discover what you need for this fish or that location and you'll be able to whittle your gear down to necessities. Remember, the simpler it is, the better it will work.

'Reading' The Water

Consistent fishing success depends heavily on being able to look at a stretch of water and 'read' it. What you're looking for are clues to the mood and whereabouts of fish, and what the most appropriate techniques might be. This skill is based on the everyday faculties of sight, sound, smell and reason. Observation is more than just registering impressions though, it involves taking the time to look around and trying to understand the significance of what you see, hear and smell. Reason is a faculty we all have and can develop, but even the sharpest reasoning depends on having solid information to work with.

Information doesn't come unbidden, but it lies all around you. What's needed is for you to set your mind to gathering it. What you can see on the water should start questions in your mind, such as, "how come that fish I just caught was right there?" or "how come that guy is catching fish and I'm not?" Straight out face to face enquiry with other anglers can yield some amazing gems of fishing lore. Most fishermen are surprisingly generous with information about 'how to', it's just 'where to'

thing between you and the fish is the fishing line and the weakest point in that line is always the knot. Any knot weakens the line it is tied in - good knots weaken it less, that's all. The better the knot, the stronger the connection, and the better your chances of landing that big one.

A range of good knots is shown in the Tackle section of this book but equally important is how you go about tying them. Take your time with knots, don't pull them down dry, or too quickly, or you'll create friction heat and accelerate the break-down process of the nylon line. You can effectively lubricate the line by moistening it in your mouth, then, by pulling the knot down carefully, you'll ensure the maximum possible strength in every rig you use.

Casting Skills

Casting skills are among the most important you can develop. Most times you need to propel the bait or lure out to the fish, and the more easily you can send it straight and far enough, the more effectively you'll be fishing. Read the chapters on fishing gear for a guide to the best gear they tend to be close-mouthed about, but some guys are even willing to divulge that.

Reading fishing books and magazines is another source of fishing education and can provide not only answers but the stimulus to enquire further and go on to bigger and better things. Don't just book-worm it though, get out on the water as often as you can, and start to make the connections between what you read and what you can see, and experiment with ideas for yourself.

Gathering Bait

If you're fishing with bait, the indisputable rule is that it should be the freshest you can get, and often, there's no better bait than a live bait. While you will have to carry baits in to some locations, the best bait will frequently be found right where you will be fishing, or close by. The skill of bait-gathering therefore is one of the foundation stones of consistently success-ful fishing.

These fishermen will stand a better chance of fishing success because they have taken the time to collect their own fresh bait

Learn how to find and catch your own bait, but also find out which baits you can preserve when they are plentiful so you will have bait when the natural supply fluctuates. Don't go in for overkill though, as some baits are perennially available, but vulnerable to over-harvesting. If the bait you're after is like that, take the long term view and only gather what you can use in a single outing.

A lot of fishing is more effective when done from a boat. A boat allows you to shift from one location to another with ease and to fish a spot from almost any direction you choose. Responsible and safe boat handling is an acquired skill though just like any other. The effective use of a boat as a fishing tool depends on you being a competent skipper, able to anchor, drift controllably, and manage lines when trolling.

Organisation is vital in small craft if you are to enjoy fishing in comfort and safety, and once again, simplicity is the key to effectiveness.

Deliberate Strategies For Success

Effective fishing strategies depend on un-derstanding the nature of the fish you are chasing, how it interacts with its changing environment, and also on developing skills in presenting baits or lures so fish find them attractive.

Working out how to approach any fish-ing situation is easier if you follow a sys-tem. The simpler the system the better, and one which I've found to work is based on the sequence shown below; for which credit should go to the USA 'In-Fisherman' magazine.

Preparation + Location + Presentation = Fish

Preparation

Find out as much as you can about your target fish and its surroundings, which rigs and what gear is best for that kind of

fishing, then work on the skills involved in using them.

Check the weather before fishing trips, not just the night before, but for several nights - weather systems generally take a few days to form and take effect before moving on.

Keep a fishing diary too. This will provide you with a reliable ready reference for what's likely to happen at certain times of the year or when a certain combination of conditions occurs.

Look at the gear of any successful fisherman. It may or may not be pretty, but you can bet that it all works. The only way fishing gear won't let you down at the crucial moment is if it receives adequate maintenance between trips. A simple washing and wipe down with a clean soft rag is adequate for most reels. Don't hose them - that drives dirt and salt inside where it can do a lot of damage.

Check your fishing line and rod runners for wear and tear, don't store rusty hooks with new ones, make sure your accessories like gaffs or nets are in good order, and that you have a knife that's sharp with the blade well protected.

Electronic gear like radios and sounders and outboard motors need looking after too. The consequences of failure here can be expensive and disastrous.

Location

This can mean choosing the right place as well as physically locating the fish within an area. This is where your ability to read the water comes into play. There are several tools you can use to help here. Polarised sunglasses cut surface glare, enhance contrasts and allow better vision into the water. Echo sounders can reveal exact water depths, show bottom contours and structures like weed, reefs and logs. They can even show fish or concentrations of baitfish. Two-way radios are not only a safety device, you can pick up some very useful information on fish whereabouts by listening closely on various channels.

Other natural signs are pointers to likely fish locations. Current lines carry food and indicate clear, if temporary, travelling paths used by fish. Sudden changes in water colour can indicate dropoffs into deep water, a rising reef, or the unmixed interface between bodies of fresh and saltwater. Seabirds often wheel in flocks over feeding pelagic species and any individual seabird in low, straight, purposeful flight is worth following a while as it may be on its way to a school of surface fish beyond your line of sight.

In freshwater, snags or rocks in streams are focal points, as are points of land, weedbeds and drowned timber in lakes. Any cuts or corners in embankments or foreshores are also good places to look. Concentric rings in the water surface can indicate a feeding trout, and on a bass stream, or in a barramundi creek, flashes, humps or boils in the water are fish signs too. Sometimes you'll hear an audible 'chop' as a bass hits the surface, or a subdued 'whump' when a barra inhales something down below. Trout generally feed more delicately, but when on 'fry' or 'hoppers' can slash with the best of them.

Presentation

What strategy is all about, is choosing the best way to present a lure, fly, or bait so that fish will take it. It covers such things as where you cast, or if trolling, how far back you set it. It also takes into account whether it's important for the angler to remain inconspicuous to the fish and if it is, involves ways of approaching to within fishing distance with stealth.

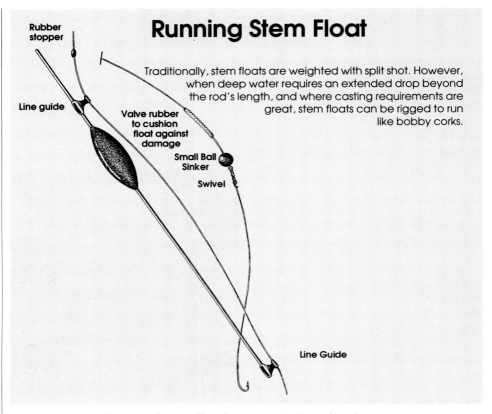

Running Stem Float

Rubber stopper

Line guide

Valve rubber to cushion float against damage

Small Ball Sinker

Swivel

Line Guide

Traditionally, stem floats are weighted with split shot. However, when deep water requires an extended drop beyond the rod's length, and where casting requirements are great, stem floats can be rigged to run like bobby corks.

Running floats allow longer casts than fixed ones.

How you rig the bait or lure is another factor, and, if you move it to prompt a strike, how you move it - and how far - and how fast.

Most of the time, fish prefer a bait that is moving. The key is, it should move in a way that the fish finds appealing, not alarming. Where possible, shy biters should be presented with a bait that moves under the influence of the surrounding water. If there is no water movement, some scavenging species are happy to pick up a motionless bait, but most worthwhile angling targets like their food mobile.

Presentation can also be aided or enhanced by such things as berley, or by visual and sonic attractors.

Berley can be scraps of solid food or a mixture of solids and liquids. Gamefishermen throw scoops of live yellowtail or slimy mackerel overboard to incite schooled tuna to feed. Trout fishermen use the same principle, scaring grasshoppers off the bank and into the water. This encourages trout to lunge at anything skittering across the surface, such as a grasshopper with a hook in it, or an imitative fly pattern.

Visual attractors work too. Fishermen in freshwater impoundments use reflective metal blades like Ford Fenders and Cowbells for trout, and bluewater fishermen use mirrored gamefish teasers. Some of that attraction is probably also based on the sounds these things make. A recent development of visual berley is the use of fluorescent dyes, squirted onto baits to make them stand out and prompt a predatory response.

A classic example of sonic berley is when a surface popper is snatched under with a jerk of the rod-tip to create a resonant 'bloop'. These 'bloops' often prompt spectacular surface strikes from a diverse range of species. On occasion, the tactic can turn up some real surprises.

Often it's not what you present but how it's served that makes the difference. These spot-tail bass took a bright green jointed minnow, while the trout (below right) took a small bait fish pattern fly. In each case the presentation was the key.

In Summary

Consistent fishing results are not the product of sheer chance. Mostly, fish fall to anglers who know enough about their target fish to assemble the necessary gear and skills to catch them under commonly encountered conditions.

The chapters which follow deal in detail with some of the fish you're likely to encounter, the gear and baits you'll need to catch them, and specific strategies for different climatic and geographic regions. Also, we've mapped out a selected national spread of regional guides with brief information on what's available, and when it bites best during the year.

Through the combined experience and skills of Australia's best fishing writers, this book offers practical fishing information in the form of 'keys' - keys which when used, can open the doors to better fishing.

Welcome to the world of fishing - come on inside!

To Follow:-

FISH SPECIES

Barramundi

The barramundi is a favourite Australian fish, highly regarded for its sporting prowess and edible qualities. Historical confusion between true barramundi and the saratogas (sometimes erroneously referred to as 'spotted barramundi')is rare these days.

Barramundi are a tropical species ranging from the Mary River in Queensland to the Ashburton River in Western Australia, but occurring in greatest numbers north of the Tropic of Capricorn. They are also found in the southern rivers of Papua New Guinea and Irian Jaya, as well as parts of South East Asia, ranging as far north as India's Bay of Bengal. Barra live in fresh, brackish, estuarine and inshore waters, rarely straying far beyond the mouths of tidal rivers, harbours and inlets. They require access to saline, tidal waters in order to reproduce, but will live for many years in land-locked lagoons and billabongs without breeding. They are a large, handsome and alert fish, commonly encountered at weights between 2 and 6 kg. Fish over 10 kg are far from abundant these days, although the occasional 20 kg monster is still a possibility in more isolated areas.

Barramundi prey on small fish such as mullet, herring and archer fish, as well as prawns and freshwater shrimp. In the

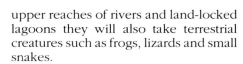

upper reaches of rivers and land-locked lagoons they will also take terrestrial creatures such as frogs, lizards and small snakes.

One of the most fascinating characteristics of this species is its ability to change sex as it matures! All barramundi are born male, but at a certain size (which appears to vary from place to place), they develop ovaries and become females.

Sadly, barramundi populations have been greatly reduced by over-harvesting and habitat destruction in many regions, particularly along the eastern seaboard of Queensland. Today, southern anglers must travel to the Northern Territory or the Kimberley region of Western Australia in order to find consistently good barra fishing.

Barra respond to a wide range of angling techniques, including bait fishing, lure casting, trolling and fly fishing.

Bass (Australian)

For all intents and purposes, the Australian bass and its cousin, the estuary perch can be treated as a single species by anglers. So similar are they in appearance and habit that most fishermen have trouble in telling them apart.

Bass and estuary perch occur in coastal rivers, creeks and lakes from the Mary River in southern central Queensland to the mouth of the Murray River, in South Australia. Their natural range extends upstream only as far as the first impassable waterfall, dam or weir, and they require winter-time access to brackish tidal waters in order to successfully reproduce.

These attractive, alert species are relatively small fish, and most anglers are happy to encounter specimens in the 0.5 to 0.8 kg range. Bass do not often exceed 1.5 kg in weight, although fish twice that size are still taken on rare occasions. Exceptional specimens – mostly estuary perch – may very rarely approach weights of 5 kg.

During the summer months, when they are more readily available to anglers, bass prefer clean, running freshwater with a reasonably high oxygen content and a diversity of food types. They prey mostly on shrimps, crayfish, frogs, insect larvae and terrestrial creatures such as beetles, cicadas and even mice or lizards.

In most areas, bass and perch represent a relatively specialised angling target, requiring the use of specific tackle and techniques. Although they respond avidly to natural baits, including live crickets, frogs and earthworms, most sport fishermen prefer to catch bass with lures such as plugs, minnows and poppers. They are also a superb fly rod target.

Although they are fine to eat, these days most of the bass and estuary perch caught by thinking anglers are released in order to preserve the dwindling stocks of these valuable native species.

Bream

There are three major bream species in Australia, each prized by anglers.

The eastern black bream or yellowfin bream occurs along the eastern seaboard of Australia, from the southern or central coast of Queensland in the north, to Wilsons Promontory in the south.

Eastern black bream are a fish of estuarine and inshore waters, occurring mostly in the lower reaches of larger tidal rivers, bays, inlets and harbours, and over reefs and gravel beds extending well offshore. They will also range upstream in coastal rivers, moving well beyond the upper limits of tides at times, entering fresh water for short periods.

In contrast, the southern black bream lives almost exclusively in estuarine and bay waters, rarely straying far beyond the mouths of tidal rivers, harbours and inlets unless pushed out of these enclosed waters by heavy flooding. Like its eastern cousin, it will also move upstream into fresh waters at times.

Southern bream range from the far south coast of New South Wales, around the southern coast (including Tasmania) to about Shark Bay in Western Australia.

Pikey bream are found in tropical waters around the northern half of Australia, preferring mangrove-lined estuaries, bays and inlets.

All three bream are very similar in appearance and each species displays considerable colour variation between individuals, dependent on habitat.

A fourth fish, the tarwhine, is similar in appearance to bream, but has a more rounded head and longitudinal rows of yellow spots along its flanks. It is found around the southern half of the Australian mainland.

Bream and tarwhine rarely exceed 1.4 kg, but eastern and southern bream over 3 kg have been caught.

They feed primarily on prawns, shrimps and crabs, as well as marine worms, shellfish and some aquatic vegetation. They will also take small, live fish at times.

Bream are all highly rated table fare, with succulent, white flesh that remains sweet and moist when cooked. Tarwhine are also a fine table fish, although they have a black stomach lining which should be removed by scrubbing when cleaning the catch.

Cobia

The cobia or black kingfish is a somewhat enigmatic fish found in discontinuous pockets throughout the tropical and sub-tropical oceans of the world. At various locations within their vast international range they are known as black kingfish, lemon fish, crab-eaters, sergeant fish and ling, although cobia is the most widely accepted common name for the species.

In Australia, cobia are mostly encountered over offshore reefs and gravel beds, around islands, bomboras and undersea pinnacles, and near navigation buoys, drilling platforms and similar structures. However, they will also show up in large estuaries, bays and harbours at times.

While most frequently found in Queensland, the Northern Territory and northern Western Australia, cobia will occasionally stray as far south as Jervis Bay on the east coast and Fremantle on the west.

Cobia are large fish, commonly reaching 1.2 m or more in length and weighing as much as 20 or 30 kg. Exceptional specimens may attain twice that weight. Their flattened, almost shark-like head, dark longitudinal bands and eight to ten stout, stubby dorsal spines separate them from most other fish, although small cobia do bear a passing resemblance to the suckerfish or remora.

Cobia prey on a wide range of fish and crustaceans, often taking large numbers of sand crabs from the sand and gravel areas adjacent to northern beaches. These fish commonly follow large sharks and manta rays, as well as frequenting man-made devices such as channel markers.

Cobia respond best to live or fresh-dead baits of whole or cut fish, squid and octopus. They will also strike at a range of lures and large flies, either cast and retrieved, or trolled behind a moving boat. Because of their variable abundance, cobia are mostly an incidental catch taken by anglers fishing for more common target species such as Spanish mackerel, yellowtail kingfish and tuna. However, in light of their striking appearance, powerful struggle when hooked, and delicious, white flesh, they are always a welcome addition to the catch.

Dart

The dart family contains several fish of interest to Australian anglers. The most widespread and commonly encountered is the swallowtail dart. These are relatively small fish, rarely exceeding 0.8 kg in weight, although very occasionally reaching almost twice that size. They occur along the eastern seaboard of Australia, from the Queensland coast to Jervis Bay.

An almost identical fish called the common dart is found on the west coast between similar latitudes. It grows a little larger than its eastern counterpart.

Dart are a fish of our estuarine and inshore waters, occurring in the lower reaches of larger tidal rivers, bays, inlets and harbours. They are especially common along ocean surf beaches, where they hunt for marine worms and crustaceans and sometimes prey on small bait fish.

Dart are usually caught by shore-based anglers casting with relatively light tackle, fine lines and small hooks. They are mostly an incidental catch taken by anglers fishing for more desirable target species such as whiting, bream and flathead.

Despite their small average size, dart provide a spirited struggle when hooked and have reasonably tasty, if somewhat dry, flesh.

Dart can be held in an area by judicious use of berley or by using soft baits like pilchards which break up when attacked, creating their own berley trail.

If anglers fish in pairs, the school can be kept excited if one fish is left to struggle in the water until the next is hooked and so on.

Drummer (Black & Silver)

Two fish commonly known as drummer are important to Australian anglers. The first species commonly known as drummer is the eastern rock blackfish, black drummer or 'pig'. This dark, omnivorous fish is confined to the east coast, although an almost identical fish occurs in smaller numbers along the south-west coast.

Another species known as silver drummer or buffalo bream occurs in greatest numbers along the eastern seaboard of Australia, from the southern coast of Queensland in the north, to Wilsons Promontory in the south. They are also present in north eastern Tasmania, parts of South Australia, and the West Australian coast to about Shark Bay.

Both silver and black drummer live in wave-washed, inshore waters adjacent to rocky shorelines, headlands and stone breakwalls. They eat a range of algae, kelp and other marine weeds, as well as worms and certain types of crustaceans.

Drummer are taken mostly by shore-based anglers casting baits such as cunjevoi, prawns, cut crab, bread and marine weed.

Both species commonly reach weights of 1 kg to 3 kg, and may occasionally grow much larger. Silver drummer have been recorded to 14 or 15 kg on rare occasions, while black drummer are known to reach 9 kg.

Both fish are exceptionally hard fighters when hooked, and often will sever the angler's line on submerged ledges and reef outcrops. The black drummer is a delicious table fish which should be filleted and skinned for best results. In contrast, the silver drummer is rather unpalatable, with coarse, tough flesh and a strong iodine flavour.

Flathead

There are over 30 species of flathead in Australian waters, although only a handful are of particular interest to anglers. The rest live in very deep water, do not grow to an edible size, or are rarely encountered.

The largest, most important angling species is the dusky or estuary flathead. It occurs along the eastern seaboard of Australia, from the central coast of Queensland in the north, to Wilsons Promontory in Victoria.

Dusky flathead live mainly in estuarine and inshore waters, rarely straying far beyond the mouths of tidal rivers, harbours and inlets. They're also occasionally found beyond the upper limits of tidal movement, in almost fresh water.

The dusky averages 1.2 kg or less, although specimens much larger are common in some areas. It has been recorded at weights in excess of 9 kg, but examples over 7 kg are uncommon. In northern and western estuary waters it is replaced by the smaller bar-tailed flathead.

Sand flathead in various forms are all very important species to offshore anglers around the southern half of the Australian continent, including Tasmania. They are found between the shoreline and sand or gravel areas in water as deep as 100 m.

Further offshore the tiger or king flathead becomes dominant although this reddish-hued, thick-bodied flathead also moves into shallower areas in southern latitudes, particularly around Tasmania.

All of these flathead species are known by a wide variety of colloquial names, including 'lizard', 'frog' and 'yank'. They are popular angling targets, pursued by large numbers of fishermen.

Flathead eat a wide variety of small fish, crustaceans and marine worms. They respond best to live or fresh-dead baits of whole or cut fish, squid and octopus. They will also strike at a range of lures and flies, either cast and retrieved, or deep-trolled behind a moving boat. The emphasis should always be on the use of moving baits presented close to the sea bed when pursuing flathead.

All of the flathead mentioned here are fine table fish, although the flesh of larger duskies tends to be a little dry.

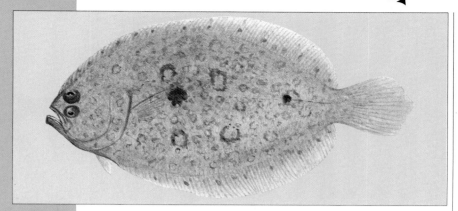

Flounder

Several species of flounder are found in Australasian waters. The most important are the large-toothed flounder and the small-toothed flounder. Flounder are occasionally confused with the other major Australasian flatfish group – the soles. However, flounder are distinguished by their body shape and distinctly separate tail. In contrast, sole have an almost continuous fin running right around their tongue-shaped bodies.

As with other flatfish, juvenile flounder swim upright in the manner of normal fish. However, as they mature, one eye 'migrates' around their head and they begin to swim on their side. Eventually, they spend most of their time on or very near the seabed, with their eyes facing upwards. Their lower flank becomes white or very pale, while the upper surface of the fish takes on a camouflage pattern of spots and mottled markings.

The two major flounder species mentioned are found in sub-tropical, temperate and cool waters around the southern half of Australia.

They are a fish of our estuarine and inshore waters, occurring mostly in the lower reaches of larger tidal rivers, bays, inlets and harbours, and less commonly over sand and gravel beds extending offshore towards the edge of the Continental Shelf. They will also move upstream

beyond the tidal influence at times.

These two flounder are relatively small fish, rarely exceeding 0.6 kg in weight, although occasionally doubling that. They prey on a variety of small fish, prawns and other crustaceans, and are quite aggressive predators for their size.

Flounder are mostly an incidental catch taken by anglers fishing for more common target species such as flathead, bream and whiting. However, some anglers target them specifically in cooler southern waters like those of south-eastern Tasmania. Because of their delicious, moist, white flesh, they are always a welcome addition to any angler's catch.

Garfish

The garfish family has many representatives in Australian waters, where it is also known as gar or 'gardie'. In New Zealand, the same fish are called piper, while Americans refer to members of this family as balao or 'ballyhoo'.

The most important and commonly encountered garfish species are the near-identical eastern and southern sea garfish, the river garfish, the robust garfish or 'three-by-two' and the snub-nosed gar. These fish occur right around the coastlines of Australia and New Zealand, but are more important as angling species in the southern half of Australia and the North Island of New Zealand.

Garfish are small, slender creatures. They rarely exceed 35 cm, and even very large specimens usually weigh less than 0.3 kg. They survive on a diet of rotting mangrove leaves, algae, tiny crustaceans and larger forms of plankton.

Despite their diminutive size, garfish are a popular angling fish, much prized as both bait and food.

Garfish are a relatively specialised angling target, calling for the use of specific tackle and techniques. They are caught mostly by anglers using light tackle, fine lines and small hooks. They respond best to lightly weighted, unweighted or float-suspended baits of bread, dough, maggots, fish flesh strips, prawn pieces, or segments of marine worm.

Because they are such a favoured food item of large predatory species, garfish can profitably be used as livebaits in the same locations where they are caught.

This particularly applies to the sea-garfish which is often caught around rough, rocky areas of the coastal shoreline where there is some shelter from the swell, and some cover in the form of kelp and/or white water.

Groper (Blue)

The eastern blue groper and western blue groper are actually members of the wrasse family, and are in no way related to the much larger Queensland groper or the 'groupers' of the Atlantic and Caribbean.

There are several colour variations of blue groper, usually known as brown groper, red groper and blue groper. These differences are related to the sex of the fish, and do not indicate separate species or sub-species.

All groper are born as females. The juvenile females are green or greenish brown, sometimes sprinkled with pale spots. As they mature, they take on either a brown or a red hue, largely dependent upon the surrounding terrain and water depth (the red variation is more common in deeper water). Later, some of the larger females transform into males, becoming bright blue or deep navy in the process.

Adult eastern blue groper are large fish, commonly reaching 90 cm or more in length and weighing as much as 15 kg. The western variety grows even larger, and exceptional specimens have been recorded at weights in excess of 35 kg.

Groper are found in temperate and cool waters around the southern half of Australia. They occur mostly in wave-washed waters adjacent to rocky shore-lines, headlands and stone breakwalls, where they feed primarily on sea urchins, shellfish and crabs.

Groper are a specialised angling target, requiring the use of specific tackle and techniques. In particular, they are taken by shore-based anglers casting crab baits on very sturdy tackle, with thick lines and double or triple strength hooks. Once hooked, they provide a powerful fight, and not all groper that are hooked are landed, as they often sever the line on a rock ledge, or bury themselves in kelp.

Larger groper are delicious eating fish, although juveniles under 4 kg tend to be a little mushy and flavourless.

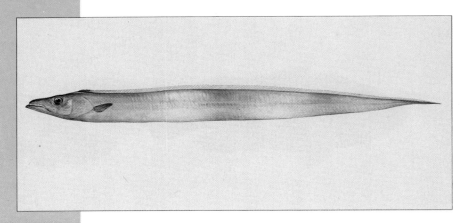

Hairtail

The enigmatic hairtail has a wide, but discontinuous, distribution through the Indo-Pacific region, occasionally turning up in areas of Australia and New Zealand where it has never before been recorded.

Hairtail, like the closely related and very similar frostfish, are thought to be deep ocean species which make occasional forays into certain estuaries and harbours along the coast. Juveniles are seasonally abundant in tropical ports such as Townsville, while adults are fished for on a regular basis in just a handful of locations on the eastern seaboard of Australia, mainly between Newcastle and Wollongong. In particular, they are targeted during the winter months in the Hawkesbury River estuary, Sydney Harbour and the deeper portions of Botany Bay.

These fish have a striking apppearance with their long, chrome-like bodies and sharp fangs. They should be handled with care, especially as they approach their maximum size of 2 m and 3 to 4 kg.

Hairtail are a specialised angling target, requiring the use of specific tackle and techniques. Most are caught at night on baits of small, live fish or whole pilchards and garfish. A wire leader or ganged (linked) hooks should be used to prevent bite-offs.

Despite their unusual appearance and mysterious nature, hairtail are prized as table fish having delicate white flesh.

They have no scales but their metallic silver sheen can be easily rubbed off with a wet hessian bag.

The flesh is best prepared for cooking by cutting into 'steaks' across the body – 10 cm to 15 cm is a good length and they should be cooked quickly over a moderate heat, taking care not to overcook them.

Jewfish (Westralian)

The Westralian jewfish or 'dhufish' is one of Western Australia's most highly-prized angling targets. It is a close relative of the eastern pearl perch, but grows much larger.

Adult Westralian jewfish once commonly reached 1 m or more in length and weighed as much as 20 or 25 kg. Specimens of those dimensions are rare today, except in very deep or lightly-fished areas.

Westralian jewfish are mostly encountered over offshore reefs and gravel beds, around islands, bomboras and undersea pinnacles. They extend offshore all the way to the edge of the Continental Shelf. Their geographic range is confined to the south-west coast, between the Recherche Archipelago and Shark Bay. They eat smaller fish, squid, octopus and crustaceans and are caught primarily by boat anglers using a variety of offshore fishing techniques. In particular, they respond to live or fresh-dead baits of whole or cut fish, squid and octopus. They will also strike at a range of lures and jigs, either cast and retrieved, or jigged vertically near the sea bed.

The Westralian jewfish is one of Australia's most acclaimed seafood dishes, and has few peers among the other temperate water, bottom-dwelling species.

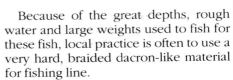

Because of the great depths, rough water and large weights used to fish for these fish, local practice is often to use a very hard, braided dacron-like material for fishing line.

It has little or no stretch, is easier to grip with wet hands than nylon monofilament and allows effective hook-setting despite the depth of water fished and the dampening effect lively water and heavy sinker weights have on the strike.

John Dory

The unusual looking John Dory is found throughout the world, and occurs in good numbers around the southern half of Australia and most of New Zealand. John Dory inhabit a wide range of marine environments, from estuaries and bays to deep, offshore waters and trawling grounds. Two closely related fish – the Mirror Dory and Silver Dory – are more abundant in deeper waters, but rarely taken by recreational anglers.

John Dory rarely exceed 1.5 kg in weight. They are characterised by their laterally compressed bodies, large, protractile mouths and the distinct 'thumb print' marking in the middle of each flank. They use their unique body shape and mouth design to drift close to unwary bait species such as yellowtail and mullet before making a lightning fast grab with their telescopic jaws.

John Dory are mostly an incidental catch taken by anglers fishing for more common target species such as flathead, mulloway and kingfish. However, because of their delicious white flesh, they are an extremely welcome addition to any bag.

Dory respond best to live or fresh-dead baits of whole or cut fish, squid and octopus. They will also occasionally strike at lures and flies, although this aggressive behaviour appears to be more

common in New Zealand than Australia.

To render livebaits easier prey for the sluggish John Dory, anglers often trim the tail fin of their baits. This enables the Dory to more easily capture the normally agile fish like yellowtail.

This species is always mentioned in any short list of the top eating fish in Australasian waters. Because of this, John Dory demands a consistently high market price, and is keenly sought by commercial fishermen.

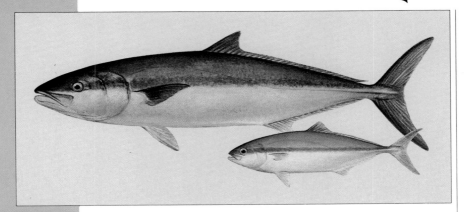

Kingfish (Yellowtail)

The yellowtail kingfish, king or 'kingy' is a member of the same group of fishes as the trevallies, amberjack and Samson fish. They are found in sub-tropical, temperate and cool waters around the southern half of Australia and the northern part of New Zealand.

Kings are mostly encountered over offshore reefs and gravel beds, around islands, bomboras and undersea pinnacles, and near navigation buoys or drilling platforms and similar structures. Small and large specimens will occasionally enter larger estuaries and harbours, especially in New Zealand.

Yellowtail kings are big fish, commonly reaching 1.2 m or more in length and weighing as much as 20 or 30 kg. Record-class specimens approaching 2 m and weighing in the 40 to 60 kg range are mostly encountered around offshore island groups such as Australia's Lord Howe and New Zealand's Three Kings and Poor Knights.

Yellowtail kingfish voraciously hunt smaller fish such as yellowtail, slimy mackerel, mullet, small tuna and even juveniles of their own breed. They are especially fond of squid and cuttlefish, and will also take prawns, crabs and marine worms at times.

Kingies are taken on live or fresh-dead baits of whole or cut fish, squid and octopus and will also strike at a range of lures and large flies, cast and retrieved, or trolled behind a moving boat. The majority are caught by boat fishermen, but shore-based anglers in deep water locations also fare well.

When hooked, yellowtail kings battle as hard as any marine species. As a result, they are greatly respected by most sport and game fishermen throughout the world.

The eating qualities of yellowtail kingfish are somewhat variable. In certain areas, particularly southern Queensland, they are prone to a milkiness of the flesh which renders them unpalatable. In other locations, especially the southern states of Australia, Lord Howe Island, Norfolk Island and New Zealand, they are highly rated table fare. Generally, smaller specimens have tastier, more moist flesh than heavyweight adults.

Leatherjacket

The leatherjacket clan represents an extensive family of fish containing several important angling species. They are characterised by their small mouths, sharp, beak-like tooth structure, sandpapery skin and the single, stout spine on their back, above the eyes.

Most of the better-known leatherjackets are found in sub-tropical, temperate and cool waters around the southern half of Australia. Among the most popular and commonly caught are the six-spined leatherjacket, horseshoe leatherjacket, Chinaman leatherjacket, toothbrush leatherjacket and the fan-bellied leatherjacket.

Most of these leatherjackets are fish of our estuarine and inshore waters, occurring primarily in the lower reaches of larger tidal rivers, bays, inlets and harbours, and over reefs and gravel beds extending offshore towards the edge of the Continental Shelf.

Leatherjackets rarely exceed 1 kg in weight, although occasionally they will reach twice that size. The yellowish Chinaman leatherjacket and the attractively marked mosaic leatherjacket are the largest species, both occasionally reaching weights in excess of 3 kg. On the other hand, the estuary-dwelling fan-bellied leatherjacket rarely tops 0.4 kg.

Most leatherjacket species are opportunistic feeders, eating shellfish, crustaceans and carrion, as well as certain forms of marine vegetation. In many regions, leatherjackets are an incidental catch taken by anglers fishing for other target species. However, they have moist, sweet, white flesh and are a welcome addition to the catch of most anglers. They are also popular with younger fishermen, who regularly encounter these fish around wharves, jetties and breakwalls.

Leatherjackets are best caught with relatively light tackle, fine lines and small, long-shanked hooks baited with prawn pieces, squid strips, octopus, cunjevoi or fish flesh. Extra length hooks or light wire leaders are needed to prevent bite-offs from these sharp-toothed little fish.

Luderick

The luderick is more widely known as the blackfish, 'nigger' or 'darkie'. In New Zealand, the same fish is called parore. Luderick are closely related to the black drummer or rock blackfish, the zebra fish, and the now rare bluefish.

Luderick or blackfish occur along the eastern seaboard of Australia, from the southern coast of Queensland in the north, to Port Phillip Bay in the south. They may also be encountered at times near Adelaide, and around the north eastern corner of Tasmania. In New Zealand, they are confined mostly to the waters of the North Island.

Luderick are a fish of our estuarine and inshore waters, occurring mainly in the lower reaches of larger tidal rivers, bays, inlets and harbours. Outside of these enclosed areas, they are also found in wave-washed, inshore waters adjacent to rocky shorelines, headlands and stone breakwalls.

Luderick are relatively small fish, from around half a kilo to one and a half kilos in weight. Occasional specimens may reach nearly twice that weight. They are omnivorous, consuming large quantities of weed and algae, as well as small invertebrates such as marine worms, shrimp and prawns.

They are a relatively specialised angling target, demanding the use of specific tackle and techniques. Luderick are mostly caught by anglers using light tackle, fine lines and small hooks, and lightly weighted, unweighted or float-suspended baits of marine weed, algae, worm pieces, peeled prawn tails, bread or dough.

Although sometimes tainted by a slightly 'weedy' iodine taste, the flesh of the luderick or blackfish is quite popular. For best results, the fish should be kept alive in a keeper net till taken home, then killed and cleaned promptly and the fillets skinned prior to cooking.

Mackerel

Several species of large, tropical mackerel are of great importance to anglers in the northern half of Australia. The biggest and best known is the narrow-barred Spanish mackerel or tanguigue. The closely related broad-barred Spanish mackerel or grey mackerel does not grow as large, but is seasonally abundant in some areas.

Smaller, but nonetheless important as angling species, are the Australian spotted mackerel and the Queensland school mackerel. The shark mackerel also belongs to the same general family.

All of these fish are found in tropical and sub-tropical waters around the northern half of Australia, although narrow-barred Spanish mackerel occasionally stray south as Jervis Bay on the east coast, and Bunbury in the west.

Narrow-barred Spanish mackerel are large fish, commonly reaching 1.6 m or more in length and weighing as much as 20 to 30 kg or even more. Exceptional examples may be almost twice that weight. Broad-barred and shark mackerel rarely exceed 10 kg, while spotted and school mackerel are commonly 1 to 4 kg, and rarely top 8 kg.

All these fish range from estuary mouths and inshore waters, out past the islands and reefs to the Continental Shelf.

They feed primarily on small bait fish such as mullet, garfish, herring and the like, but will also take squid and crustaceans at times.

They are all very popular angling targets, pursued by large numbers of fishermen. Most are caught from boats using fishing techniques such as live or fresh-dead baits of whole or cut fish. They will also strike at a range of lures and large flies.

Tropical mackerel have powerful jaws and sharp teeth, so wire leaders or ganged hooks should be used to prevent bite-offs, and extreme care exercised when handling them in a boat or on shore. The teeth of even a dead mackerel can inflict a nasty gash.

The flesh of tropical mackerels is white, firm and delicious, although shark mackerel are not as highly rated. Larger specimens of narrow-barred Spanish mackerel have been linked with cases of ciguatera poisoning. Check with local anglers before consuming any mackerel over 8 or 10 kg in weight.

Mangrove Jack

The mangrove jack is also known in some areas as red bream, dog bream or red perch. It is closely related to both the fingermark bream and the red bass. Almost identical fish in American waters are known as snapper, mangrove snapper or red snapper.

Mangrove jacks are found in tropical and sub-tropical waters around the northern half of Australia, south to about Sydney on the east coast and Shark Bay in Western Australia. They live mainly in estuarine and inshore waters, rarely straying far beyond the mouths of tidal rivers, harbours and inlets, although very large specimens are sometimes taken in reef waters well off the coast. Mangrove jacks are also capable of moving upstream into flowing fresh water at times.

Jacks commonly reach weights of 1.5 kg, and may occasionally grow much larger. Exceptional examples from offshore reefs may weigh between 8 and 10 kg.

These handsome, aggressive fish use their powerful jaws and canine teeth to capture and eat a variety of small fish, prawns and crabs. They respond to a wide range of fishing styles. Many are taken by sport fishermen casting lures or small live baits around snags, rock bars and other structural elements within tropical estuary systems. Some also suc-cumb to the prawn, crab, yabby or fish flesh baits of bream and whiting anglers.

When hooked, jacks are powerful fighters which immediately dive towards the line-cutting protection offered by submerged mangrove roots or oyster-encrusted rock ledges. Sturdy tackle and leaders of heavy nylon or light wire are recommended.

Mangrove jacks have delicious white flesh. However, it should be noted that the very similar red bass is often toxic. The clearest distinguishing feature of the red bass is a distinct 'pit' in front of each eye. This pit is not in evidence in man-grove jacks. However, if there is any doubt at all about the identification and separation of these fish, the flesh should not be consumed.

Marlin

Belonging to the same general family as sailfish and spearfish, marlin are large, active marine predators. There are three species in Australian waters – black marlin, blue marlin and striped marlin.

The black and blue marlin are the true heavyweights of this family, and among the largest fish in the sea. Both have been recorded at lengths of more than 4 m and weights in excess of 600 kg.

Striped marlin have been recorded to 200 kg and more, especially in New Zealand waters.

Marlin are mostly encountered in deep oceanic waters, near the edges of the Continental Shelf and beyond. However, favourable currents and water conditions occasionally carry them close to shore. They prey mainly on fish, including quite large tuna and mackerel, but also take quantities of squid in deeper water.

Black marlin are more common in tropical and sub-tropical waters. In Australia, they are encountered in sizes from 10 kg, right up to mature female spawners of 400 to 600 kg.

Striped marlin tend to take over from blacks as the most common inshore species off southern New South Wales, Tasmania and the North Island of New Zealand. Most examples caught in these areas weigh between 60 and 150 kg.

Blue marlin range throughout the oceans of the world and prefer the deep, oceanic currents. Most of those encountered in Australia and New Zealand are mature female specimens, weighing anywhere from 90 to 500 kg.

Marlin are caught primarily by boat anglers using a variety of offshore fishing techniques including live or fresh-dead baits of whole fish and squid. They will also take lures or large flies trolled behind a moving boat. Sturdy game fishing tackle and leaders of heavy nylon or wire are needed to withstand the powerful struggle and repeated jumps of a hooked marlin.

Marlin flesh is pinkish white and has a pleasant flavour, although larger specimens may also carry accumulations of mercury and other heavy metals. The striped marlin has darker pink or orange flesh and is more highly rated than either the black or the blue, especially for the preparation of sashimi and other raw or marinated fish dishes. All marlin are well suited to smoking.

Morwong

The morwong family contains several species important to anglers in Australia and New Zealand. The best known of these are the common blue, grey or silver morwong which is sometimes called the 'rubberlip' and the somewhat smaller jackass fish.

Other morwong of some importance to anglers are the queen snapper or southern blue morwong, the dusky morwong which is also known as the strongfish or butterfish in certain areas and the red morwong. Several other morwong species, including the magpie and banded morwong, are more often encountered by divers than anglers.

Morwong are found in sub-tropical, temperate and cooler seas around Australia and New Zealand. They are mostly encountered over offshore reefs and gravel beds, although they occasionally enter harbours and large estuary mouths. Red, banded and dusky morwong occur mostly in wave-washed, inshore waters adjacent to rocky shorelines, headlands and stone breakwalls.

Most morwong species commonly reach weights of at least 1.2 kg, and some may occasionally grow much larger. The biggest are the dusky morwong and the queen snapper or southern blue morwong, both of which are capable of growing to 1 m in length and 10 kg or more in weight. Silver or blue morwong may reach 5 kg, while the other species rarely top 2 kg.

In many areas, morwong are an incidental catch taken by anglers fishing for more desirable target species such as snapper and flathead. However, both the silver ('rubberlip') and jackass morwong are regarded as fine table fish, and are usually a welcome addition to the bags of offshore fishermen. They are commonly sold at market under the title of 'sea bream', and command reasonably high prices. The big blue morwong or queen snapper is also a top quality eating fish, and is actively sought by many southern anglers. Red and banded morwong have reasonable edible qualities, but are not taken by line fishermen as frequently as the other species under discussion. In contrast, dusky morwong have coarse, unpalatable flesh and are not often consumed.

Mullet

The mullet family is a widespread one, found throughout the salt, brackish and fresh waters of the world. The group is well represented in Australian and New Zealand waters, with at least three species being of importance to anglers. These are the sea or bully mullet, the sand or lano mullet and the yellow-eye mullet or pilch. Flat-tail, diamond and pop-eye mullet are also of regional significance.

Most of these mullet are relatively small fish, rarely exceeding 0.6 kg in weight, although sometimes reaching twice that size. The exception is the sea or bully mullet, which is regularly encountered at weights of 1 kg and more, and occasionally approaches 5 kg.

The most easily captured of the mullet species is the yellow-eye or pilch, which is common around the southern half of Australia and much of New Zealand. It is a small fish, but one which bites well on baits of prawn pieces, marine worms, shellfish and even fish strips. Sand mullet are also taken in reasonable quantities, especially on the east coast of Australia. Sea mullet, on the other hand, are notoriously difficult to catch on a baited line, surviving for the most part on a diet of microscopic plants and animals.

Most mullet are caught in estuaries and bays or along ocean beaches. They rarely

range far from shore, even when undertaking migrations along the coast.

Mullet are fair to very good table fish, and are also important to anglers as a bait source, used either alive, dead, or cut into chunks and strips.

Sometimes regarded as a 'kids' fish, mullet can be sweet meals in their own right or used as baits and berley for larger game. They are also enthusiastic biters, available in sufficient numbers to provide the fast-paced fishing kids like.

*Sand mullet will also take
small white flies*

Mulloway

Mulloway are a very popular angling target, however, consistent catches are only made by specialist anglers specifically targeting this species.

Mulloway are taken by shore-based anglers casting from beaches, breakwalls and rock platforms, and by boat fishermen using a variety of offshore fishing techniques. In particular, they respond to live or fresh-dead baits of whole or cut fish, beach worms, squid and octopus. They will also occasionally strike at lures and large flies, especially at night or in flooded river mouths. Sturdy tackle is required to land larger specimens.

Rocky shorelines both along the coast and within estuaries are good places to look for mulloway. They are often relatively inactive during the day but are definite propositions at night.

In flood time however, mulloway can be taken from creek junctions, breakwalls and headlands near beach corners.

Several fish are caught each year on lead-headed feather lures, when floods discolour the water.

Despite their relatively strong and distinctive odour, larger mulloway are a highly rated table fish. In contrast, very small specimens tend to be soft and rather flavourless, thus earning the nickname of 'soapy' jew or 'soapies'.

Mulloway are not lone hunters all the time. They will school up offshore around islands in late winter and early spring and can also be taken in large numbers during floodtime when they congregate around river entrances and adjacent headlands to hunt fish washed out by the fresh water.

When lurefishing for mulloway (in estuaries), large minnow type plugs should be cast repeatedly into areas where tidal flow creates eddies around rocky corners, bridge pylons, or deep holes. The best retrieve is a slow steady wind.

Lures with sonic attractors built-in, like rattles, are generally successful.

Baitfishing for these big fish often requires the angler to allow plenty of time after the initial pickup of the bait before striking. At other times, such finesse is not required as the fish will tear off and hook itself.

41

Murray Cod

The Murray cod is Australia's largest freshwater fish, and among the three or four biggest freshwater species in the world. It once grew to weights in excess of 100 kg, but these days, any cod over 30 kg is an exceptional fish. Most Murray cod encountered by anglers today weigh between 1 kg and 15 kg.

Murray cod or 'goodoo' (an Aboriginal name for the fish) are native to the Murray/Darling system and its many tributaries in western Queensland, New South Wales, northern Victoria and south eastern South Australia. They have also been introduced into rivers, lakes and dams outside this natural range, with varying degrees of success.

The smaller, but closely related, trout cod or blue nose was once reasonably abundant in the cooler headwaters of some rivers, but is today present in just a handful of isolated localities.

Similarly, the various east coast cod (which are yet to be accurately described in scientific terms) are now rare – possibly endangered – in their native waters along the upper Clarence, Richmond and Mary River systems. As a result, they are now totally protected by law.

Murray cod are caught mostly in warmer, turbid outback rivers, lakes and man-made impoundments. They also

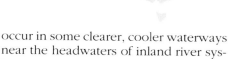

occur in some clearer, cooler waterways near the headwaters of inland river systems.

Cod eat yabbies (freshwater crayfish), shrimps and small fish, as well as occasionally taking terrestrial creatures such as frogs, lizards, snakes and even juvenile waterfowl!

Cod respond to a wide range of angling techniques, including bait fishing, lure casting, trolling and even fly fishing. Traditionally, they were caught on heavy set-lines baited with yabbies, small fish, bardi grubs and worms, even galah breast, rabbit pieces and strips of kangaroo meat. Today, sport fishermen recognise the challenge and excitement of targeting Murray cod on modern casting tackle and relatively light lines.

Murray cod from slow moving waterways may have a high fat content. The tastiest cod of all are 2 kg to 6 kg fish from clean, flowing waters.

Nannygai

The nannygai, 'gai, 'goat' or redfish is a common reef species around the south eastern corner of Australia. Very similar fish, including the swallow-tail nannygai and the red snapper or 'Bight redfish' take over from the common nannygai in Tasmanian, South Australian and Western Australian waters.

Nannygai are mostly encountered over offshore reefs and gravel beds, around islands and near undersea pinnacles. They occasionally enter deeper harbours and bays in cooler, southern waters, but are more common on offshore grounds.

Nannygai are relatively small fish, rarely exceeding 0.6 kg in weight, although occasionally reaching twice that size. The swallow-tail nannygai and red snapper both grow considerably larger than the eastern nannygai, sometimes attaining weights in excess of 3 kg.

All of these nannygai species have extremely large mouths in relation to their body size, and are voracious little hunters, preying on a range of smaller reef species, crustaceans, octopus and squid.

Although they are an important commercial species, most nannygai or redfish taken by recreational anglers are an incidental catch, boated while fishing for larger and more desirable target species such as snapper, flathead and morwong. They are caught primarily by boat anglers using a variety of offshore fishing techniques. In particular, they succumb to bottom-fished baits of fish flesh, pilchards, cut squid or prawns. They will also strike small lures and multi-hook bait jig rigs.

Nannygai are a tasty table fish with sweet, pinkish white flesh. Their small overall size and large heads result in a high degree of wastage, but this is offset by the fact that they are commonly caught in large numbers. Live nannygai are also a superb bait for large yellowfin tuna, yellowtail kingfish and even marlin.

Pearl Perch

The pearl perch or 'pearly' is a bottom-dwelling fish confined to a relatively small stretch of coastline between about Fraser Island, in southern Queensland, and Port Macquarie, in northern New South Wales. It is closely related to the much larger Westralian jewfish.

Pearl perch are deep sea fish, rarely encountered in water shallower than about 40 m. They are mostly caught over rock, reef or rubble sea beds, particularly near pinnacles and undersea peaks.

Pearl perch commonly reach weights of 1.5 kg, and may occasionally grow to twice that size. They are mostly taken while bottom fishing for snapper, teraglin and other reef species.

Pearl perch are one of our most delicious table fish and, like the Westralian jewfish, usually appear in any short list or 'top ten' of Australia's best eating species.It is a popular myth but a rarely seen event that snapper fishermen will trade two snapper for every single pearl perch.The eating quality is very good certainly but most snapper fishermen are notoriously unwilling to trade their fish for anything. However, given the choice, most enthusiastic fish-eaters do prefer the pearlies.

They take baits of fish flesh or occasionally, large peeled king prawns or squid, when these are naturally plentiful.

Pearl perch tend to school over rubble beds, often aggregating in nearly vertical columns above the sea bed.

While a depth sounder may indicate the profile of a school of pearl perch that looks like a patch of kingfish, kings are usually over reef, while such a sounder tracing over a flat seabed is almost always perch.

When pearl perch are thick, you can sometimes hold the school beneath your boat and improve your catch by keeping them feeding well – this can be as simple as using offal and scraps for berley but may require the investment of a better class of ground bait like fresh, cut pieces of pilchard.

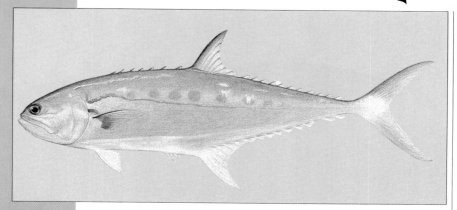

Queenfish

Although there are several very similar species of queenfish, leatherskin or 'skinny' in Australia's tropical seas, the common or *lysan* queenfish is by far the largest and most important.

The queenfish is a big, active saltwater sport fish, much prized by anglers for its fighting ability and acrobatic jumps when hooked. It is found in tropical waters around the northern half of Australia, living mainly in estuarine and inshore areas, but occasionally straying well beyond the mouths of tidal rivers, harbours and inlets to frequent reef passes, bomboras and the tidal rips around offshore islands.

Although growing to well over a metre, queenfish have laterally compressed bodies and are therefore quite light for their length. Most of those encountered by anglers weigh between 2 and 7 kg, although exceptional examples in excess of 12 kg are occasionally reported.

Queenfish prey on small fish and prawns, and respond to a wide range of angling techniques, including bait fishing, lure casting, trolling and fly fishing. They are taken by both shore-based and boat anglers, and provide exceptional sport when hooked on relatively light tackle.

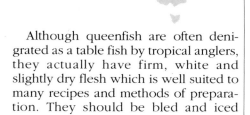

Although queenfish are often denigrated as a table fish by tropical anglers, they actually have firm, white and slightly dry flesh which is well suited to many recipes and methods of preparation. They should be bled and iced promptly after capture.

Salmon (Australian)

The Australian salmon or 'kahawai' is a popular angling species throughout the southern half of Australia and around much of the New Zealand coastline.

Australian salmon are in no way related to the true salmon of the Northern Hemisphere. The only close relative of the Australian salmon is the much smaller Tommy ruff or Australian herring.

Salmon or kahawai are a schooling species which occur mostly in wave-washed, inshore waters adjacent to rocky shorelines, headlands, breakwalls, jetties and beaches. Juveniles, which are called 'salmon trout' or 'bay trout' in Victoria, are common in bays, harbours and larger estuaries.

There are actually two sub-species of Australian salmon: an eastern and western population. Both strains commonly reach weights in excess of 2 kg, and may occasionally grow much larger. They have been recorded to weights of almost 10 kg in exceptional cases. The largest specimens tend to occur in the Great Australian Bight, Western Australia and New Zealand's North Island.

Salmon eat a variety of small bait fish such as pilchards, herring and anchovies, as well as small squid, krill and prawns.

Salmon are a very popular angling target, pursued by large numbers of fisher-men. They are taken by both shore-based and boat anglers using a variety of techniques. In particular, they respond to baits of whole pilchards or garfish, cut fish flesh, prawns and marine worms. They will also strike at a wide range of lures and flies.

Slow retrieves work best for salmon as their bite can be a fumbling affair – even on lures.

Silver or chrome spoons work, as do poppers and small blue and white minnows.

Salmon have dark, reddish-grey flesh with a prominent blood line and a reasonably strong flavour. They are best suited to casseroles, fish cakes and similar dishes. They are also popular for canning and smoking.

Samson Fish

The samson fish is closely related and rather similar to both the amberjack and the yellowtail kingfish. It can be differentiated from these two fish by its deeper body, blunter head and darker, blotchy or barred colouration, although fin ray counts are sometimes required to separate juveniles of the three species.

Samson fish are confined mostly to the sub-tropical and warmer temperate waters of Australia's east and west coasts, although they also range through south western waters into the Great Australian Bight. Generally, they are more common in Western Australia where they are often called 'sea kingfish'.

Samsons are large fish, frequently reaching 1.2 m or more in length and weighing as much as 20 or 30 kg. Exceptional examples may approach 2 m and 50 kg.

Samson fish are caught by both land-based and boat anglers using live and dead fish baits, squid or lures. They are strong, active fighters and demand sturdy tackle in their larger sizes.

Semi-regular catches of small samson fish are taken from reefs on the mid-north east coast. Such places as Port Stephens, Laurieton and Port Macquarie are consistent producers of juvenile fish often in catches of other species.

Samson fish make fine table fare, although very large specimens tend to be somewhat dry and coarse.

47

Saratoga

Saratoga are primitive, freshwater fish belonging to a family which also has isolated representatives in South-East Asia and South America. Two similar looking, but geographically separate, species occur in Australia. They are the northern saratoga and the Dawson River saratoga. Both are erroneously referred to in some older literature as 'spotted barramundi', although this confusing habit appears to be dying out.

The saratoga ranges from the Jardine River, on the north western tip of Cape York, to the Darwin area of the Northern Territory. It prefers billabongs and water holes, but is also found in some slower moving rivers. A similar fish occurs in Papua New Guinea and Irian Jaya.

The Dawson River saratoga was originally confined to the Dawson-Fitzroy system in central Queensland, but has now also been stocked in several man-made dams, most of which are close to Brisbane. It prefers relatively clean, running fresh water with a reasonably high oxygen content and a diversity of food types, although it will also survive in still waters.

Both species attain lengths in excess of 90 cm and weights of at least 4.5 kg, although the northern saratoga is larger, occasionally reaching weights in excess of 6 kg on the Australian mainland and 10 kg in Papua New Guinea.

Both species of saratoga are 'mouth brooders'. The female holds fertilised eggs in her mouth until they hatch, and also allows the fry to swim back into her mouth for protection during the days and weeks after hatching.

These fish feed on insects and terrestrial creatures such as frogs, lizards and small snakes, as well as various bait fish, shrimps and freshwater crayfish.

In recent years, the saratoga has developed a well-earned reputation as a sport fish in its own right, and is now avidly pursued on a largely catch-and-release basis. Both species are particularly attractive targets for fly fishermen.

Saratoga are an inferior quality table fish, with many bones and coarse, tasteless flesh. For this reason, most of those caught are returned to the water alive.

Snapper

The snapper is also known as the pink snapper, red, 'reddie', red bream, squire and 'pinkie'. It is, without doubt, one of the most popular saltwater species in Australia and New Zealand. In Australia, snapper are found around the southern half of the mainland, from about Rockhampton in Queensland to Carnarvon in Western Australia. They are rare in Tasmania.

In New Zealand, the fish is found right around the North Island and as far down the east coast of the South Island as Christchurch. Snapper are also found at Lord Howe and Norfolk Islands.

Snapper from different regions vary considerably in body shape and colouration. Fish from the Australian east coast are typically brick-red and develop distinctive humps on their heads as they attain maturity. In contrast, specimens from South Australia and New Zealand tend to be a lighter, silvery pink and rarely exhibit a hump, regardless of their size.

The largest snapper are caught in South Australia, Norfolk Island and New Zealand. Exceptional examples to 20 kg have been recorded, although any fish over 12 or 13 kg is a real prize. On the east coast of Australia, the species rarely tops 10 kg these days.

Small snapper called cockneys, red bream, squire, pinkies or ruggers in various locations, are often encountered in bays and estuaries. Larger snapper move offshore, although they return to shallow bay waters periodically to feed and spawn. Generally, snapper of all sizes prefer bottom strata of rocks and gravel, or transition areas between reef and softer seabed materials. They are opportunistic feeders, consuming crabs, shellfish, prawns, squid, octopus and small fish.

Snapper are a very popular angling target, pursued by large numbers of fishermen from both boat and shore. In particular, they respond to baits of cut fish flesh, whole, small bait species such as pilchards, garfish and herring, squid, cuttlefish, octopus and prawns. They will also take lures and flies on occasion, especially jigs fished on or near the seabed.

Snapper are highly-rated table fish and command premium prices.

Sooty Grunter

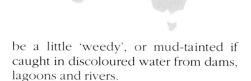

The common sooty grunter is just one member of a relatively large group of tropical fresh and brackish water species of the grunter family, some of which are still to be fully described by scientists.

Sooty grunter are also known as black bream, khaki bream and 'blubberlips'. They occur in the tropical rivers, swamps and billabongs of northern Australia, occasionally ranging downstream into brackish areas. They generally prefer clean, running water with a reasonably high oxygen content and a diversity of food types, but will also be found in turbid lagoons, dams and water holes in some areas. They prey mainly on freshwater crayfish, shrimps, small fish and insects, but will also consume aquatic and terrestrial vegetation, including fruit, such as wild figs, which falls into their home streams from bankside trees.

Sooty grunter rarely exceed 1.4 kg, although they can reach twice that size. They are often taken incidentally by anglers fishing for barramundi, but are today highly regarded as a sporting species in their own right, being one of our hardest-fighting freshwater fish on a kilo-for-kilo basis.

Sooty grunter respond to a wide range of natural baits, lures and flies. They provide reasonable to good table fare when taken from clean, flowing water, but may be a little 'weedy', or mud-tainted if caught in discoloured water from dams, lagoons and rivers.

Look for concentrations of fallen timber along creek margins or for any shaded area close to the bank. They also frequent areas where shallow flats drop into deep holes or where a wide bend deepens into a channel.

Sooties love to reside anywhere there is cover and structure and are obliging enough to move considerable distances to strike any small wobbling lure.

When they are plentiful which is often, they can be prompted into competitive behaviour, often barging one another out of the way to grab the lure.

Sweetlip

The red-throated sweetlip, sweetlip emperor or 'lipper' is a very important tropical and sub-tropical reef species taken in large numbers by party-boat customers and other anglers fishing the bottom in northern waters. The closely related grass and gold-spotted sweetlip are also of some importance as angling species as, of course, are the various emperors, particularly the red and spangled emperors.

Sweetlip stray as far south as the New South Wales border at times, but are much more prolific in northern reef waters; from about Rockhampton in the east to Carnarvon in the west. They are also taken in massive numbers around Norfolk Island.

Red-throated sweetlip commonly reach weights of 1.5 kg, and may occasionally grow to 4 kg. The scarlet colouration in their fins, throat area and mouth lining is characteristic, and helps prevent confusion with other tropical species, including closely-related members of the emperor clan.

Sweetlip inhabit reef areas and prey on a range of crustaceans, molluscs and smaller reef fish. They are caught primarily by boat anglers using offshore reef fishing techniques. In particular, they respond to weighted lines baited with fish flesh, small whole fish, squid or prawns.

Sweetlip are a highly rated table fish, not quite in the league of red emperor and coral trout, but extremely tasty nonetheless.

Many anglers in the tropics fish a strip of bait on a leadheaded jig, bouncing their offering close to coral walls or in deep holes. Sweetlip don't strike half heartedly either, so a strong arm approach will work better than giving them line when they run.

Tailor

Tailor are widespread throughout the temperate and sub-tropical seas of the world. An identical fish called bluefish occurs on the eastern seaboard of the United States, while in South Africa the species is known as elf. Here in Australia, tailor are sometimes called choppers, skipjack or 'skippies', and often their common name is misspelt as 'tailer'.

Tailor are found in sub-tropical, temperate and cool waters from southern central Queensland to Carnarvon, although they are uncommon in western Victoria and extremely rare in Tasmania. Tailor are not found in New Zealand.

Tailor commonly reach weights of 2 kg, and may occasionally grow much larger. Exceptional specimens in excess of 1 m and 10 kg have been recorded, mostly in Western Australia, although any tailor over 6 kg is a prize catch.

Smaller tailor or choppers are a fish of our estuarine and inshore waters, occurring mostly in the lower reaches of larger tidal rivers, bays, inlets and harbours. Larger specimens are usually found over reefs and gravel beds extending offshore, towards the edge of the Continental Shelf. They are also prolific at times in wave-washed, inshore waters adjacent to surf beaches, rocky shorelines, headlands and stone breakwalls.

Tailor form schools of varying sizes. Juvenile to mid-size specimens often congregate in very large numbers, feeding voraciously on shoals of pilchards, whitebait and other small forage fish. This activity attracts seagulls, terns and other sea birds from great distances.

Tailor are a very popular angling target, and many are taken by shore-based anglers casting baits of whole pilchards, garfish, whitebait or fish flesh strips, often presented on ganged or linked hooks.

They also respond avidly to lures and flies of all types, either cast and retrieved or trolled. Linked hooks or a wire leader are advisable to prevent bite-offs.

Fresh tailor which have been bled and cleaned promptly after capture are very tasty. They are also well suited to smoking and pickling. However, tailor bruise easily and deteriorate when frozen.

Teraglin

The teraglin or trag is a relative of the mulloway. Many recreational anglers have difficulty in telling these two fish apart.

The key differential features of these species are their tail profile and scale size. The trailing edge of the teraglin's tail is concave or inward-curving, whilst that of the mulloway is convex or outward curving. In addition, the scales of the teraglin are noticeably smaller than those on a jewfish of similar length and weight.

The mouth of the teraglin is yellow or yellowish-orange. While a similar colouration is sometimes evident in the mulloway, it is never as bright and obvious as in teraglin.

Teraglin are relatively small fish, averaging anywhere from 1 kg to 3 kg and rarely exceed 5 kg. However, exceptional specimens may rarely approach lengths of 1 m and weights of 9 kg.

The geographic range of the teraglin is strictly limited in comparison with mulloway, extending from southern Queensland, down the eastern seaboard to about Montague Island, off Narooma. However, within this range they are much more likely to be encountered between Yamba in northern New South Wales, and Kiama, just south of Wollongong.

Almost all teraglin taken by recreational anglers come from offshore grounds in depths between 20 and 80 m.

Teraglin feed primarily on small fish, crustaceans, squid and octopus. They appear to travel and hold in schools, and once located, large catches are often possible. However, teraglin spook easily and a school may disperse if hooked fish escape or excessive noise is made by boats above the school.

Most good hauls of teraglin are taken at dusk, dawn or through the night. Unweighted handlines and relatively large, sharp hooks are much favoured by experienced 'trag' fishermen along the coast.

The teraglin is a highly-rated table fish, and is regarded by most seafood fanciers as having superior flavour and texture to mulloway.

Trevally

Several species of this large family of fish are important to Australian anglers. Silver or white trevally are found in southern Australian and New Zealand waters, and giant trevally, big-eye trevally and golden trevally in the tropics and northern temperate zones. Silver trevally, called skipjack or 'skippy' in parts of Western Australia, are commonly 1.5 to 3 kg, and may occasionally grow much larger. The biggest specimens have come from Lord Howe Island, and weigh in excess of 11 kg.

Trevally are a popular angling species, taken mostly in larger estuaries, harbours, inlets, bays and over inshore reefs. They are captured by both shore-based and boat fishermen on pilchards, whitebait, cut fish pieces, prawns, squid, worms and cunjevoi. They will also strike small lures and flies at times.

Bled and cleaned promptly after capture, silver trevally are a fair to good table fish, although their flesh sometimes contains harmless parasites.

The tropical trevallies tend to grow larger than their southern counterparts. Giant trevally commonly reach 1.2 m or more in length and weigh as much as 20 or 25 kg. Exceptional specimens may occasionally top 1.6 m in length and 45 kg in weight.

Very big tropical trevally are still erroneously called 'turrum' by some people. The only true 'turrum' – more correctly known as the gold-spotted trevally – rarely tops 9 kg.

Tropical trevally respond to a wide range of angling techniques, including bait fishing, lure casting, trolling and fly fishing. They are often an incidental catch taken by anglers fishing for species such as mackerel, tuna, coral trout, cobia and even sailfish. However, large tropical trevally are much prized as sporting opponents, providing one of the toughest tussles of any fish on a kilo-for-kilo basis.

Smaller tropical trevally – particularly goldens – are very good table fish. Larger specimens of giant trevally may be a little dry and coarse.

Trout (Brown)

Originally, brown trout were introduced to Australia and New Zealand from the British Isles during the second half of the 19th century.

They thrive in many Australasian waters, especially cooler alpine and sub-alpine streams and hydro-electric storage dams.

Brown trout in streams and smaller rivers are relatively small fish, rarely exceeding 1.5 kg in weight, although they can reach twice that size. Generally, they grow larger in lakes and dams, very occasionally approaching 10 kg in some waters. However, any trout over 4 kg is a real prize.

Trout prefer clean, running fresh water with a reasonably high oxygen content and a diversity of food types. They need such conditions in which to spawn and obtain their maximum growth potential, although they will also survive in some 'marginal' waters that were once considered to be too warm or turbid.

Trout eat a wide range of aquatic and terrestrial insects, shrimps, crayfish and small fish such as gudgeons, smelt and whitebait. They will also consume juveniles of their own breed.

In Australia, trout are confined to the highlands and western slopes of New South Wales, Victoria, south-eastern

South Australia and the southern corner of Western Australia. They also thrive throughout Tasmania. Trout have found New Zealand waters even more to their liking, and this island nation now boasts some of the finest trout fishing in the world. Although most Australasian trout stocks are land-locked, small sea-run populations do occur, mainly in western Victoria, Tasmania and New Zealand.

Trout (Rainbow)

Rainbow trout are another very popular angling target. Most are caught by anglers using relatively light tackle, fine lines and small hooks, lures or flies. They respond to a wide range of angling techniques, including bait fishing, lure casting, trolling and fly fishing.

Rainbows of all sizes are highly regarded food fish, although some people prefer the taste of browns. The tastiest trout are generally those with orange or pink flesh – a result of dietary components such as shrimp and freshwater crayfish. Rainbow trout flesh is also well suited to smoking, salt or sugar curing and pickling.

Rainbows respond well to wet flies fished deep in fast water – a longer leader than normal (say up to 4 or 5 m) is sometimes necessary to get the fly down to where the fish are lying close to the bottom.

Unlike brown trout, rainbows are predisposed to chase lures or flies which are made to skitter or move erratically across the current. Sometimes, when the fish are feeding on active prey like smelt or caddies this technique is deadly.

They are generally more aggressive fish than browns of a similar size and in many locations this leads to their ease of capture and a somewhat diminished reputation as an angling challenge.

However, once hooked there is speed and power aplenty as the rainbow leaps and burrows vigorously in its attempts to escape.

Large rainbows are in fact very much a fish to be reckoned with in fast water, quite capable of stripping line from anglers' reels and defying capture for extended periods.

In particular, a hybrid strain of rainbows, known as 'triploid' fish are phenomenal fighters. These are found in selected waters where they have been stocked, particularly at Dee Lagoon in Tasmania.

Tuna

There are many species of tuna in Australia and New Zealand - albacore, dogtooth, northern bluefin, mackerel tuna, southern bluefin, striped tuna, and yellowfin tuna. Another species, the big-eye tuna, is mainly of interest to commercial fishermen.

Striped tuna are small to medium-sized fish which average 2 to 4 kg in weight, with occasional specimens exceeding 7 kg. They are mostly taken by boat anglers trolling or casting small lures and flies but will also respond to small live and dead fish baits. Striped tuna make excellent bait for a wide range of fish.

Southern bluefin tuna are caught in Australia from temperate and cool seas in southern latitudes and they occasionally reach 2 m and 170 kg. These tuna respond to trolled or cast lures and flies, but will occasionally take live and dead bait fish and squid.

Yellowfin tuna are found in tropical and sub-tropical waters around the northern half of Australia, but make seasonal forays into cooler southern waters, ranging as far south as Tasmania and New Zealand.

Yellowfin are a fish of the deep ocean near the edges of the Continental Shelf and beyond, however, favourable currents and water conditions occasionally bring them inshore, within reach of small boats and land based anglers.

These are large tuna, regularly attaining weights of 50 to 100 kg in our waters and occasionally approaching 120 kg. Smaller yellowfin in the 2 to 30 kg range form large schools, but very big fish are more likely to be encountered singly or in small groups.

Yellowfin respond best to live or fresh-dead baits of whole or cut fish and squid. They will also strike at a range of lures and large flies, either cast and retrieved, or trolled behind a moving boat. In some deep water areas, they are available to shore-based sport and game fishermen.

Yellowfin have pinkish-red meat that cooks to near-white. They are second only to albacore in the quality of their flesh, and are rated ahead of albacore for the preparation of raw fish dishes such as sashimi.

Wahoo

The wahoo is a fast, exciting game fish found in tropical and sub-tropical waters around the northern half of Australia, as well as elsewhere in the world. It also makes seasonal forays into temperate and cool waters, occasionally travelling as far south as Perth, Eden and the northern tip of New Zealand's North Island.

Although similar to the Spanish mackerel in body shape, wahoo are distinguished by their more cylindrical cross section, short, upright tail lobes and the even height of their first dorsal fin.

Wahoo regularly attain lengths approaching 2 m and weights in excess of 20 kg. They have been recorded to 50 or 60 kg around Fiji and Tahiti. In Australia, most of those caught weigh between 8 and 30 kg.

Wahoo are mostly encountered in deeper, oceanic waters, near the edges of the Continental Shelf. However, favourable currents and water conditions occasionally carry them close to shore.

These fish will often be found in late spring and early summer working rocky spines of reef shoreline, particularly under schools of frigate mackerel.

These fish have wickedly sharp teeth set in scissor-like jaws and should be handled with extreme care at all times, even when dead. They feed on pelagic bait species such as small tuna, flying fish, dolphin fish, sauris and rainbow runner. They may also consume squid at times. Wahoo respond to a wide range of angling techniques, including bait fishing, lure casting, trolling and fly fishing. They are caught primarily by boat anglers using a variety of offshore fishing techniques. In particular, they are taken as an incidental catch while trolling for marlin and tuna.

Wahoo have delicious white meat and are at least the equal of the tropical mackerels in the culinary department. The slug-like intestinal parasites often found in their gut have no detrimental effect on these fish.

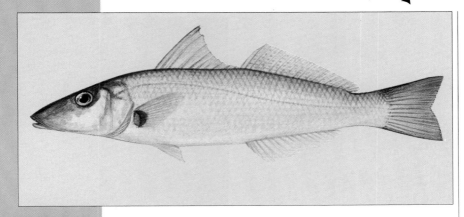

Whiting

Two species of whiting are especially important to Australian fishermen. They are the King George or spotted whiting of cool, southern seas, and the sand, silver or yellowfin whiting of warmer temperate and sub-tropical waters. Other species such as Queensland's winter whiting and Western Australia's yellow-finned whiting are of regional significance. The King George whiting is by far our largest representative of this family, occasionally exceeding 1.2 kg and even reaching 2.5 or 3 kg in very rare instances. This is in contrast to the other whiting mentioned, which rarely top 0.5 kg.

King George whiting are found in temperate and cool waters around the southern half of Australia, being most prolific in Victoria, South Australia and Western Australia. They live mainly in estuarine and inshore waters, particularly favouring the relatively shallow sand and gravel flats or sea grass beds found in southern bays, harbours and inlets.

Sand or yellowfin whiting, on the other hand, are most prolific along the eastern seaboard of Australia, from the southern or central coast of Queensland in the north, to Wilsons Promontory in the south.

Yellow-finned whiting occur between similar latitudes on the west coast. As well as occurring in estuaries and bays, both these fish are found in the surf line along ocean beaches.

All of these whiting eat marine worms, prawns, shrimps, small crabs and various invertebrates. They are very popular angling targets and are caught mostly by anglers using relatively light tackle, fine lines and small hooks. Best baits include marine worms, cockles, pipis, peeled prawn tails, saltwater yabbies or 'nippers' and even squid strips. Whiting will very occasionally take small lures or flies.

All the whiting species are highly rated table fish, none more so than the King George whiting, which is rated by many experts as Australia's most delicious fish species.

CHAPTER

3

TACKLE & TECHNIQUES

Rods & Reels

Flyrods are generally two piece and are from 2.4 to 2.7 m long. They bend or 'load' with a gradual curve to deliver the flyline smoothly. Flyreels are simply centrepins with a check or 'clicker' to prevent over-runs when line is stripped from the reel to cast. They are also often drilled to lessen their weight and to enable the flyline to dry.

Spinning rods can be 1.8 to 2.4 m long, and one or two piece. They have light tips for casting small baits and lures, and the mid section stiffens quickly into the butt. A spinning or 'threadline' reel suits line classes up to 6 kg. They are simple to operate, can cast a variety of weights and can have good drag systems and fast retrieve speeds.

Baitcast rods are used to cast heavier lures and baits from small revolving drum reels mounted on top of the rod. Most have magnetic cast control, level winding mechanisms and superb drag systems. Larger types of these 'overheads' are favoured for snapper and mulloway bait-fishing. The rods are 1.5 to 1.8 m long with the power spread evenly. They have slightly heavier tips and more moderate curves than spinning rods, so they unload or straighten less violently during a cast to minimise line over-runs.

Centrepin or 'blackfish' outfits comprise long slender rods and simple, free-running centrepin reels, which require some skill to master. The long soft rod gently swings the weighted float and rig which is allowed to pull line from the reel. The angler prevents over-runs by applying light finger pressure to the rim of the spinning spool.

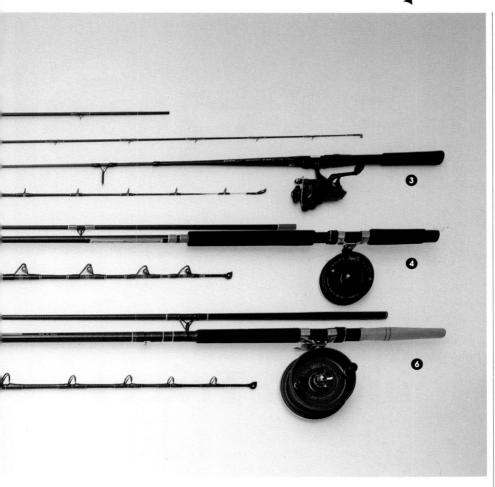

Roller-runnered gamefishing rods with straight or bent-butts are designed to apply maximum leverage to large powerful gamefish. They can be as short as 1.6 or as long as 2.1 m and the curve is moderate and even throughout the rod. Gamefishing reels are large overheads, with enormous line capacity and efficient, heat-dissipating drag systems.

Sidecast rods are 3.4 to 4.4 m long with the reel mounted close to the butt. Depending on the size of the reel and power of the rod, you can put together a sidecast rig for a variety of fish. Moderate to fast tapered rods are needed for big baits and powerful fish. Slow tapered rods suit small, soft baits and float rigs. The sidecast reel is a simple, powerful winch with a turn-table enabling the spool to be rotated 90 degrees. Even unweighted baits on

1. Fly rod and reel
2. Baitcast rod and reel
3. Spinning rod and reel
4. Blackfish centrepin rod and reel
5. Bent-butt rollered game
   rod and reel
6. Sidecast rod and reel
7. Jig/troll rod and reel

heavy line can then be cast from the side of the spool.

A good jig/troll/livebait outfit generally consists of a moderate to fast-taper rod some 1.6 to 2.0 m long, carrying either a smaller lever drag overhead reel or one of the larger star drag models. If the reel can be cast with, as well as troll baits and lures, and drop jigs to the bottom, it makes a very useful blue-water outfit.

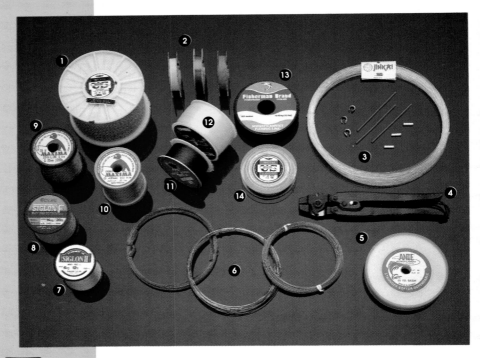

Lines & Traces

There are several kinds of fishing line. The choice of materials is determined in part by whether the line is to serve as main line or trace material.

Traces can be hard-drawn single strand wire, as is used for rigging game-fishing baits and sometimes tropical lure fishing, or soft wire, as is sometimes used when bait-fishing for toothy species like tailor, mackerel or hairtail. Cable-laid wire in 7 strand or 49 strand is customary for shark-fishing and heavy co-polymer nylon traces are popular when bait and lure-fishing for marlin and tuna. Some of these nylon traces have special crimping sleeves, armour springs, and eyelets to provide quick, strong connections.

Main-lines can be made from low stretch braided dacron, sophisticated co-polymer nylons with supple cores and tough outer skins, or co-filament nylons, which can combine differing line characteristics within a unified extrusion. Other specialty lines are oval, or slightly flattened in section.

Most fishing lines however are simple extrusions of single strand nylon, called monofilament, or 'mono'.

The different forms taken by this basic fishing product are staggering. It comes in an astonishing variety of colours, hardnesses, breaking strengths, durability, stretch factors, diameters, and knot strengths. Most people however can get good fishing performance from lines with moderate diameter for breaking strain and a fair mix of suppleness and toughness, provided the line also ties a good knot. Such lines aren't cheap, but they are worth the little extra.

Unless you're dissatisfied with your line, there's no point making a change just for the sake of it. Like most things in fishing, if it's not broken, don't 'fix' it, but if you're missing bites, or the line seems unduly cranky, or if you'd like to cast further, it may pay you to look at a higher grade of fishing line. Perhaps you'd like to pack more yardage onto a given sized reel. Remember though, you only benefit from using fishing line that suits your needs. It may come as a surprise that no one type of line is perfect for every job. Some however, will do certain jobs better than others.

Limp lines suit spinning reels and baitcasters but they're usually limp because they're soft, and that can mean they are subject to abrasion damage. Springy lines are often quite hard-wearing, but these suit large diameter game reels or sidecasts better than spin or baitcast reels, on which they can be uncontrollable. Low stretch mono suits fishing around rough country because there, if you let a hooked fish move too far, you can lose it. That same line though can lose resilience and break on the strike after extended off-shore trolling, or after a hard fight on a strong fish.

This means you may need to balance the disadvantage of line stretch against the fact that it can be a form of insurance, especially with light line where margins for error are slim.

That doesn't mean that high or low stretch lines are no good, just that you pay for every advantage with balancing factors. Fluorescent lines can deteriorate in sunlight for example, but while fresh, work very well and offer better line visibility when fighting a fish, or watching trolled lures and baits. The thing is to choose a line which offers the greatest range of features that your fishing requires.

People readily see bait as a consumable item, but seldom understand that fishing line is the same. Fishing line doesn't disappear with use like bait, but something does disappear – in part at least – and that is the line's performance. Besides elongation fatigue, other things can destroy fishing lines. Cracked runners can shred it, or threadline reels with no bail roller, or bail rollers that have seized can simply melt the line with heat build-up.

Knots are always a potential source of trouble as the very process of tying a knot tends to apply friction and compression to the line, two things nylon just doesn't like at all. You can minimise your knot problems by learning knots with higher strength ratings (expressed as a percentage of the line's un-knotted breaking strength). Tie them carefully and properly and don't rush your knots, give them the attention and time they deserve. Always lubricate the knot before you pull it down, (moistening the knot in your mouth will lubricate it very well). Pull your knots down slowly, never jerk them tight, as this causes intense friction damage where you don't want any at all.

Despite these shortcomings, fishing line is still the only thing between you and a hooked fish, so it pays to make some effort to look after it. With sensible care, like washing it down after use and storing it out of direct sunlight, and away from excessive heat, fishing line will last for considerable periods instead of 'mysteriously' letting you down when you can least afford it.

To get the best from your fishing line, come to terms with which line types suit you best, and when buying line, don't make false economies, buy the best you can afford. Lastly, always fish with the best part of the line you've got.

1. *Dacron*
2. *Top-up spools*
3. *Jinkai system*
4. *Jinkai pliers*
5. *Heavy mono leader dispenser*
6. *(left to right) Hard drawn, soft drawn and cable wire*
7. *Fine diameter low stretch mono*
8. *Fluorescent trolling mono*
9. *&10. Different coloured lines provide camouflage in different light conditions*
11. *Fine diameter hard surface line*
12. *Soft fluorescent line*
13. *Soft moderate stretch line*
14. *Lead-core trolling line*

65

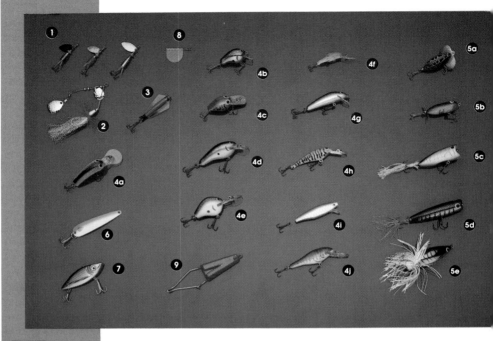

Lures & Flies

Freshwater

Freshwater lures include (1) bladed spinners (2) spinner jigs, (3) cobras, (4) swimming minnows and plugs, (5) surface lures, (6) metal spoons, and (7) bibless noise-makers. The clear plastic 'D'-shaped keel (8) minimises line twist when trolling bladed lures. It is often not required for spinning. The lure retriever (9)

is dropped down on a heavy cord to engage the lure body, then the cord is pulled to straighten or tear the hooks free and recover the lure.

Dry flies (1) (2) (3) in the photo below left, float to imitate mature winged insects. Nymphs (4) (5) and (8) are fished underwater to represent immature aquatic insects. Wet flies (7) mimic baitfish and other large sub-surface prey, while the Black Muddler (6) can be used as a wet or dry fly.

Lures like spinners and swimming plugs work well either cast or trolled, but all of them require some movement to draw strikes from fish. Flies are cast to fish, often needing only the stream's flow to carry them past waiting fish. In still water, wet flies need to be moved to attract fish.

Swimming lures are effective if fished in a series of stop/start movements, like a small crippled creature providing easy prey. Freshwater surface lures work best when used to create a surface commotion in small, localised areas.

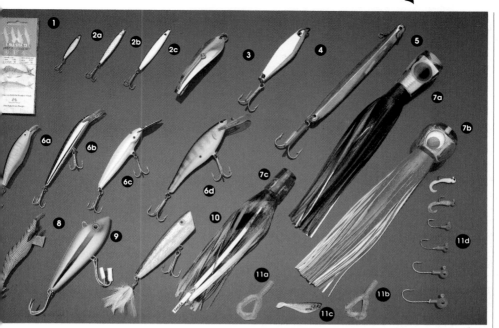

Saltwater

Saltwater bait-chaser rigs (1) are sets of small flies on droppers, rigged with a sinker and lowered over a school of bait-fish or into a berley trail over reef to catch live bait. Slim, metal baitfish imitations (2) can be cast, jigged or trolled for a variety of predatory fish. The thin spoon (3) is trolled and the coffin lure (4) can be cast, jigged or trolled.

The big metal lure (5) is a deepwater jig. Saltwater minnows (6) are more robust than freshwater types to imitate saltwater bait and withstand larger saltwater fish. Plastic-skirted acrylic head lures (7) are trolled for kingfish, wahoo, tuna and mar-lin, and the multi-pronged lure (8) is a squid jig, fished over inshore shallows.

The bibless minnow (9) is a high speed trolling lure, the big cigar shaped popper (10) can be cast and 'blooped', or trolled, and the small plastic tails are used on the single hook lead-head jigs (11) for flat-head and various reef fish. Saltwater flies (small photo this page) generally imitate small forage fish and can be cast and stripped in by hand, or trolled.

Above:
1. *Deceiver*
2. *Bonefish*
3. *Pink Thing*
4. *Dahlberg Diver*

Opposite page:
1. *Elk-hair Caddis*
2. *Royal Wulf*
3. *Adam's Irresistible*
4. *Green Nymph*
5. *Pheasant-tail Nymph*
6. *Black Muddler*
7. *White Rock Streamer*
8. *Bitch Creek Nymph*

Hooks, Sinkers & Connectors

Sinkers

Sometimes it seems there are as many different hooks, sinkers, and swivels as there are fish swimming in the water. Most fishermen use only a handful of patterns and sizes to suit local conditions and species, and you too can choose a path through the confusion with some thought.

Sinkers are there to provide casting weight and help position the bait near feeding fish. Choosing sinkers depends on how far you have to cast, and how they will influence the bait's behaviour in local water conditions.

Pictured on the opposite page and beginning at the top left corner, the helmet sinker is used for beachfishing because it casts well and can resist rough water movement enough to hold a swinging bait in a feeding area. The large bomb-shaped snapper sinkers are used for deep sea fishing and the smaller ones for casting off the rocks.

The ringed sinker with the small bumps is also for beach fishing. The two containers below and to the right of that dispense split-shot which is crimped onto the line and often used in float rigs. The bean sinkers on the left are used as trolling weights inside plastic squid, or as fixed live-baiting sinkers, and as running sinkers in drift rigs.

Below those, there are: a barrel sinker, a bug, a spoon sinker and two channel sinkers. Barrels are flattened and painted white to be used as small lures, or rigged between a float and swivel for float fishing ballast. Bugs are just small, flattened bean sinkers, and spoon sinkers suit rocky bays and deep holes off surf beaches where turbulence can sweep the bait around within feeding zones.

Channel sinkers have large holes in the upright ends so line can be fed freely to timid biters. This rig has hooked some very large bream when alternative sinker set-ups would have just lost the bait, and the fish been dismissed as a 'tiddler'.

Ball sinkers suit casting rigs very well. For bream, rig them to run right down onto the hook and for whiting, to a swivel above a trace of about half a metre.

Connectors

Stainless steel split-rings are for attaching hooks to lures. Snaps come in more sizes and types than the two shown here and allow quick convenient changes of rigs or lures. Use ball bearing snap swivels for trolling, and barrel types for casting, and don't use a snap so large that it affects the action of a lure or bait. If it's as strong as the main line, it's strong enough.

Simple barrel swivels without snaps serve as stoppers for running rigs or convenient attachment points for rigs with traces or droppers. Most don't actually 'swivel' too well at all under a direct line of pull, but they will take some line twist out of a rig that has been tumbled or rotated by water movement. Ball bearing swivels are the only way to eliminate this problem entirely and are ideal for trolling or gamefishing rigs, but aren't warranted in all fishing situations.

Slim swivels suit light line, and float rigs benefit from slim swivels to minimise water drag and prevent unbalancing the rig when casting. If a running sinker with a large hole is used, a slim swivel can get caught in the hole and jam the sinker - in such cases it would be better to use a brass ring instead.

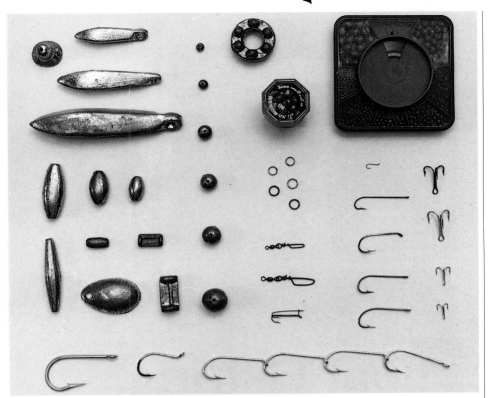

Hooks

Fish hooks vary in design and size to suit particular fishing situations and the physical attributes of different fish and baits. To carry appropriate baits and present them attractively, hooks need the right shape and shank length. They must also fit inside the fish's mouth and be strong enough to hold the fish on the tackle being used.

For example, the little safety pin hook shown is perfect for live-baiting with mudeyes or grasshoppers for trout, but would be totally unsuitable for larger, more powerful fish.

The hooks on the far right are all trebles for use on lures and those in the next row left, are from the top: (1) a tiny fly hook, suitable for dry trout flies; (2) a long shanked pattern, good for leatherjackets and yellowtail, or in larger sizes, for whiting and flathead. The next hook down has a forged shank for strong-jawed fish, and both hooks below that will neatly present baits like prawns and yabbies.

Linked hooks can carry long baits such as whole garfish or pilchards, while short, recurved 'suicide' hooks in various sizes can suit bream, snapper, or live-baiting for kingfish. The last hook on the bottom left is a Tarpon hook, sometimes used on large gamefishing lures.

To determine the size and pattern of hook you need, consider the mouthsize of your target fish, and the size, shape and nature of the bait likely to attract that species. It also helps to match the hook size to the hook-setting ability of your chosen outfit. It's hard to set big hooks on light line, and while small hooks can land big fish, using a hook so small that it simply buries in a big bait is useless. A fish with powerful jaws can pulp a soft bait and allow entry of the point, but with large, firm baits, even on big fish, the point should stand well clear in order to take hold. Lastly, most hooks are not sharp enough when first bought, but a little work with a file or sharpening stone can make a dramatic difference to your hook-up rate.

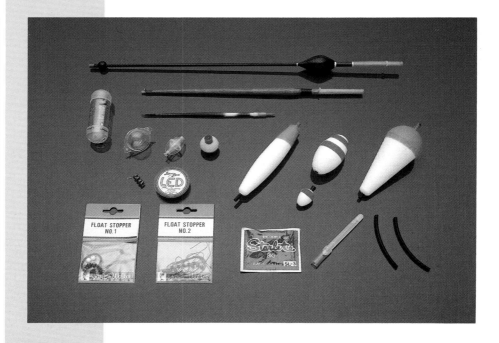

Float Fishing

Floats are used to present baits to fish by suspending them at depths where fish are feeding, or drifting them into a feeding zone. Sometimes they are also used as part of the casting weight in a rig.

The float's weight, shape, and degree of buoyancy should be appropriate to the bait and rig in use and should take into account whether conditions are rough or calm, or if there is any run in the water.

The other very important function of a float is as a bite indicator, so above all else, a float must be visible. Generally, this means they should be brightly coloured, such as fluorescent red or orange. Oddly enough however, the easiest colour of all to see against a white foamy sea, is black. For this reason, stemmed blackfish floats for rockfishing are sometimes tipped with a length of black rubber tubing.

Just as fish can be put off by a bait weighted down unnaturally by too much lead, they can also shy off if the float is too hard to submerge when they take the bait.

You should match the float to the line and bait size, and weight the rig so that the float stays visible until a fish takes. The float should then slide smoothly under without resistance so the fish does not become alarmed and drop the bait before the hook can be set.

For shy biters such as estuary blackfish, or bream and garfish, use slim floats like quills and pencil floats. Both bream and blackfish off ocean rocks however, willingly pull under onion-bodied stem floats or small bobby corks.

To float-fish at night, you can attach a chemically activated 'star-lite' to the float stem with the small piece of tubing provided in each packet (see photograph on opposite page). Just 'crack' the light tube, slip it into one end of the tubing then put

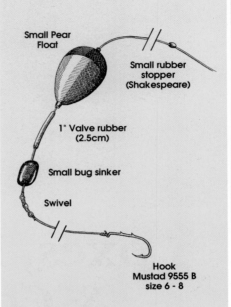

the tubing onto the float and it will light the float-top all night.

A torpedo shaped float suits live baiting off the rocks because tuna and other gamefish are likely to eject a bait if they feel it's tethered unnaturally. On the other hand, a tailor, black drummer or snapper in rough water is likely to hit the bait so hard that float buoyancy doesn't matter, and may even help set the hook. Large, pear-shaped floats suit big baits for these fish in rough seas.

It's thought that trout mistake bubble floats for natural bubbles on the surface, but tiny bobby corks can work as well. The real advantage of the bubble float is that you can let water into it and provide casting weight without limiting the free movement of the bait with sinkers on the trace.

A small weighted berley bomb can be used to localise fish under your rig, either as part of the rig or separately.

Small coils of strip lead make adding and subtracting weight on a rig easier and quicker than either using split-shot or changing running sinkers.

Running Float Stopper Rigs

Small Pear Float

Small rubber stopper (Shakespeare)

1" Valve rubber (2.5cm)

Small bug sinker

Swivel

Hook
Mustad 9555 B
size 6 - 8

Running floats need a stopper system so the float can be pulled under and signify a bite. There are a variety of float stopping systems available.

Small rubber stopper beads, can be slipped onto the line with the fine wire loop threader provided, or stopper knots can be tied in fishing line or wool. You can also loop the line twice through a short length of rubber tube, which, as it is pulled tight, twists the tubing into a neat little 'bead'.

If it doesn't work, the piece of rubber tube is probably too long. Just trim it a bit and it will behave nicely. For fixed floats, use short collars of plastic spaghetti or rubber tubing slipped over the stem.

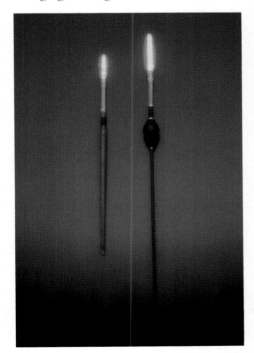

A Star-lite fitted to the float stem will illuminate it all night

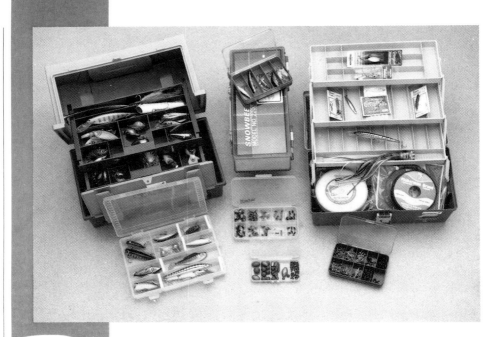

Boxes, Bags & Containers

Hardcase Tackle Boxes

Tackle boxes can be square, oblong, deep, flat, high, or slender, and can have just one, or several layers or drawers. Generally, they all have differing sized compartments to allow gear to be separated by size and type for organisation and easy access. A handy tip is to pack multi-tiered boxes with the heaviest items down low as this will improve their stability when open.

Some boxes are too big to take fishing every time, but are great for home storage or extended trips. Others are ideal for slipping into a pocket or a small soft bag when mobility and lightweight are the keynotes. Regarding the perennial problem of not being able to fit in all your gear no matter how many boxes you have, try to formulate a short list of 'must-have' tackle items for each kind of trip.

Nymph and wet fly boxes (below) have ripple-strips of foam in which the flies can be separately embedded, while dry fly boxes segment the space into deep compartments to protect the hackles.

Soft-packs & Specialised Containers

Don't overlook the value of simple shoulder bags. Beach fishermen and stream walkers find a small soft bag or haversack useful, provided it has a few separate compartments and is robust enough.

Gamefishermen can carry their lures in roll-up soft packs with clear plastic windows. These provide compact storage and easy, quick selection without the traces and hooks tangling. Expensive reels justify the protection of a padded bag or reel wallet against impact damage.

Soft padded strips of material with self-closing velcro tabs make bundling rods an easy job. Once you've used these to transport rods you'll wonder how you got along without them.

Good fishing rods are quite expensive, and it's worth slipping at least a soft bag over them to protect them from the scuffs and gouges of transport. Anglers travelling longer distances by air or over rough

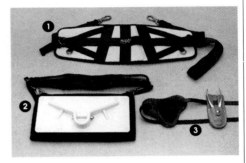

country will see the wisdom of specialised rod tubes like the one pictured.

Rod-belts, Harnesses & Gimbals

For extended fights or brutal encounters with big fish on heavy gear, you can take some of the strain off your back with a suitable harness (1). These are used in conjunction with a gimbal fitted rod bucket (2) and can make all the difference in the world on really big, stubborn game fish.

A lightweight approach that works well to relieve the discomfort of a rod being buried in your groin or stomach is this simple leather rod bucket (3). It is very suitable for small boat work or rock and beach fishing as the strap can double as a belt for carrying tools like knives and pliers in pouches.

Things you should look for in a tackle box are:

1. How well they close and seal
2. Are they corrosion proof?
3. How much abuse they can stand.

A tackle container which shatters or falls apart is useless.

Fishing Clothes

You may not have thought so, but clothing can influence how effectively you fish. Concentration and alertness depend largely on angler comfort, so clothing should be loose fitting, well ventilated and suit the local climate.

For protection, long sleeves are best and can always be rolled up, but short sleeves suit some kinds of fishing better. Colour is important too. Sombre greens and browns will camouflage you on a trout stream, but in the tropics or out in a boat all day, light colours reflect heat and keep you cool. Hats insulate your head in cold weather and protect you from heatstroke and sunburn in summer. They also reduce eyestrain, which is a major cause of angler fatigue.

Properly specified high contrast polarising sunglasses filter harmful radiation as well as cut surface glare, enabling you to spot fish. Attach a buoyant keeper strap to your glasses and if dropped in the water, they'll float. Highly reflective lenses suit saltwater fishing, but for freshwater, amber lenses are better choices.

Specialised fishing vests carry a surprising amount of gear, but regular shirts and trousers will do, provided they are a roomy cut and have enough pockets.

Every fisherman needs wet weather gear, even summer showers can leave you soaked to the skin, and at risk from chills.

Ultra-light spray jackets can be folded into a small bundle, are easy to stash and carry, but their rain-proofing is limited to light showers. Specialty lightweight materials such as Goretex (tm) are much more waterproof and tough, and don't create the perspiration and chafing problems of plastic raincoats. They're more expensive, but they work better too.

Ventilated baseball caps are cooler than full-brimmed stetsons but do not offer as much sun protection.

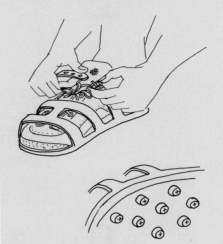

Special Purpose Footwear

Cleated plastic sandals will improve your footing on slippery rocks. Buy one shoe size larger than normal so they'll fit over your standard footwear.

Blackfish anglers especially, who frequent the ocean rocks, are well advised to use these, as without them a nasty fall may result in being swept in. For really slippery conditions, full cleats bolted through the soles of sturdy sandshoes may be needed.

Stocking foot waders have come into their own in recent times coinciding with the advent of affordable, purpose designed wading shoes. Even with ordinary (and much cheaper) sandshoes, the new lightweight reinforced nylon waders have transformed high country streamwork from an uncomfortable slog to an enjoyable exercise, and make stream crossings safer and more sure footed than was possible with the older style moulded-boot waders.

These come in both chest and thigh lengths and are much tougher than earlier products.

For colder water, nothing beats the insulation and wearer comfort of quality neoprene waders. These are a bit like a diver's wet suit, except they incorporate a waterproof membrane which keeps the inside dry and warm. They don't suit high summer stream work, but for winter surf fishing or cold alpine lakes and deep wading they are superb.

Booted waders (right) still have a place where a robust, low cost wader is required and waterproofing is more important than covering long distances over rough terrain.

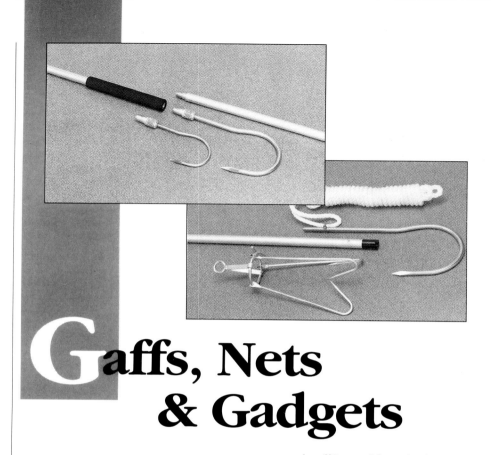

Gaffs, Nets & Gadgets

Gaffs

Gaff hooks are used to lift spiny or heavy fish which won't fit into a landing net. This combination rock gaff (1) uses screw-in connections. It changes easily from small to large fixed heads, or can be extended. It can also be used as a flying gaff (2). The grapnel gaff is used from high cliffs. The line is clipped into the frame, then the unit is lowered on a cord to the fish below. The hooks are jiggled into place and once in, provide a secure method of lifting the fish.

Nets

Nets come in fixed and folding designs, (left) your choice depends on your storage needs and how the nets are transported. Stream fishermen and small boat anglers can benefit from a net which folds away when not in use, but prawn scoops or landing nets for bigger fish are better with fixed frames. Keeper nets (right) are used to keep fish alive and fresh until you're ready to clean them.

This laminated timber landing net (next page, top) can be clipped onto your belt, slipped into the back pocket of a fishing vest, or attached to an elastic cord and suspended behind your back out of the way.

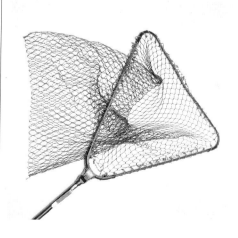

Gadgets

Various lotions and potions required for fishing can be carried in small handy containers. You can get insect repellent in a roll-on pack, while sunscreen and fluorescent bait dyes come in squeeze-packs. There's also an an oily paste to make flies float and another to make them sink.

Some fly-line manufacturers sell their lines on specially designed spools which allow easy rewinding should you need to change from say, a floating flyline to a sinking line.

Instead of juggling innumerable spools of leader material, carry a dispenser rack of various leader diameters. A clip-on mini torch with a flexible head leaves both hands free for night fishing, and a pair of surgical artery forceps can be locked onto hooks safely to remove them from the fish. Various tools can be hung from a small retractable pin-wheel. This one carries a mini line snipper.

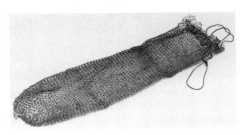

Fish smokers (above) can turn even quite ordinary fish into culinary delights. Large fish can be scaled and filleted or cut into strips, (leave the skin on unless the fish is a herbivore). Small fish are best scaled, cleaned, the gut cavity scrubbed and lightly salted, then smoked whole.

This stainless steel hot smoker uses methylated spirit for fuel in a tray beneath the smoke box. A handful of sawdust is sprinkled inside the smoke box and the drip tray and smoke rack carrying the fish is placed on top of that. Close the box, light the metho and give the fish about 20 minutes a kilo. You can buy smoker sawdust or make your own from suitable timber. Any dry, close-grained timer is acceptable. Don't use timber with a high resin or sap content, or with any paint or oil on it.

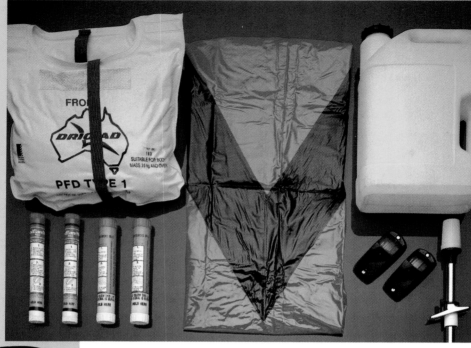

Basic Gear for Fishing Boats

Boating regulations vary from State to State, but some basic items of equipment apply to all boating situations. Life jackets are a legal requirement as well as being advisable. Hand-held distress flares come in two types - 'rocket' flares which shoot a brilliant light into the sky and should be used at night, and 'smoke' flares which release a dense cloud of orange smoke - these are for day-time use.

Orange and black 'V' sheets are carried so craft in distress can be seen from considerable distances.

Water containers should hold enough water for everyone on board for a minimum of two days, and navigation lights serve at night to alert other vessels to your boat's position or direction of travel.

Two types of fishing anchors are commonly required. These are a grapnel type called a reef pick, and a bladed or Danforth type, called a sand pick. Both require sufficient rope to work properly, and also about half a boat length of heavy chain. The chain positions the anchor correctly, allowing it to dig into the bottom and preventing it from being lifted away.

Canoes are versatile small water craft ideal for calm freshwater and estuaries.

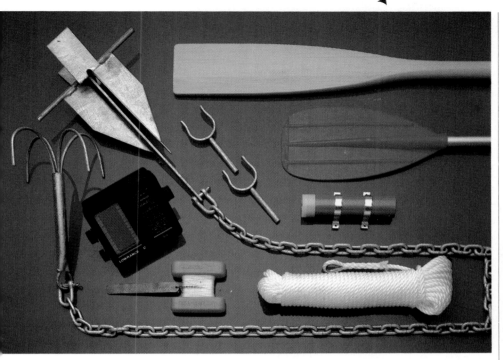

Paddles are best suited to canoes while larger open craft should be fitted with oars and rowlocks, or have auxiliary motors. Even the smallest boat can benefit from simple rod holders. The type shown is usually positioned vertically or at a slight angle to help hold the line clear of the boat when trolling or on the drift.

Echo sounders can indicate bottom depth and also show any schools of fish or bait beneath the boat. The weighted float is dropped over the side to mark the exact position over a reef or school of fish. The boat can then be anchored accurately over the fish which is important for fishing success.

Medium sized boats like this seaworthy centre console are good enough to venture offshore with an eye on the weather.

Small aluminium dinghies are good family boats in most sheltered water situations.

Large gamefishing boats can make extended offshore journeys. In capable hands they are safe and comfortable at sea and can handle much larger fish as well.

Essential Accessories

Hand Tools

Knives with sturdy blades are needed to prepare bait, as this often involves cutting bones and gristle. Filleting knives are slender and flexible to steer the knife around bone and avoid wasting meat. A quality folding knife is safe to carry and can handle simple cleaning duties.

Sharp knives cut easily and cleanly, but the effort needed to use a blunt knife can result in loss of control with disastrous results. Carpenters' oil-stones are adequate for sharpening knives and nylon cutting boards save knife edges.

Hook removers can be simple plastic disgorgers, a loop of strong wire on a handle, or a pair of specialised pliers. Use side cutters for wire and heavy nylon, engineers' pliers for heavy work, and long-nosed pliers to remove hooks from small fish. Those shown here have a small projection at the tip for opening split rings, which is the sole use of the flat-handled pair beneath them.

You can scale fish with the back of your bait knife, a serrated metal scaler, or one like this plastic model with loosely fitted pegs in the head.

Spring balances can tell you how much your catch weighs, and also take the guesswork out of setting the drag pressure on your reel, especially important when fishing light line.

Bait Gathering Gear

Bait-pumps are used to gather squirt worms and yabbies from sandflats exposed at low tide. If the flats are covered by water you can pump them into a sieve which retains the baits and allows the sand to fall through.

Mullet can be caught in traps baited with bread. These three types will all catch small baitfish. Use a berley cage to attract

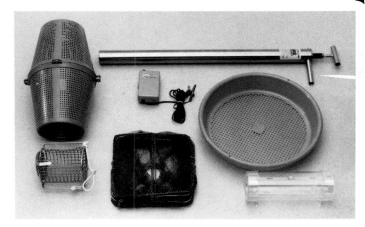

yellowtail or slimy mackerel to an area then fish for them with light handlines and small baits of fish flesh.

Baitfish can be kept alive in a bucket of water if the water is periodically exchanged. You can enhance their survival by replenishing the oxygen in the water with a battery operated aerator, powered either by 1.5 volt torch batteries or a 12 volt car or motor cycle battery.

Maps, Charts and Directories

The cornerstone of successful fishing is information. The better the quality of that information, the better your fishing prospects. You can do a lot yourself to make your fishing trips effective by studying area maps or charts.

Saltwater fishermen can obtain the 'AUS' series of Admiralty charts from good chandleries and specialty mapping outlets. These are required by law for outside fishing and show depth contours in metres or fathoms (one fathom = six feet). They also show reefs, navigation hazards and prohibited areas.

Various private concerns produce fishing and tourism maps and some have helpful detail and tips for an area. Your local tackle store and fishing club are good sources of 'mud-maps' and fishing 'marks'.

Topographical maps from the Central Mapping Authority or State Lands Depart-

ments show freshwater rivers and other landforms in detail where there can be wild and productive fishing. You can check who owns the land through the Cadastral map register and you should approach the land-owner by phone or letter for permission before entry.

Books and Tables

Reading good fishing publications can accelerate the fishing education that would take several years to acquire in the field. Fishing videos focus on action more than information but can prove helpful too.

Tide charts are the saltwater fisherman's bible. Compiled by scientific bodies such as the Flinders University of South Australia, they are reproduced throughout the country by various local agreements. They indicate moon phases, show approximate times and levels of high and low tide and also indicate local variations for where the tide is earlier or later than times stated on the tables.

Last century, an American named John Alden Knight devised a system of tables which took into account the movement and cycles of the sun as well as the moon. He reasoned that the sun influenced the behaviour of fish and game just as the moon did. With allowances for regional and international differences these 'Solunar Tables' have proven themselves accurate enough to gain the worldwide support of fishermen.

Knots

Knots are a necessary evil in fishing. Evil because even the best knots weaken the line they're tied in — necessary because without them you can't attach lures, hooks, floats or baits to the rig. Good knots mean better fishing though, so time spent learning to tie them is a wise investment.

Locked Half Blood

This simple and strong knot is ideal for tying hooks and swivels to lines testing up to 25 kg breaking strain. It is an especially firm favourite with whiting and snapper fishermen.

1

Thread the eye of your hook or swivel and twist the tag and main line together.

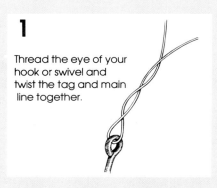

2

Complete three to six twists and thread the tag back through the loop formed by the first twist.

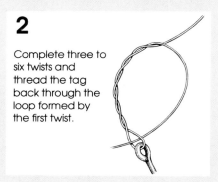

3

Pull the main line just enough so that the knot begins to form. Do not pull it up tight yet or you will have an un-locked half blood which may slip; particularly if you're tying new line to a shiny hook.

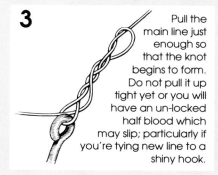

4

To lock the knot, thread the tag through the open loop which has been formed at the top of the knot.

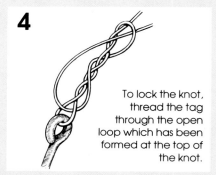

5

Pull the knot up firmly and the result should be something like this. Should a loop form within the knot, simply pull on the tag until it disappears.

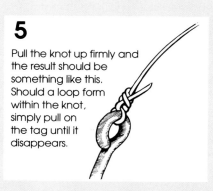

1

Pass the leader through the
eye of the hook and make a
loop against the shank so that
the tag protrudes a
short distance past
the curve.

Common Snell

*Originally developed for hooks
with flattened eyes, the snell is still
appropriate when it is desirable to
align the leader with the shank of
the hook. Whether or not the leader
passes through the eye of the hook
(as illustrated), is optional.*

2

Roll the loop around
the shank of the hook
and tag, encircling
the curve and
spear.

3

Continue in this manner until
the required number of
wraps are in place.
(The dotted line and
arrow indicates the
passage of the loop
around the hook.)

4

B

The snell is closed
by pulling on the tag
(A) against the main
line (B). Additional
pressure will lock the
snell securely on
the shank of
the hook.

A

5

When using hooks with roughly
turned, or partially open eyes,
it is safer to lock the snell
just short of the eye
where it will stay even
under the pressure of
playing a fish.

Double Overhand Loop

The Double Overhand Loop is a quick and useful way of attaching droppers to a main line. Its strength is adequate with medium to heavy tackle.

1

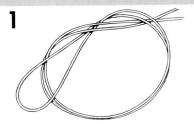

Form a loop in the end of your leader and make a simple overhand knot with the doubled strand.

2

Wrap this doubled strand through the loop a second time so that this configuration is shown. It is this second wrap which gives the knot its strength.

3

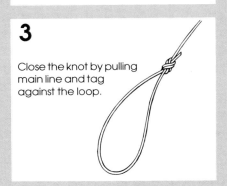

Close the knot by pulling main line and tag against the loop.

Tying a Tagless Dropper Loop

This dropper loop can be tied anywhere along your line enabling the fisherman or angler to use multiple droppers. It has applications in both recreational and commercial fishing.

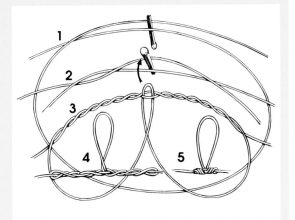

1. Make a circle or loop in your line and insert a match to one side of the crossover.

2. Rotate the match putting a twist in the line. This is what your loop will look like after rotating the match half a turn. Continue to make either three or four complete rotations so that a series of twists are made each side of the match.

3. Taking care not to lose your place, remove the match and pull the doubled section of your loop through exactly the same twist from which the match was removed.

4. As you pull the knot tight, you will notice the sequence of twists reverse so that the loop feeds from the centre of the knot rather than from the outside as you might expect would be the case.

5. The finished knot looks something like this. It is neat, strong, and - most important of all - can be tied at any point along the main line.

Opposed Rolls

Also known as 'Grinner', 'Universal', and 'Four Turn Water Knot'

This join is widely used by freshwater and saltwater anglers alike and works well in heavy or light lines. However, when tying with heavy, or stiff lines, use only three turns instead of four.

1

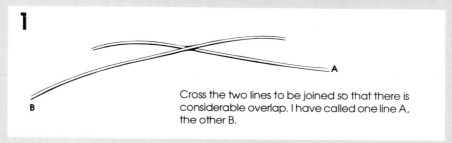

Cross the two lines to be joined so that there is considerable overlap. I have called one line A, the other B.

2

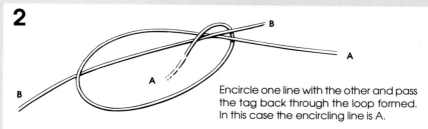

Encircle one line with the other and pass the tag back through the loop formed. In this case the encircling line is A.

3

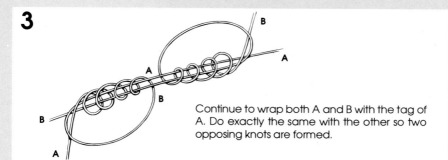

Continue to wrap both A and B with the tag of A. Do exactly the same with the other so two opposing knots are formed.

4

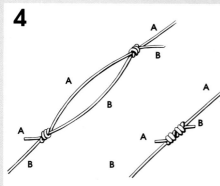

Close both of the knots but do not pull them tight. If you do, damage to the line will occur as you pull them together.

Lubricate the line with saliva or powdered graphite, then pull the knots together gently. Exert additional pressure on the tag and main line of each knot before pulling both knots together once more.

For best results, one line should encircle the other as described in step 2. Simply looping one line, laying it beside the other and wrapping both strands with the tag, causes the tags to stick out like spurs.

Albright

This is a simple knot for tying a heavy leader to a light main line. It is particularly useful in sportfishing where the leader has to be wound in through the runners of the rod and onto the reel.

1

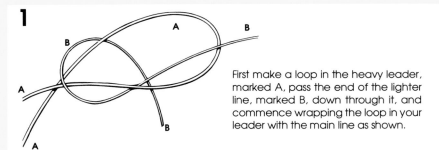

First make a loop in the heavy leader, marked A, pass the end of the lighter line, marked B, down through it, and commence wrapping the loop in your leader with the main line as shown.

2

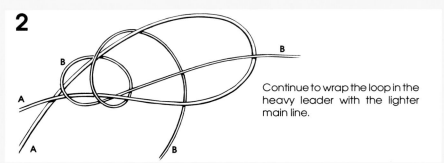

Continue to wrap the loop in the heavy leader with the lighter main line.

3

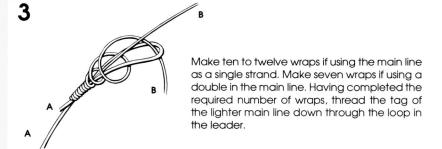

Make ten to twelve wraps if using the main line as a single strand. Make seven wraps if using a double in the main line. Having completed the required number of wraps, thread the tag of the lighter main line down through the loop in the leader.

4

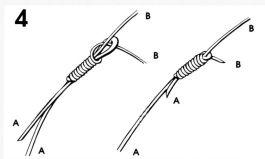

Reduce the size of the leader loop by pulling the short end back through the wraps you have made around it.

Having reduced the loop so that it fits tightly around the leader tag, pull the knot tight by exerting tension on the main line. It is important not to trim the tags until the knot is fully formed.

Harrison's Loop

Introduced to Australian anglers by fishing writer Rod Harrison, this method of attaching a lure with a loop is strong and secure and does not diminish the action of the lure.

1

Make an overhand knot in the leader, thread the eye of the lure with the tag end, then pass the tag back through the overhand knot.

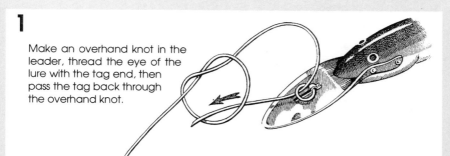

2

Wrap the leader with the tag three times.

3

Pass the tag back through the overhand knot first formed.

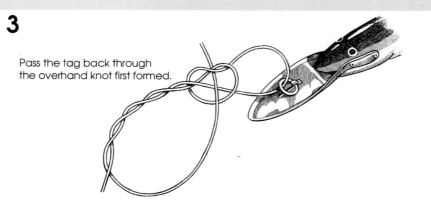

4

Form the knot by pulling the mainline against the tag, and finish off by pulling on the mainline against the loop.

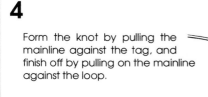

Spider Hitch

Possibly the easiest method of securing a double, the Spider Hitch is widely used in sportfishing.

1

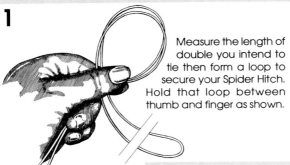

Measure the length of double you intend to tie then form a loop to secure your Spider Hitch. Hold that loop between thumb and finger as shown.

2

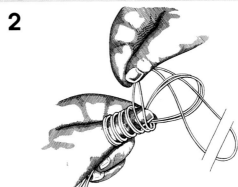

Begin by wrapping the loop and your thumb with the double. Do this five times and feed the double through the loop.

3

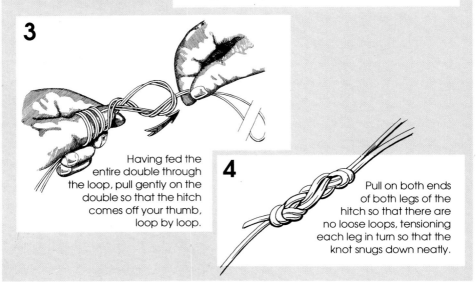

Having fed the entire double through the loop, pull gently on the double so that the hitch comes off your thumb, loop by loop.

4

Pull on both ends of both legs of the hitch so that there are no loose loops, tensioning each leg in turn so that the knot snugs down neatly.

Rigs

Presentation is the key to attracting fish and rigs are the means of achieving that presentation. The other function of a rig is to secure a hookup on the fish.

Running Floats

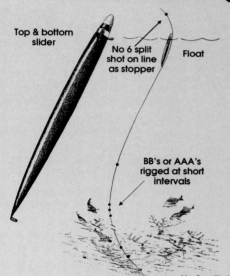

Top & bottom slider

No 6 split shot on line as stopper

Float

BB's or AAA's rigged at short intervals

No 8 split shot rigged above hook

Slider Floats

There are two types of sliders. Those with eyes at the top and bottom for close range fishing in flowing water, and those which are only eyed at the bottom, designed for casting longer distances.

Top and bottom sliders are made completely from balsa and will carry between two and six AA shot. Bottom sliders have balsa or plastic bodies and fine cane stems known as 'peacocks'.

Sliders work as running floats to present baits at depths between 2 and 10 m. The short drop from the rod tip also allows casts to be made despite surrounding bankside foliage that would severely restrict casting fixed floats with long drops.

Running Float

The most basic running float runs between two stops on the line. The float rests on the bottom stop when the rig is cast out, and as the bait sinks, the float slides up the line, coming to rest beneath the top stopper.

Stopper knot

Bobby cork or large pear float

Small ball sinker

Wooden bobber-type floats are favoured by some pier and rock fishermen because they are heavy enough to cast without additional weight. Because the central hole is large, they slide without difficulty. Styrene floats are more widely used however and some have inbuilt casting weight.

The size of the bottom stopper is of little consequence and can be a swivel, valve rubber stop, or even a small sinker. However, the top stopper must be small enough to be wound in through the rod guides.

A stopper small enough to pass through the rod guides may also pass through the hole in a large float, so a small bead is threaded onto the line between the top stopper and float to prevent this.

Fixed Floats

Float is positioned on line between two
closely spaced split shot

Waggler Floats

Wagglers are either made
from balsa and cane, or from
clear plastic. Those made from
clear plastic are called 'crystal'
wagglers and are favoured when the
shadow of an opaque float could frighten fish.

Those made from cane, or with cane stems and
balsa bodies, are called 'peacock' wagglers.
These may be straight like the clear plastic
wagglers or 'bodied' at the base
to give added weight for casting.

With a single eye at the base, the
wagglers are threaded onto the
line and locked in position with two split
shot crimped onto the line; one each
side of the eye.

The attitude of the float, and presentation of the bait, are determined by
the 'shotting' pattern. That is to say;
what size of shot, how many, and
where they are attached to the
drop below the float.

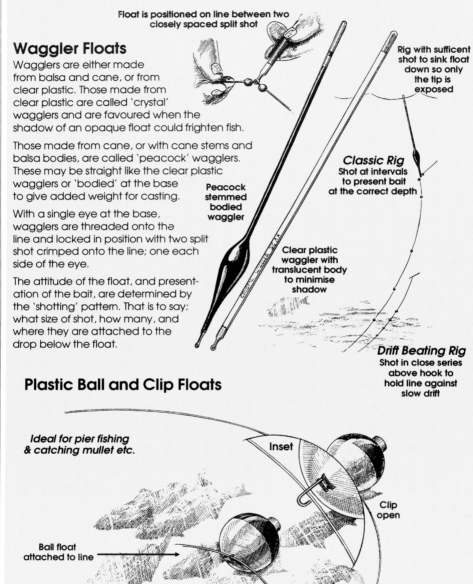

Rig with sufficent
shot to sink float
down so only
the tip is
exposed

Classic Rig
Shot at intervals
to present bait
at the correct depth

Peacock
stemmed
bodied
waggler

Clear plastic
waggler with
translucent body
to minimise
shadow

Drift Beating Rig
Shot in close series
above hook to
hold line against
slow drift

Plastic Ball and Clip Floats

*Ideal for pier fishing
& catching mullet etc.*

Inset

Clip
open

Ball float
attached to line

No 6 - 8 hook

Large split shot
or small sinker

Used by pier anglers in conjunction with long trevallia poles on which the line is retained
with a cleat. In telescopic versions, line is tied directly to the top guide.

In this application, the float governs the depth of bait presentation on a fixed length of
line. Mullet dominate the bags of anglers using the plastic ball and clip float.

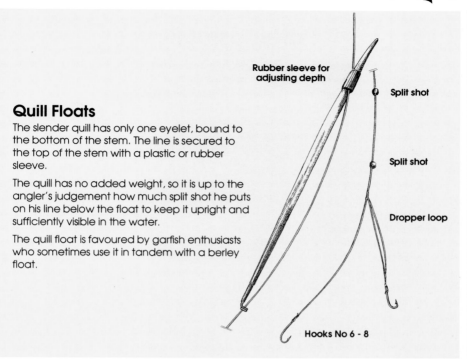

Quill Floats

The slender quill has only one eyelet, bound to the bottom of the stem. The line is secured to the top of the stem with a plastic or rubber sleeve.

The quill has no added weight, so it is up to the angler's judgement how much split shot he puts on his line below the float to keep it upright and sufficiently visible in the water.

The quill float is favoured by garfish enthusiasts who sometimes use it in tandem with a berley float.

Running Sinker Rigs

Running sinkers are used for finicky fish because they can pick up the bait without feeling the weight of the sinker. Sinkers designed to be rigged this way include the ball, bean, barrel and pyramid types.

The simplest running sinker rig is a sinker running on the line all the way down to the hook. While this is effective up to a point, is does have limitations, which are: there is no provision for a separate leader, and only small sinkers can be used because large sinkers tend to crush any bait above the hook, or even jam over the hook eye. When using large sinkers, a small sinker or bead should be placed between the eye of the hook and the sinker to prevent this happening.

In other running rigs, the sinker runs on the line to a solid ring or swivel to which a separate leader of suitable material can be tied.

Paternoster Rigs

Paternoster rigs are those with a sinker tied to the end of the line and droppers coming off the main line at intervals. Sinkers used on Paternosters include snapper lead, star, bomb and teardrop.

Paternoster rigs can be used on both heavy and light rigs and work well in a variety of situations. Main line droppers may be contrived simply by tying a dropper loop in the line and threading the eye of the hook with the loop, or a loop to loop arrangement can be used to add hooks already on leaders.

Sometimes swivels and rings are incorporated into the rig to achieve stronger tying off points. Three-way swivels are a popular choice but take some care with their alignment.

Primarily used for whiting snapper & flathead

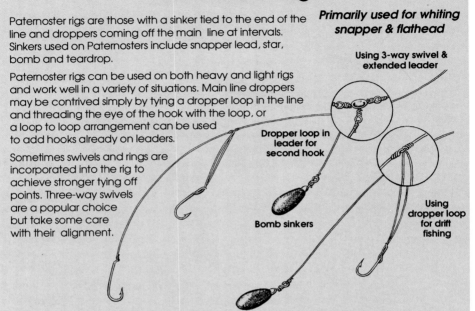

Using 3-way swivel & extended leader

Dropper loop in leader for second hook

Bomb sinkers

Using dropper loop for drift fishing

Paternoster Style Running Sinker Rigs

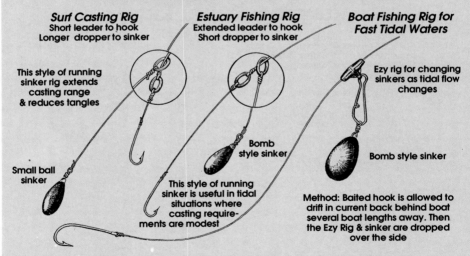

Surf Casting Rig
Short leader to hook
Longer dropper to sinker

This style of running sinker rig extends casting range & reduces tangles

Small ball sinker

Estuary Fishing Rig
Extended leader to hook
Short dropper to sinker

Bomb style sinker

This style of running sinker is useful in tidal situations where casting requirements are modest

Boat Fishing Rig for Fast Tidal Waters

Ezy rig for changing sinkers as tidal flow changes

Bomb style sinker

Method: Baited hook is allowed to drift in current back behind boat several boat lengths away. Then the Ezy Rig & sinker are dropped over the side

These rigs are suitable for situations where standard running sinkers are limited. For example – in strong currents or where long casts have to be made and where soft or weedy bottoms could entrap conventional rigs. Where long casts are an advantage, short droppers above the sinker are required.

When fishing over weed or on soft muddy bottoms, standard running sinkers may block up, become fouled or snagged. A short dropper to the sinker, preferably of a much lighter line than the main rig will solve this.

In strong tidal situations it is an advantage to extend the leader some metres behind the main line and sinker. By threading a clip swivel in the line, any amount of leader can be let out behind the boat in the tide before the sinker is allowed to drop to the bottom.

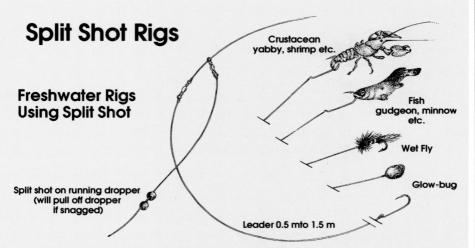

Split Shot Rigs

Freshwater Rigs Using Split Shot

Crustacean
yabby, shrimp etc.

Fish
gudgeon, minnow
etc.

Wet Fly

Glow-bug

Split shot on running dropper
(will pull off dropper
if snagged)

Leader 0.5 mto 1.5 m

In freshwater fishing, split shot offers a number of advantages over other methods of weighting the line. Its use is extended to bottom fishing, particularly over snaggy ground.

In a variation to the running Paternoster rig, stream fishermen – particularly when fishing running water – sometimes run a sliding dropper weighted with split shot.

Not only does the method offer considerable scope for weighted adjustment, but the shot rarely snag, and when they do, tend to pull free of the dropper freeing the rig with the loss of only one or two shot.

The versatility of the rig is such that live baits like yabbies and small fish can be used as well as wet flys.

Split Shot Rigs for Saltwater Fishing with Floats

In both salt and freshwater, split shot is used on the line below floats – to present baits at the correct depth, to position the float correctly in the water, and in some cases, add additional weight for casting.

Usually, a series of fairly small sizes are used in preference to a single large shot because minor adjustments to float position can be made, the bait can move around more freely, and bites are registered more clearly.

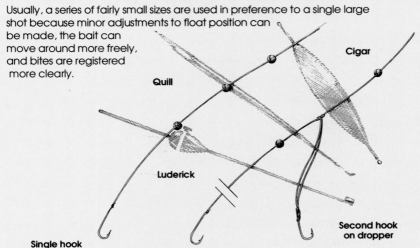

Cigar

Quill

Luderick

Single hook

Second hook
on dropper

Baits

Baits are most attractive to fish when they are fresh and well presented. Different baits work on different fish too and while there is some overlap of choice for differing species, all fish prefer a bait to look, behave, and smell as enticing as possible.

Estuary

Frustration and failure are often the experiences of people who lack the basic knowledge to collect live estuary baits. A few items such as bait pump, fork hoe and scoop net however, will enable several prime baits to be gathered at low tide from sand and mud flats.

Yabbies or nippers live in large communities on sand flats and are prized baits for bream, whiting and flathead. The bait pump is operated amongst their numerous large holes and the contents discharged onto the sand. Pump three times in each hole to explore the deeper chambers for yabbies. Discharge the mud and sand from each pump into a floating sieve if there is water over the flats.

Yabbies should be handled carefully and the water in their container changed regularly. Discard any that are dead as these will foul the water.

Sharp clicks heard in the weed beds towards low tide are made by another crustacean called a green nipper, which has one large claw similar to the yabbie. Puddle your feet up and down in the weeds until a muddy pool forms and you will find it easy to catch them. They rise to the surface to escape their sullied environment and are detected by their movements, usually around the edges of the dirty pool. Green nippers are stronger than yabbies and are a top attractor for bream and whiting.

Squirt or tube worms are deadly on bream, whiting and mullet, and during the spring months, luderick too. Profuse small holes, and sometimes the tips of their papery tubes on mud and sand flats indicate their presence. An empty fruit tin, inverted and forced down over the holes will pressure them out, or a bait pump can

Cockles (right) and pipis (left) make suitable estuary baits for bream.

*Above Left: Whitebait rigged
with single and double hooks
Above: Green Weed
Left: Blood worms*

be used. Squirt worms are very fragile and difficult to handle without damaging them.

Blood worms are hardy baits as they are fairly tough and not easy for the fish to get off the hook. You can dig for them on the tidal mud flats using a four pronged fork hoe with a short handle. Protective footwear such as a pair of laced gym boots fitted high around the ankles is necessary. Lowcut shoes can be lost in the gooey mud.

You can catch prawns in the daytime with a scoop net pushed through weed beds. A bed of fine ribbon weed with about 30 cm of water over it is a likely place. Prawns can also be scooped or drag-netted by conventional methods during the dark of the moon. Live prawns are great for flathead, bream and whiting.

Tiny shrimps that thrive in weed beds can be scooped from under bridges, wharves, jetties and various spots which provide shade and shelter. These are excellent bait for fish species with small mouths, such as as garfish. sand mullet, luderick and whiting.

Gather green weed for luderick around the shores of estuaries, lakes, rivers, creeks and in tidal pools, drains and backwaters. It grows on rocks, piles and virtually any other structure that offers attachment, as well as in mud or sand.

Other baits such as squid, yellowtail and small mullet (for catching mulloway) are also obtained in the estuary. Suitable

*Left to right: Live prawn rig – Peeled
prawn rig – Whole dead prawn – Rig for
two small live prawns – Peeled prawn
pieces– Small shelled sections of prawn*

Baiting a Yabby

Yabbies are gathered using a yabby pump on mud or sand flats when the tide has gone out far enough to expose their holes.

The yabby is soft, rigging it live with the hook just through the tail creates difficulties. The fish will usually just pull it from the hook.

A useful method of baiting a yabby is to pass the hook through its tail like a sewing needle before anchoring it in the carapace.

Bait-holder hooks like the Mustad 9555B are preferred for yabbies.

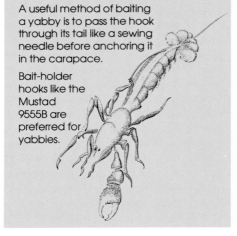

baits for bream include cockles and pipis, (found in weed beds) and soft shelled clams (dug from the mud flats). Satisfactory commercial baits for the same species are mullet and fowl gut, or green and frozen prawns. 'Green' prawns are simply dead, uncooked prawns. When fresh, these are better than frozen prawns, but even frozen prawns can be used to catch fish. However, good live baits will always make fishing less of a gamble.

Dead slimy mackerel belly-rigged on ganged hooks as troll bait for Spanish mackerel

Tropical Baits

Travellers to the tropics can take bait with them, buy it when they get there or catch it on site. Excellent bait can be bought in all the larger tropical towns and include West Australian pilchards, local prawns and squid. IQF quality (individually quick frozen) baits are common, and there may be regional variants like mullet and garfish.

Local fishermen in the tropics are well aware of the value of fresh bait, so it's common for tackle stores and bait outlets to have fresh bait on offer, especially at weekends.

While using lures in the tropics gets justifiable publicity, bait-fishing opens up a more versatile approach to species like mangrove jack, cod, javelin fish and threadfin salmon, or even black jewfish in the deeper holes at the bottom of estuaries.

Northern locals catch a good deal of their own bait using cast nets or drag nets for prawns, several species of herring and also garfish. A strong light off a jetty at night will attract squid in close where they can be speared.

The best time to gather daylight bait is early morning on a rising tide. While cast-netting from a boat is safe enough, using a drag net involves getting into the water, where crocodiles may well be present. For this reason, drag netting on an open beach with good visibility is safest. In summer, the danger of sea stingers is also very real but this can be minimised by wearing full length clothing. For obvious reasons, nobody goes into the water after dark.

In estuaries, yabby or nipper pumps can be used with success. Around stony headlands there are plenty of small crabs which make good bait for parrotfish and cod. A number of types of small worms live under broken rocks in the intertidal range, and these make great bait for small whiting, which are plentiful, and excellent live bait for barramundi.

At the upper limit of tidal influence, giant Machrobrachium prawns can be caught at night using a strong torch and a scoop, and will also enter the same type of shrimp trap used in southern inland waters. This magnificent bait can also be eaten, and with a body length of up to 30 cm, it doesn't take many to make a meal!

Freshwater Baits

There are many and various baits available to the freshwater angler. They range from natural grubs and insects, to live fish and even some manufactured baits.

A properly presented live bait is just about the best method you can use to fool a big trout or Murray cod and these can be fished under floats, on a drift rig, or as part of a bottom fishing set up. The important thing with bait-fishing is not to use line that is so heavy that it impairs natural presentation or alarms the fish so that it drops the bait. Line of 2 to 3 kg is ideal for trout, redfin, and small native fish. For Murray cod, you may need 4 to 8 kg line. Some popular freshwater baits include:

Mudeyes: These are the nymphal stage of dragonflies and when suspended under a bubble float or mudeye waggler float are one of the deadliest trout baits

around. A number 12 fly hook should be placed through the mudeye's small, undeveloped wings. This will allow the bait to swim unimpeded.

Grasshoppers: In the summer months, grasshoppers are a sure fire bait when free-drifted down the river, or cast to fish, much as you would a lure or fly. Hook them under the back edge of the hard shell covering the back and shoulders of the insect. Black crickets can be rigged the same way. Both baits are very effective when fished under a bubble float.

Bardi Grubs: The best bait for Murray cod and many other native fish, especially yellowbelly. Bardi grubs attract fish with their characteristic odour and for this reason can be effective even when fished inactively on a bottom rig like a Paternoster. Use a Mustad *540 hook in a 1 or 1/0.

Shrimp: Great baits for native fish like bass, silver perch and golden perch, and introduced fish like trout and redfin. They are gathered in traps baited with bread or soap and are simple to rig. Pass the hook once through the tail of large shrimp, or hang several on the hook if they're small.

Yabbies: Also known as crayfish, the small ones will take trout and redfin, and

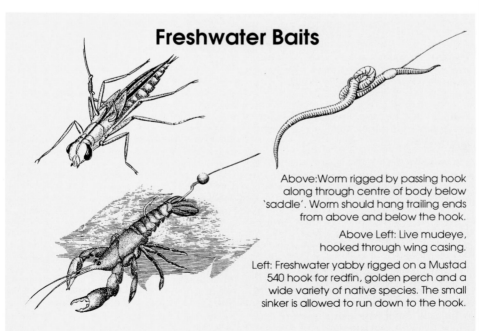

Freshwater Baits

Above:Worm rigged by passing hook along through centre of body below 'saddle'. Worm should hang trailing ends from above and below the hook.

Above Left: Live mudeye, hooked through wing casing.

Left: Freshwater yabby rigged on a Mustad 540 hook for redfin, golden perch and a wide variety of native species. The small sinker is allowed to run down to the hook.

Hook live fish such as slimy mackerel and yellowtail above lateral line as shown

Mullet rigged as swimming bait (top), shown with fillet removed (centre) and fillet trimmed into large and small strip baits

Slimy mackerel cut as cube or 'chunk' baits

larger ones are superb for Murray cod. Hook them through the tail, and if required, remove their nippers.

Worms: The most popular and universal freshwater bait of all. Collect them by digging around soaks or looking under rotting timber in wet areas, and keep them in cool, dark places. They are dynamite on trout and native fish, especially after heavy rain has the fish looking for drowned worms. Thread them singly onto a hook, or use a number and bunch them with the ends waggling enticingly. They can be fished under floats, with running sinker rigs, free drifted or trolled behind flashing attractors like Ford Fenders.

Other baits include manufactured paste baits like XL long life bait, or Catchit, or you can use small live fish.

If using live fish for bait, don't transport them to a waterway where they don't already have a natural place.

Offshore Baits

A fundamental element of the marine food chain is that big fish eat little fish. For this reason, successful offshore baits consist in the main of whole fish, or pieces cut from fish. Offshore baits commonly in use include pilchards, garfish, and mullet. Small members of the tuna family also make prime cut baits for larger tuna or bottom fish such as snapper.

Few marine fish will reject a pilchard or garfish bait. These are generally fished on ganged hook rigs which, provided they're sharp, have excellent hooking characteristics. Both gar and pilchards, like mullet, are also fished as cut baits in strip form on single hooks, but the oily flesh of mullet and pilchards has more attraction.

Garfish and small mullet also make effective trolling baits for offshore gamefish. They can be rigged to swim enticingly or to splash along the surface like a fleeing baitfish.

With the notable exception of pilchards which are generally sold frozen individually (IQF style) or in blocks, fish regard most frozen baits with less enthusiasm than something that is perfectly fresh. There is no fresher bait than a live bait which for offshore anglers usually means securing some live yellowtail and slimy mackerel prior to fishing.

These can be located over shallow reefs and around structures like navigation beacons. Small baited hooks fished on light line are effective, especially if used with a berley mix of soaked bread and sardines. In deep water, baitfish can be located with

Pilchards rigged whole and as 'chunks'

an echo sounder and will respond to multi-hook baitfish jigs. As one fish goes for a jig, others compete with it, and several baitfish can be boated at once.

Live-bait requires careful handling with wet hands to avoid it being fatally stressed before it can be used. A supply of clean, well oxygenated water is necessary and dedicated offshore fishing boats often have special live-wells with recirculating water systems for that purpose. However, a plastic garbage bin can suffice, provided the water is changed frequently.

Bigger species such as Striped tuna and Mackerel tuna can be bridle-rigged and trolled live for marlin or big Yellowfin tuna, or rigged whole as dead baits, and drifted down deep for sharks.

Inshore Baits

Because some offshore species also frequent inshore waters many offshore baits are suitable here also. The abundance of bait close to the coast also means you can obtain fresh or live bait quickly and be fishing as soon as you arrive.

Inshore fish respond to some estuary baits too, one of which is 'pudding'. This is a mixture containing bread, salami, sardines and cheese and an almost endless variety of other ingredients. This minced mixture is kneaded into a pudding consistency and moulded onto the hook like putty.

Pudding suits bream, drummer, garfish, yellowtail and sweep, and will also occasionally take snapper and morwong. The traditional bait for morwong is peeled prawns, but as these get a bit pricey, fish baits spun out with a bit of pudding can be more affordable.

Other estuary baits that work on inshore grounds are yabbies, green nippers, cockles and blood worms - if you can keep them away from rubbish fish such as mado and trumpeter.

Of all the baits you can purchase for inshore fishing, WA pilchards are undoubtedly the most popular, and can be fished whole on ganged hooks, cut into chunks or mashed for berley.

Baits that are naturally abundant inshore are garfish, yellowtail, slimy mackerel – and squid. These fish make excellent strip or live baits and can be line caught on small baited hooks or baitjigs, although squid respond best to special squid jigs. There are many types of squid jigs, but none as reliable for the casual

Garfish rigged whole on ganged hooks and as strip bait.

Mullet strip baits – the large bean sinker has heavy leader looped through it and can be slid up and down the rig as desired, holding its set position by friction. The small running ball sinker provides casting weight and a slow sink rate for 'floater' baits in white water or a moderate run.

amateur as the 'prawn' style, sometimes called the 'Yo-Zuri' type.

Baitfish congregate over shallow reefs, around harbour entrances, docks, and navigation beacons and usually bite best on a rising tide. Good squid water is generally 2 to 5 m deep, very clear, and where sand runs into reef, or any sudden change in bottom material occurs. The jig is cast over the weed and reef, allowed to sink close to the bottom then retrieved in a series of slow lifts and drops. When you feel a slight increase in weight, simply lift the rod tip and the squid will become impaled on the lure's forward facing prongs.

Squid can be used as bait in strips cut from the hood or cape of the main body or, in autumn, a deadly snapper bait is to impale the complete head and tentacles on a suitable sized hook, and drift it un-weighted down a berley trail near exposed reef and a wash area.

Berley can attract fish from some distance and hold them in the area immediately beneath or down current from your boat. Good berleys are chicken pellets, boiled wheat, a mix of bread, poultry mash and tuna oil, or mashed up fish of species with oily flesh - like tuna, pilchards, or mullet.

If you are intending to use live bait, you'll need to set up a system to keep those baits alive. This can be done simply with a large plastic bucket or small garbage bin. If you change the water frequently and increase the oxygen content

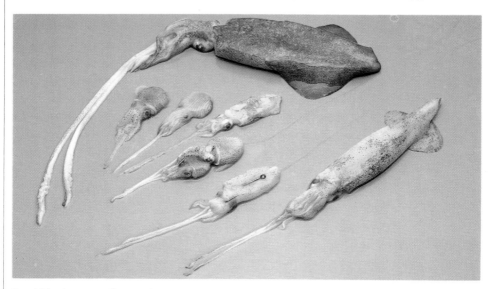

Squid baits – small squid can be rigged whole or doubled up as shown. Larger squid are best cut up into strips and the dark skin peeled away to present an attractive white bait.

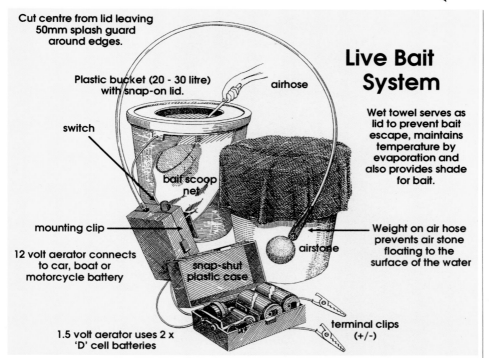

Cut centre from lid leaving 50mm splash guard around edges.

Plastic bucket (20 - 30 litre) with snap-on lid.

airhose

switch

Live Bait System

Wet towel serves as lid to prevent bait escape, maintains temperature by evaporation and also provides shade for bait.

bait scoop net

mounting clip

Weight on air hose prevents air stone floating to the surface of the water

12 volt aerator connects to car, boat or motorcycle battery

airstone

snap-shut plastic case

1.5 volt aerator uses 2 x 'D' cell batteries

terminal clips (+/-)

---

of the water with an aerator, you can keep baits alive for much of the day. A system which fully exchanges the water is preferable but not necessary. If you've timed your run right and are over the right spot, you won't have to keep those baits alive long anyway.

When fishing close to the rocks or in behind a beach, it sometimes pays to have some standby beach and rock baits like cunjevoi, beach worms or cabbage. Snapper, mulloway and drummer frequently prowl the drop-offs, a mere cast behind the surfline, or over shallow reefs which might be hard to reach from the shore and don't get much fishing pressure.

Beach and Rock Baits

One of the most common questions asked by fishermen interested in getting into beach or rock-fishing is "What type of bait should I use?" While bait selection is critical to success, freshness and suitability to the species being sought is also very important.

There are many different baits that will catch fish for the beach fisherman and also work on the rocks. These can be baits you can catch or collect, or some which must be bought.

Being able to catch your bait has several advantages, not the least of which is economy. Self-caught or gathered bait is fresh, it can be fun to catch and it's also a way to involve the kids and make fishing more of a family affair.

Baits You Can Catch or Gather

Cunjevoi: This brown rubbery growth on the inter-tidal rocks looks like a plant but is in fact an animal and one of the family of sea-squirts. It is safest to gather cunje during calm seas at low tide. Use a strong bladed knife to cut through the leathery casing and remove the soft pink inner flesh, or as some anglers do, use a small hoe to chip the whole growth from the rocks and clean the flesh out later. This bait is excellent for black and silver drummer, luderick, bream, groper and trevally. Even snapper fall for it occasionally.

Above: Octopus makes excellent bait, either whole for big mulloway or snapper, or in strips and tentacle sections for smaller fish like bream, flathead and teraglin.
Left: Cabbage Weed grows plentifully along flat, ocean-front rocks and is the favoured bait for ocean run blackfish.

Crabs: Red or Black crabs are the most commonly used. Red crabs are caught at low tide by going through patches of red weed and under ledges with your hands. This is not for the faint hearted and can involve being nipped by crabs or eels, so light gloves can be a help. Black crabs are easy to collect with a crab spear from under ledges or between rocks, anywhere from the low to high tide marks.

This activity requires you to have your back to the sea, so never do it when the seas are rough, as red weed patches and ledges are also where the most wave action takes place. Crabs are best fished as floating baits in gutters, or on the bottom with minimal lead. They are a prime bait for bream, groper and snapper.

Squid: Can be caught at many rock locations or even in estuaries prior to a rock-fishing trip. Use a prawn-type squid jig to catch them by casting out, letting it sink and winding it back in a series of slow lifts. When a squid takes and you feel some extra weight, just lift against it to hook up. Squid can be rigged whole if very small, but the hoods or tentacles of larger calamari can be slit into strip baits. For snapper, it sometimes pays to rig the whole head and tentacles on a 6/0.

Octopus: These can be difficult to catch from the rocks but small specimens can sometimes be found in rock pools - be careful to avoid the deadly blue-ringed octopus however as it's bite can be lethal. Both octopus and squid are good tough baits able to withstand the attacks of small pickers. It helps to skin the bait, exposing the white flesh beneath.

Fish-baits: Most rock and beach locations have a good supply of small baitfish which can be caught and used either live, or cut up into strips or fillets. Yellowtail, tailor, small whiting and garfish all frequent the foamy wash areas of beaches and rock platforms, with slimy mackerel a bonus for the rock fisherman. All these baits will attract bream, snapper, tailor, salmon, flathead and mulloway.

Beach Worms: Require some practice before they can be caught. The worms are located by the use of a stink-bait. This can be any old fish frames or such on a string which is dragged along a foot or so inside the wave line. As the waves recede, the odour of the bait draws the worms out of the sand and you can spot them by the tiny 'V' made as the receding water parts around their protruding heads. It involves teasing the worm from the sand with a finger-bait of pipi or fish flesh, then seizing it from behind with the other hand before it can zip back into the sand again. Some anglers use peg-jawed long nose pliers but these tend to break the worm up, killing it prematurely.

Fished whole and live in a bunch, these are deadly on mulloway and big bream. For whiting, you can cut the worms into sections as you need them and feed the whole length of the piece onto a small, long-shanked hook.

Pipis: These smooth-shelled bivalves (called cockles in South Australia) are found between high and low tide marks on clean, less trampled beaches. Sometimes you can detect them by a flat, circular mound in the sand, but more often than not they are buried deeper than that and the way you gather them is fun for adults and kids alike. Choose a spot where the waves wash up about ankle to knee deep, then start to twist your feet back and forth like the silly dance craze of a generation or so back. As you twist, your feet will sink into the waterlogged sand and if there are any pipis there, you'll feel them with your bare feet. Just reach down and pick them up, it's that simple. (Doing this on metropolitan beaches however is regrettably inadvisable due to the risk of broken glass and discarded syringes.)

To rig them, split the shell open with a strong knife and remove the firm yellow-white flesh. This can be cut into thin strips for whiting, larger pieces for bream, or several slipped whole over a 7/0 hook or similar for jewfish.

Baits You'll Have to Buy

Pilchards: These are one of the most popular baits around and are commonly

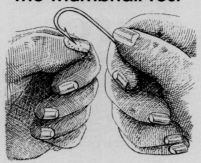

The Thumbnail Test

To test how sharp a hook is, drag it across your thumbnail. A sharp hook will catch and start to dig in. If the hook just skids off, it isn't sharp enough.

The test is a good one because many fish mouths are at least as hard as human fingernails and if you're to get a hook-up, the hook first has to take hold.

used with success from beaches and rocks, both as bait and berley. The most readily available are the blue pilchards trucked in from Western Australia. These are either block frozen or I.Q.F. (Individually Quick Frozen) which are more expensive, but less wasteful.

Fish them whole or in halves on linked hooks, or cut into strips or chunks. They can be fished under a bobby cork, or on the bottom, as their oily flesh attracts fish from quite some distance, or cast and retrieved in much the same way as you would a whole garfish bait. The fish they'll take from the beach or rocks include bream, snapper, mulloway, flathead, salmon, tailor, and kingfish.

Garfish: You can use the smaller slender River garfish but most anglers prefer the stouter, firm-bodied Sea garfish, believing them to be a better bait. Some bait shops stock garfish in frozen packets, but it's better to buy them by the kilo from the markets, fresh and unfrozen. Rig them the same as for pilchards for the same species. Garfish have the advantage of being able to withstand repeated casting.

Lures

Man has been successfully fishing with lures since ancient times. The search for food provided the developmental impetus for early designs and the predatory nature of many fish did the rest.

Reasons Why

Fish strike these artificial offerings out of a sense that they are some form of food but it was the presentation of the lure, not its substance which was the essence of the deception. It remains the same today.

Fish instincts that lead it to strike a lure involve more than just hunger. Territorial considerations provide an often irresistible catalyst for a fish to strike. The lure is seen as an intruder in the three dimensional zone some fish claim as their own. The Murray cod is a prime example.

Competition between feeding fish is another reason. When schooling fish are actively feeding, aggression overrides natural caution. Tuna, kingfish and kahawai are much easier to take on lures in schools than when encountered as solo fish.

Outright curiosity is sometimes the undoing of fish that do not really fit the predatory role. Often they become hooked when venturing too close to investigate a lure.

In today's consumer society, the available lures form a cast of thousands. There are lures for every conceivable fishing situation, every fisherman's whim and every fish mood. When these variations are multiplied by the range of sizes and colours in popular use, the total list of lures would need a tackle box the size of a house.

Materials

Lures are made from metal, wood, hard plastic, soft plastic and feathers. Each has advantages and disadvantages which de-

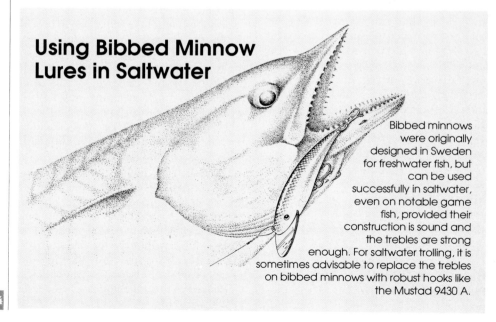

Using Bibbed Minnow Lures in Saltwater

Bibbed minnows were originally designed in Sweden for freshwater fish, but can be used successfully in saltwater, even on notable game fish, provided their construction is sound and the trebles are strong enough. For saltwater trolling, it is sometimes advisable to replace the trebles on bibbed minnows with robust hooks like the Mustad 9430 A.

Lure Fishing with Trebles

3567 or 9430A

9430A

3565

73028

3567

The treble hooks on lures are the most vulnerable part of the rig and should be replaced regularly. Also, the correct choice of treble must be made for the lure to be used to its best advantage.

For example, the large metal jig in the drawing needs a robust treble, so too does the hexagonal bar lure designed for long casts and fast retrieves from land-based platforms by anglers seeking saltwater pelagics like tuna and kingfish.

The choice for this pair would be the Mustad 3567, or 9430A if used on heavy tackle. The minnow could also wear a pair of Mustad 9430A trebles if the lure was intended for heavy saltwater use.

For the small lures, the 3565 series would probably suffice, while a size 10, 73028 pattern should fill the bill nicely for the little 7 g casting jig.

However, the overriding factor with choice of trebles is the weight of tackle the lure will be used with.

termine both the performance character-istics of the lure and the fishing situations it is suitable for.

Metal lures provide casting weight for long distance presentation and a fast sink rate so anglers can fish any water level between top and bottom. Compared to wood and plastic lures, their action is min-imal.

Factors which determine the action of metal lures include; shapes that react with water pressure, rod action imparted by the angler, and sheer speed.

Wood is an easy lure making material to work with, and with few exceptions provides a degree of buoyancy which gives a distinctive action. The majority of wood lures are elongated and fish-like 'minnow' types fitted with metal or plastic bibs. This 'bib' makes the lure dive and

together with the buoyancy and shape of the body sets up the basis for the lure's action.

Lures made from hard plastics and two part foams have slightly different perfor-mance characteristics to those made from timber. Injection moulding processes make it easy to produce hard plastic lures quickly and simply. Soft plastic lures are generally made in a split-moulding pro-cess.

Types and Uses

Sling Jigs
This group includes high speed types such as WK Arrows, Jensen Pirks, Stingsildas and their lookalikes, as well as the celebrated Half by a Quarter from the

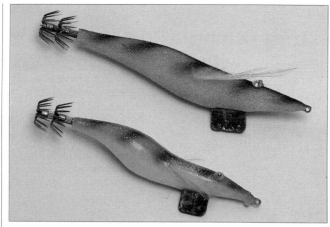

Left: Prawn-type squid jigs such as these, though expensive have rapidly become the dominant design in popular use. They are best retrieved with a slow sink and draw technique

NSW Central Coast and the tuna slugs evolved in Moreton Bay.

These have little built-in action, relying on high speed retrieves to induce that fish-catching wobble. Fast reels are essential - and these lures are at their best when surface fish are actively feeding. The technique is to cast it amongst the splashes and wind like hell.

Pelagic fish will often feed exclusively on a certain type and size of baitfish, depending on what is prevalent at the time. Success then often depends on lures matching the dimensions of the baitfish, especially the length.

Deep Jigs

These metal lures generally have a little more built-in action and are bottom jigged over reef. Bottom jigging is simply dropping lures straight down to the bottom and retrieving them in a variety of ways - flat-strap, sink and draw, or as erratically as you can. A sure-fire kingfish technique, deep jigging also works on many other surface and bottom fish.

Lures representative of this range include the Irons, Mavericks, Jensen Pirks and Grim Reapers.

Spoons

These are effective in both fresh and saltwater. They can be cast, jigged or trolled and they're cheap. Perhaps the best known spoons are the Australian made Wonder Wobbler and ABU's Toby. If trolled or retrieved too quickly, they will gyrate and produce significant line twist,

Skirted lures are suitable for billfish or tuna. This one is a 'pusher' style

so always use a quality swivel. They are best retrieved in a slow, irregular motion.

Thread-Ons

The concept of the thread-on lure is simply that the line is passed through the lure body to tie the hook on. Thread-on lures are used in both salt and freshwater. Saltwater examples include skirted billfish lures, and the basic feather jig trolled for smaller pelagics - and used to spin for mulloway when rivers are in flood.

Some of our most effective trout lures are thread-on types. Baltic Minnows and the Tasmanian Devils are among Australia's most used lures. A new floating thread-on called the Jensen Killroy has added the attraction of minnow performance to the genre. Killroys and Tassie Devils work best when trolled some distance behind the boat, especially over gently sloping banks in large freshwater impoundments holding trout.

When using Tassie types and Baltic Minnows a small rubber buffer in front of the hook will protect the knot and make a world of difference to the lure's action.

Bladed Spinners

Bladed spinners are freshwater lures which work better in rivers than lakes. They range in size from huge 'aeroplane' spinners - once used extensively for Murray cod prior to the advent of wobbling lures - down to some tiny ones with fingernail-sized blades. Small, stream size spinners such as Celtas, ABU Droppens, Mepps and Jensen Insects are specialist small water trout lures which will also take silver and Macquarie perch, redfin and bass.

Small bladed spinners work best around rapids and where there is a moderate flow. The whirring blade has a sonic effect and its flashing may simulate the flash of baitfish scales. The combined effect is very effective on feeding fish.

Bladed spinners can cause line twist if trolled for any distance, so a quality swivel should be used to keep this problem under control.

Spinner Baits

Not widely recognised yet, these lures are the coming thing - especially when fishing impoundments for Murray cod, golden perch and redfin. The lure has a single lead-head jig hook, dressed with a many-legged rubber skirt and carrying one or more rotating blades mounted on an integral wireframe. These are basically a casting lure with considerable anti-snag qualities. An effective use is to cast them amongst cover, and after they've sunk to the bottom, commence a slow retrieve.

Lead Head Jigs

Lead head jigs come either dressed with bucktail or similar fibre, or as blank hooks to which you can add various soft plastic tails. The most well known type is the

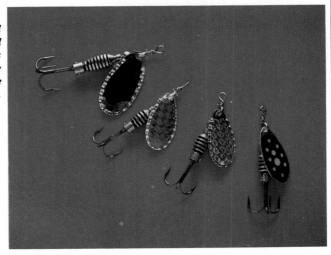

Right: Small bladed spinners are best used in freshwater lures around rapids where there is a moderate flow.

double tail Mister Twister popular in flathead fishing.

Like spoons, lead head jigs are versatile but are at their best when yo-yoed or hopped slowly on the bottom. This takes a degree of patience, difficult for anglers accustomed to faster lures, but the fact that small lead head jigs are part of military survival kits says something for their effectiveness.

A reason for the success which lead head jigs have on flathead is their ability to be slowly jinked across the bottom. This puts them on a collision course with a flathead, a confrontation is forced, and the outcome is often a hook up. Another successful example of the type is the Vibrotail which works well on tidal water barramundi.

Poppers

The slanting and cupped faces of these poppers from Rebel make them suitable for trolling or high speed retrieval. Trolling poppers such as these is a good exploratory technique when looking for species such as kingfish in temperate waters over reefs – or trevally in the tropics around islands and fringing coral shelves.

Surface Lures

Surface lures come in various types and with peculiar names. These are: poppers, fizzers, stick baits and paddlers, all of which reflect the way each lure works.

Poppers can be skippers or bloopers. Skippers are high speed lures, at their best when large predatory fish are rampaging through baitfish schools on the surface. The lure has a slanted face and tapered front to facilitate a rapid retrieve - or trolling at a fair clip. Trolling skipping poppers is a great way to locate trevally, queenfish and Spanish mackerel.

In contrast, bloopers have large cupped faces designed to catch water and air when moved with a sweep of the rod tip. The resulting 'bloop' explains the name. Bloopers can draw predatory fish from considerable distances but require a patient approach and slow and deliberate rodwork.

Fizzers are cigar shaped lures with small propellers mounted at either end. Like bloopers, they require painstaking rodwork. The secret is to use the rod to move the lure just enough to kick the propellers over, pause, then repeat the process. A practiced hand at 'fizzing' may bring a lure to life a dozen times without having to retrieve line.

Fizzers work best in freshwater, on barramundi and sooty grunter in the tropics, bass in temperate freshwaters and some alpine lakes for trout at night. Heddon's Tiny torpedo is an enduring fizzer type.

Stick baits are fizzers without the propellers. They focus on a lure fishing truism - the less fittings a lure has, the more skill is required to use it. To manipulate a stick bait properly requires experience, but they can be deadly on barramundi encountered over shallow mudflats.

Paddlers are so called because of the way special fittings make them behave. Heddon's Crazy Crawler and the Arbogast Jitterbug are prime examples which produce explosive strikes from bass on summer evenings. They can be worked with straight retrieves or with a little judicious rodwork, especially just after the lure lands. Making the lure simulate a stunned insect is sound bass-fishing strategy.

Trolling with Skirted Lures

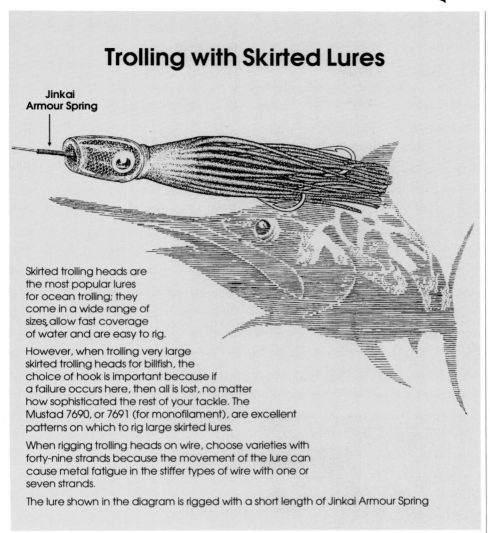

Jinkai
Armour Spring

Skirted trolling heads are
the most popular lures
for ocean trolling; they
come in a wide range of
sizes, allow fast coverage
of water and are easy to rig.

However, when trolling very large
skirted trolling heads for billfish, the
choice of hook is important because if
a failure occurs here, then all is lost, no matter
how sophisticated the rest of your tackle. The
Mustad 7690, or 7691 (for monofilament), are excellent
patterns on which to rig large skirted lures.

When rigging trolling heads on wire, choose varieties with
forty-nine strands because the movement of the lure can
cause metal fatigue in the stiffer types of wire with one or
seven strands.

The lure shown in the diagram is rigged with a short length of Jinkai Armour Spring

Bibless Lures

Bibless lures have slender frontal areas, allowing them to be drawn through the water with minimum resistance, and hence at speed. They are also very responsive to short rips of the rod when used in a sink and draw fashion.

They have a tight vibrating action which increases tempo with speed. This makes them popular for high speed trolling in tropical offshore waters. Many informed bluewater veterans now use them in preference to skirted lures. Prominent examples of offshore bibless lures are the Masta Blasta and Casta Blasta, designed by well-known angler Malcolm Florence.

Another type of bibless lure contains metal spheres in sonic chambers. These rattle when the lure vibrates and the type has become known by the generic name of the 'rattling spot'. That name actually belongs to an original of the type made by the Cotton Cordell company in the USA.

Barramundi are the fish that put 'spot' type lures on the map. Initially this came about through 'spots' (which are sinking lures) being lowered and jiggled amongst snags and rock bars where barra often hole up when not actively feeding. This technique resulted in strikes where other methods with other lures failed. From there, use of the lures snowballed, with various spot-type lures used widely in normal cast and retrieve fishing and even for trolling.

Minnows and Plugs

Minnows and plugs are far and away the most popular lure type in current use. Their body shapes vary from elongated to squat, and they are mostly buoyant, floating at rest and diving when moved through the water. Some are designed to sink at a controlled rate.

Both types rely on the bib to plane the lure down as motion is applied. The inherent buoyancy of the lure material provides a counteracting force, and this resistance accounts for much of the lure's action.

The live baitfish or 'shimmy' action is reproduced in the longish minnow type of lure of which the Finnish made Rapala and Nils Master range are outstanding examples. Baitfish actions are appropriate to saltwater fishing, and barramundi - whatever the location.

The slower, wider wobble of the 'crippled fish' action is more pronounced in plug types which are best for inland fishing. Legendary inland lures such as the Flopy and Flatfish provide perfect examples of this lazy action that works so well on Murray cod and golden perch. Australian made lures are increasingly well represented in this group.

The shape, size and angle of the bib has a major bearing on the lure's action. The greater the angle of the bib to the direction of the pull, the greater its resistance on the water and the shallower it will run. True deep-runners are identified by large, flattened bibs. The effective and popular Mann's 'depth-plus' range have such a bib design which provides deep running characteristics to both minnow and plug types.

Fundamental rigging differences exist between minnows and plugs. Plugs often come fitted with an articulated tow point mounted on the bib. A conventional 'hard' knot will suffice in all cases where this kind of arrangement exists. Many minnow types have fixed towing links fitted to the front of the lure body. For optimum action these must be rigged with a non-slip loop knot. A snap or split ring may act as an alternative but can unbalance lighter lures.

Priorities

Any fish that eats other fish will eat a lure. With that sweeping statement we've probably included at least 90% of the fish kingdom as potential candidates for lurefishers. However the real essence of lure fishing comes from not only knowing the characteristics and performance envelopes of the various kinds, but also some knowledge of the priorities of lure fishing.

The priorities of lure performance are: running depth, speed, action, size, visual contrast, shape and colour. Some anglers put colour at the top of the list, however fish may not perceive colours as we do; and it is proven that colours wash out as depth increases. Aspects of presentation, which will be covered in the strategy sections of this book also have a critical bearing on fishing results, regardless of the lure type.

This Murray cod fell for the strong action and fat profile of this deep diving plug

*Sometimes the rewards of successful lure fishing
can be spectacular, like this 12 kg kingfish*

4

STRATEGIES
FOR
SUCCESS

Estuaries & Bays

Temperate Zone

Our east coast estuaries and bays host a good variety of fish, some easy to catch, others requiring patience and a little more expertise. Most are seasonal and even if available for much of the year will have a peak month or two. Observation, good use of tides to fish and gather bait, and employing the most suitable tackle and strategy for each species achieves top results.

Tides dominate fishing in the estuaries and bays. They affect the movement and feeding pattern of the fish and the availability of bait. Spring tides (which have the maximum rise and fall) reach a maximum height of about 2 m on the New South Wales coast. This allows the fish additional feeding areas, consequently making them harder to locate. On the credit side, the extreme spring lows, (sometimes zero tides) uncover vast areas of weed beds and flats, allowing baits to be more easily gathered. Neap tides (which have less rise and fall) are best because of the slower water movement and the fact that the fish are more concentrated.

A making or rising tide is generally favoured for most species but they can bite strongly on the ebb as well. Choice of a suitable tide for particular species at different locations is arrived at through local knowledge, enquiry and experience.

Study an estuary at low tide from a high vantage point to get a idea of the layout and to spot any likely boating problems as the tide advances. This is the time to check out exposed weed beds, as well as sand and mud flats for bait. If you can, buy a map that shows the water depths and any other helpful information about the waterway.

Wind is often a problem to overcome, especially in open bays. Estuaries usually have a number of arms and channels however, which are sheltered from the prevailing wind by undulating shores, hills or even buildings. When fishing on the drift, places can be found where the wind has minimum effect. A light wind blowing against a strong tide may slow a drifting boat to an ideal pace, whereas one

When the wind and tide oppose each other, this can slow the drift which is good for flathead fishing.

Yo-yoing on drift for flathead

Sinker stirs up sand on each drop

that blows from the same direction accelerates the boat's movement.

When fishing from a boat which is anchored fore and aft, face the bow into the wind as this will avoid any waves breaking over the stern. In calmer water you can face the bow in the direction of passing boats to combat their wash as they pass.

Drifting is a time-proven strategy, used mainly to catch flathead, but sometimes adapted to whiting or to locate bream. Several lines are trailed from a boat drifted side-on to the current or breeze, the craft being kept under control and on course by using the oars. This allows the baits to cover the full length of a channel or bay and gives the fish a better chance to find

them. When a few fish are encountered, the boat can be anchored or you can drift over the same spot again.

Another ploy used for flathead in deep water is to yo-yo from an anchored or drifted boat. To yo-yo, a heavy sinker is used to keep the line vertical while the bait is jigged up and down to entice the fish.

Handlines should not be overlooked, especially when fishing from a boat. They are ideal for flathead, bream, whiting, mulloway, hairtail, blue swimmer and mud crabs, and for catching bait such as yellowtail.

An excellent strategy when fishing tidal channels for bream is to use a handline with a 3 m trace rigged below a channel

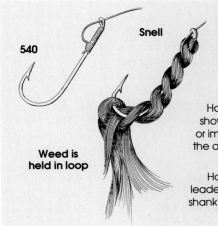

540

Snell

Weed is held in loop

Baiting with Weed

Various weeds are used to catch luderick and putting them on the hook is quite an art. A popular hook for presenting weed baits is the Mustad 3331 Sneck because its square gape holds the weed very well.

However, a Mustad 540 with a turned down eye is shown in the diagram this allows the use of a simple or improved snell. This method secures the hook with the additional benefit of creating a clasp to hold the weed against the shank of the hook.

Having passed the weed through the bulge in the leader under the eye, the weed is wound around the shank and secured with a tie in the curve of the hook.

Fishing with live bait such as yabbies can result in fast clean hookups like this on bream. The take is positive and the removal of hooks easier if you are alert enough to set the hooks quickly. This is especially important on small fish which should be released. This large specimen is bound for the table.

sinker. The trace and about 6 m of mainline is fed into the current before the sinker is allowed to slide down the line. This positions the bait well down stream but with very free movement of the trace. This lack of resistance when the line is pulled through the sinker's large holes means few fish are missed. The technique catches lots of bream, whiting and sometimes luderick.

Bream feature largely in estuary catches both from shore and from boats, but tactics vary with different locations and types of water. When fishing from a boat in fast flowing water, a 2 m trace gives better results than something shorter. A number of rods can also be used from a boat. The bait is cast upstream against the flow of the tide so it can be washed along by the current. This gives the bream more chance to find it before it settles roughly at right angles to the boat.

Bream will hook themselves, against a lightly set drag or ratchet during the fast moving spring tides, but are more timid in slower moving water. Bream love oysters, so anchoring in a channel adjacent to an oyster lease on the ebbing tide can pay dividends as the fish move into deeper water.

Berley (used judiciously) will attract fish. Luderick anglers regard it as being almost as essential as bait, the basic ingredients for luderick berley being finely chopped weed and sand. A range of commercial mixtures suitable for bream include chicken pellets and varying percentages of tuna oil and pilchard oil. Homemade recipes are most popular however. These usually consist of boiled wheat with a number of additives. A berley of minced fish frames, pilchards or sub-standard bait helps to entice not only bream, but also flathead, mulloway and hairtail.

The scope is wide for lure fishing in estuaries, tailor being the obvious target. Diving terns and gulls, or even a single bird circling, can indicate their presence. Try lure casting around patches of floating

Small black crabs gathered from under rocks at low tide are excellent bait for big bream

weed as there is a good chance that tailor could be seeking bait fish which might be sheltering under it.

Surprisingly, flathead often chase lures in preference to bait. They are caught by this means from the shoreline at both high and low tide, but a boat will give you access to their entire habitat.

Bream also respond to (small) lures which are cast from the shore and slowly retrieved. Spinning from a boat or canoe around oyster leases and other vicinities where bream feed or shelter also gets results. Flathead and mulloway will also take lures at night, in illuminated water around bridges.

You can utilise floods to catch mulloway, which congregate around the mouths of creeks and estuaries to feed on fish being moved out with the fresh water.

The majority of estuary anglers have their sights set on bream, flathead, whiting or luderick, but often, they disregard a wealth of other species, such as leatherjacket, garfish, mullet, tailor, flounder and even big fish like kingfish and mulloway. Having an open mind and some hard local knowledge can result in your estuary fishing being very worthwhile indeed.

Whiting Strategy in Port Phillip Bay

Every Port Phillip Bay whiting fisherman worth his salt ignores the small sand whiting and concentrates on the famous King George whiting. Catches can be in the dozens, even the hundreds on a good day.

Use a mussel rake to get mussels from man-made structures like jetties and channel pylons. The mussels provide both bait, and shell for berley.

Whiting shelter in weed beds and amongst light reef, but feed over adjacent sand patches. Sometimes these are visible from the surface, at other times a glass bottomed viewer is helpful in locating them. Having located such a spot, the boat is anchored fore and aft to prevent it swinging. Should the spot be productive, shore marks or other fixed alignments are taken to ensure a quick return to the spot another day. However, should the spot yield no fish after fifteen minutes or so, it's a good idea to move on until the fish are found.

Whiting in tidal areas tend to be larger, and have wider bait preferences. Squid and cuttlefish replace mussels and other molluscs and hook sizes increase to No 4 and larger.

Mussels are a soft bait requiring a sharp knife to trim them neatly. Rigged with a small red bead or length of red spaghetti tubing, they are deadly baits on whiting.

Positioning Boat Using Shore Marks

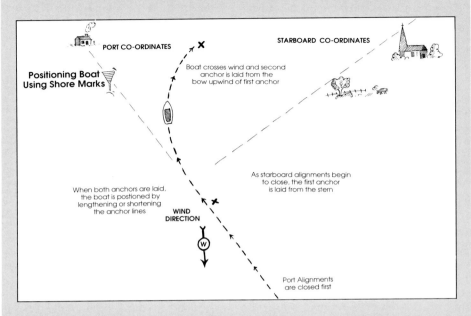

PORT CO-ORDINATES

STARBOARD CO-ORDINATES

Positioning Boat Using Shore Marks

Boat crosses wind and second anchor is laid from the bow upwind of first anchor

As starboard alignments begin to close, the first anchor is laid from the stern

When both anchors are laid, the boat is postioned by lengthening or shortening the anchor lines

WIND DIRECTION

Port Alignments are closed first

Accuracy in positioning the boat on productive marks is a strategy which separates anglers who consistently return with big catches from those who don't.

When approaching a mark with a known set of co-ordinates, the alignment nearest the direction from which the wind is blowing is closed first. As the second set of co-ordinates close, the first anchor is laid from the stern and the line paid out. Still under power, the boat swings across the wind and lays the second anchor upwind from the first.

With the second anchor fast from the bow and the boat laying back dead on the line, the first anchor line is retrieved from the stern until the boat is firmly positioned between the two anchors.

NB: This fore and aft anchoring method only suits relatively sheltered waters. In open waters or where strong winds and swells combine, it can be hazardous.

Baiting with Soft Shelled Clams

For bream, soft shelled clams are baited on the hook, shell and all. A metal barbeque or meat skewer is handy to place in the eye of an up or down-turned hook to push it through the bivalve.

❶ First insert the point of the hook beside the hinge and push it in as far as you can.

❷ Next, use your skewer to push the rest of the hook inside the clam so that the whole of the gape emerges from the shell.

❸ The bait is completed by pulling back on the trace so that the point of the hook overlaps the shell.

Tropical Zone

The one simple strategy for tropical Australian estuaries and bays is to have your own boat.

Without a boat of some kind, your choices are narrowed down to more open waters. Without a boat, the mangrove regions are beyond your reach.

This is why so many travellers take car-toppers, canoes and even inflatables along. These increase the fishing opportunities in sheltered estuary waters and winding mangrove creeks. They should not be aimed at the deceptively mild-looking northern oceans, which have complex and extensive tidal ranges. Wind strengths in the north are variable and advice should always be sought from locals before setting out on any new area.

Lack of a boat need not stop successful fishing. Harbour walls and rocks at centres such as Mackay, Bowen, Townsville, Mourilyan, Cairns, Cooktown and Darwin, produce splendid fishing for everything from fingermark and barramundi to trevally, queenfish and mackerel.

Jetties also attract fish at night and are widely patronised by locals and visitors who enjoy the tropical evenings under the lights, or in some cases, the stars.

An advantage to the more civilised fishing around the towns is that it's easy to check out. Tides in these places are the key, and a rising tide or even a high tide in a harbour at first light or late afternoon will find the local fishermen in business.

Queensland

Cooktown provides a good example. Locals will be found on the wharf there at first light on those rising tides, seeking (and often catching) queenfish, mackerel, golden trevally and barramundi.

The estuaries of major rivers can be examined best on a very low tide, to establish the pattern of channels and deeper holes. The rising tide will then bring the food, primarily prawns and baitfish, that starts fish feeding.

As a general rule, the first deep hole inside a creek or river mouth, or the first mangrove junction onto which a rising tide strikes, provide the logical places to drift a bait or cast a lure. Running channels

Gutters which drain tidal mudflats often hold baitfish and prawns which attract barramundi to feed on a falling tide. Fish may patrol the deep water at the mouths of these gutters and creeklets, or in some cases, even 'camp' right in the gutter, bottling the food up and preventing its escape to deeper water.

For this reason, it may pay to either spin or troll these areas, but a cautious approach and some exploratory casts up into the gutters in the early stages of the tide fall may be advisable.

Tropical estuaries are often loaded with well defined features like sand and mud-banks, deep holes on the outside of bends, and snags. All these can indicate probable fish locations

between the deeper holes can be worked for grunter (javelin fish) threadfin salmon, bream, whiting and even flathead - though flathead become scarcer as you move further north. It is worth noting that an incoming tide may also produce larger species, including queenfish, barramundi and school mackerel. Trevally are always possible.

The important thing is to stay alert for bait movements, as a patch of bait often attracts larger company.

In calm estuary water where rays can be seen working, stirring sand from the bottom, other predators may be following. These may range anywhere between barracuda and flathead.

One eye must be kept on the height of the tide, which can be substantial. Sharks and crocodiles use the tides in the same way fish do, and may be attracted to places where food scents are present. Those people who are observant and careful are quite safe. In fact the safety rules are fundamentally the same as those the fisherman applies at home!

The Northern Territory

The Territory's coastline is vast, extending for over 3000 km. Although there is excellent fishing in the many bays and estuaries along this coast, access is limited by a number of factors.

The seasonal weather pattern and its effect on roads has a significant bearing on access, particularly to remote locations. In the Top End, there is no summer

or winter, but two dominant climatic periods known as the Wet and Dry seasons.

The Wet occurs from December to April and is hot and humid, moderated often by cloudy periods and tropical downpours. The Dry is from May to September with fine, dry conditions and mostly cloudless skies. During the transition from the Dry to the Wet, the humidity increases, with regular afternoon and evening thunderstorms.

Many Territory rivers flood during the wet season and fishing is restricted to locations accessible by all-weather roads. Often, the only way to get to remote bays and estuaries is by sea or air travel.

Access is further restricted by the need to obtain permission before visiting many areas. In respect of Aboriginal lands, a permit must be obtained from the relevant Aboriginal land council acting on behalf of the traditional owners. For pastoral leases, permission must be obtained from the manager or lessee. A number of pastoral properties have formalised arrangements for public access to fishing spots. In some cases, this access will be conditional upon payment of a fee. For detailed information on access to Aboriginal lands or pastoral properties, contact the NT Department of Primary Industry and Fisheries, GPO Box 990 Darwin NT 0801.

Understanding and working the tides can be critical to successful Territory fishing. In some locations and for some species of fish, the best fishing occurs on a particular movement of tide and at a specific time during that tide. Some species concentrate their feeding for short periods during spring tides when the tidal range is several metres, others are more easily caught during neap tides, when the range may be less than 1 m.

Barramundi can be caught in the mangrove-lined creeks all year round, but the best time is during the transitional period between the Dry and Wet seasons. In salt water, barra fishing is best a couple of hours either side of a low spring tide, especially around snags, creek junctions, submerged rock bars, tidal run-offs where there is a colour change in the water, and across clear, shallow mudflats.

Although the creeks offer the best chance of catching a barramundi, bigger fish are sometimes encountered in open bays near isolated rock outcrops and well away from creeks.

Threadfin salmon and mangrove jacks are often caught side by side with barramundi in creeks. Both will take lures or baits, but sometimes a live bait is needed for barramundi.

Northern Territory estuaries and bays also offer excellent fishing for some reef species. Golden snapper, also known as 'fingermark bream', are mostly taken on fresh bait, but will also strike lures, particularly in shallow water or creeks and as a rule, on an incoming tide.

Estuary cod turn up anytime and anywhere, scarlet sea perch are sometimes caught in deep water and small whiting inhabit sandy creeks in good numbers.

Pelagics like queenfish and various trevallies patrol rocky headlands and sandbars most of the year, but Spanish mackerel and longtail (Northern bluefin) tuna are seasonal, moving inshore from May to September. Cobia and sailfish are spasmodic.

Above: Queenfish will take all manner of lures and baits and are real excitement machines on saltwater fly tackle.
Left: Black jewfish, (a local version of the southern mulloway) prefer deep water with some structure as protection from strong currents. Rock drop-offs and deep holes in estuary and creek mouths are good spots, as are submerged wrecks and artificial reefs such as those in Darwin Harbour.

Rock Fishing

East Coast

Rockfishing strategies and techniques are remarkably similar along the east coast, right from Green Cape in the south to Double Island Point, in the north, and this is despite covering a variety of land types and several climatic zones.

That similarity is due to the effect of the East Australian current – really a broad system of eddies which flow generally southwards. This current minimises variations in water temperatures and maintains higher averages than would otherwise be the case. As a consequence, many species of fish and aquatic life are found in common throughout its length.

Bread and butter fish like bream, tailor and flathead are common targets of rockhoppers. As the water cools, there's a generally northward seasonal movement of many species, the migration of tailor to Fraser Island being a good example. Other species move inshore and feed close in to the rocks at certain times and there are also frequent general movements of fish as they seek out favourable conditions and food supplies. Most species tolerate only a narrow range of temperatures, and understanding how this affects migrations can help you fish the best periods and areas.

A common feature of inshore water south of Port Macquarie, is that it tends to be deep and reef-strewn. Further north, the water is generally shallow, with the sandy bottom well within casting range. While this makes for easy fishing, it also has disadvantages. If sand is stirred up too much by big seas it will send fish out into deeper water.

All rockfishing tackle must be rugged and capable of withstanding the punishing conditions encountered on the ocean rocks. The sidecast reel reigns supreme with rockhoppers. Anglers prefer a rod about 4 m long, as this helps to keep their line above any rock ledges and enables them to stand back from the water's edge. A rod with a flexible tip and powerful butt is recommended, as fish often have to be lifted from the water.

Along the south coast of New South Wales, land-based game fishermen target tuna and kingfish wherever deep water is found. Some of the top spots in the country for this type of angling are in the Jervis Bay area. Rockhoppers also use high-speed reels, with gear ratios of up to 6 to

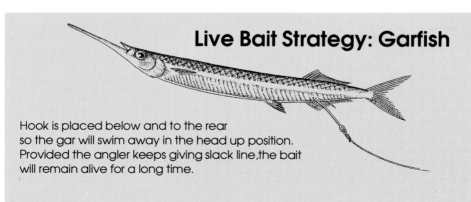

Live Bait Strategy: Garfish

Hook is placed below and to the rear so the gar will swim away in the head up position. Provided the angler keeps giving slack line, the bait will remain alive for a long time.

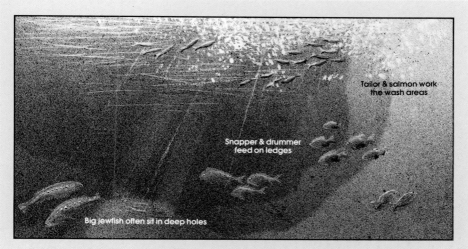

Tailor & salmon work the wash areas

Snapper & drummer feed on ledges

Big jewfish often sit in deep holes

Most fish prefer to have some cover from predators which encourages them to congregate in wash areas found around the rocks. This aerated white-water is caused by waves washing over sections of low rock before foaming back into the ocean. This also washes in food, which is often held in a back eddy, attracting bait fish and predators alike. Using a berley mix of bread or chicken pellets will attract fish from nearby reefs, which would otherwise be out of casting range.

1, to spin for fast-swimming pelagic species. This is an active and exciting sport, although fish numbers have severely declined since the halcyon days of the sixties and seventies.

The secret of successful rockfishing is to understand fish behaviour and how this is influenced by sea conditions, the stage of the tide, the strength and direction of the wind, the time of day, and the stage of the moon.

Many species of fish prefer the run-up tide as this allows them to feed over flooded flats or else washes food from rocks. If you inspect cunjevoi beds or vegetation areas below low tide mark you'll often see signs of where fish have been feeding.

A high tide, near to sunset or sunrise, is a prime time. This coincides with a change in light conditions when fish become more active. Conversely, there are areas that fish well on a falling tide, or that can only be reached with a low tide. To accommodate such local variations you need to gain personal experience of each area, or do some research such as reading or talking to other anglers.

The effect which different phases of the moon have on fishing cannot be overstated, although this effect varies on different species. For example, fish such as luderick won't bite well with a full moon, yet other species such as tailor do. Again, it's a matter of trial and error, subject to local variations.

Pot-holing is an effective method of fishing shallow water-covered flats at night. You need to be skilled in handling your gear and finding your way around in the dark, but fish move into very shallow water at night to prospect for food and fishing results can be excellent.

A prime spot is where ocean rocks meet a beach. Here, you can encounter both rock and beach dwelling species. Generally you fish from the rocks and cast your bait into the feeding zone, which is behind the waves breaking on the beach. If you hook a large fish you can sometimes walk it back around to the beach to land it in safety. Tailor, bream and mulloway are regularly caught in such areas.

Rockfishing often improves as conditions begin to settle after rough weather. The increased food supply stirs fish into a

Rock shelves like this one are deceptively dangerous. Although flat and level, that weed growth is slippery underfoot and its presence indicates the rocks are regularly under water.

feeding mood, and many species, such as drummer and luderick prefer slightly discoloured water, presumably as it gives them some cover from predators.

If conditions are dangerous in more exposed areas, you can generally find a protected corner behind a reef to soak a bait. Fish often move into such areas in search of food washed off more exposed rocks, and if your bait is fresh and something the target species will accept, you can fish productively and in safety.

Rock fishing means frequent tackle losses. Many species prefer rocky areas and you cut down your options if you avoid these places, but tackle losses can be minimised by using simple rigs, such as a small ball sinker running down to the hook, or using an unweighted bait or a float rig to keep things off the bottom.

Tragically, many rock fishermen are swept to their deaths each year – generally because they were foolhardy, or fished dangerous places unnecessarily. Always treat the sea and the rocks with respect and commonsense and remember that no fish is ever worth dying for.

South Australia

Rock-fishing in South Australia offers few if any pelagic species, but snapper and salmon are plentiful, impressive in size and regularly caught.

Snapper frequently top 10 kg and salmon run from 4 to 5 kg, so they are well worth the angler's effort. Local techniques differ from elsewhere, based mostly on geography and local fish behaviour.

North of Whyalla, the rugged Lowly Peninsula turns on hundreds of giant snapper for rock fishermen each season, but they bite best when it's freezing cold and the wind is so strong you can barely keep your feet.

Rock ledges in this area front very shallow water. This lack of depth doesn't deter the fish though, in fact you can often see the tips of their tails protruding from the surface as they fossick along the bottom.

Pilchards, squid heads, small octopus or fish fillets are fished on linked suicides and 24 kg trace, with casting weight usually being a snapper lead of 100 g or so.

The lead is rigged on line lighter than the main line so that if fouled on the bottom, the rig can be retrieved by snapping the sinker trace.

South of Adelaide, particularly in winter and spring, numbers of big salmon can be caught by bobby-corking with baits of fresh pilchard. A few dedicated spin-men catch fat salmon by casting to the edges of the school bringing the lure past the fish in a steady slow retrieve.

Incidental species available from the rocks include sweep, leatherjacket, parrot fish, silver drummer and trevally. In summer, squid and garfish are popular targets.

The rocks facing the turbulent Southern Ocean are quite steep and slippery, and tragically, lives are lost every year when fishermen fail to give this stretch of coastline the respect and caution it deserves. In rough weather, use gear heavy enough to swing fish up, rather than having to go down into the teeth of the sea to land them.

In quieter gulf waters, species such as snook, tommy ruffs and whiting can be taken from rocks, particularly if there are substantial weed beds nearby. These shel-tered platforms are safe and very popular with anglers of all ages.

Western Australia

Rock fishing in Western Australia can be divided into two distinct areas: the south-west corner, and the upper west coast. The first is typified by the smooth, sloping rocks of the Albany region, while the second is best known for the steep cliffs of the Quobba and Shark Bay coastlines.

The popular species for rock fishermen in the southwest are herring, salmon and silver trevally. Blue groper, samson fish and the occasional jewfish provide welcome alternatives.

For herring and silver trevally, berley is a great help. A common rig is simply a berley cage with a whole whitebait in tow half a metre behind.

For all of the other species, a whole pilchard on linked hooks is fine, with as small a sinker as suits the location. Salmon are also great lure takers.

Great care must be taken in choosing a safe location along the south coast, as the

Big mulloway like this can be caught from Western Australian rock ledges.

Sailfish caught from the rocks on helium balloon rig - Steep Pt., WA

Weighted Stem Float

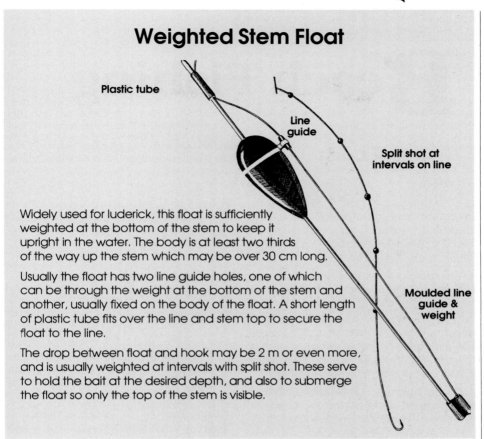

Plastic tube

Line guide

Split shot at intervals on line

Moulded line guide & weight

Widely used for luderick, this float is sufficiently weighted at the bottom of the stem to keep it upright in the water. The body is at least two thirds of the way up the stem which may be over 30 cm long.

Usually the float has two line guide holes, one of which can be through the weight at the bottom of the stem and another, usually fixed on the body of the float. A short length of plastic tube fits over the line and stem top to secure the float to the line.

The drop between float and hook may be 2 m or even more, and is usually weighted at intervals with split shot. These serve to hold the bait at the desired depth, and also to submerge the float so only the top of the stem is visible.

rocks can be very dangerous in any sort of swell. A long gaff is necessary for any of the larger species.

In the north, the rocks harbour a great diversity of species, but the two most popular are Spanish mackerel and norwest snapper (spangled emperor). Catches of other fish are virtually incidental.

There are three techniques for taking spaniards from the rocks: ballooning, baitcasting and spinning.

Ballooning requires some specialised tackle, including a reel capable of holding at least 500 m of 10 or 15 kg line.

A large whole bait, on linked hooks and wire trace, is suspended under balloons which are lowered into the sea and blown out with a land breeze. This method consistently accounts for the biggest fish, and often the most as well.

Spinning requires a lighter casting rod, and a high-speed reel loaded with 10 kg line. Lures are usually in the 25 to 60 g range, and both bibbed and bibless minnows are successful, as are leadhead jigs.

Baitcasting uses similar tackle, but pilchards on linked hooks replace the lures. A small sinker may be necessary to achieve casting distance.

Traces for both lures and pilchard rigs are half a metre of 30 kg wire.

Baitfishing is best for bottom fish such as emperor, and wire is not necessary unless there are a lot of mackerel about. It is advisable to use an absolute minimum of sinker weight to avoid repetitive tackle losses on the bottom.

A rope gaff is often the only way to get fish up the cliffs, as many of the locations are more than 5 m off the water and even a long pole gaff may not reach.

Beach Fishing

East Coast

Beach fishing is seen by some fishermen as something of a mystery. Most of their uncertainty arises from being unsure what to fish for, how to identify the productive areas of a beach, and the way in which fishing is affected by the tides.

The most important thing when fishing a beach is to concentrate your efforts in locations with the most potential to produce fish. Water doesn't just surge up and down a beach, it also moves through channels and scours out depressions and holes before leaving a beach, often some distance from where it came inshore.

Forage fish like bream and whiting move around and hunt on the edges of deep areas where the sand is fretted away by water movement and food is flushed free. Predatory species like tailor, salmon and mulloway patrol the deeper sections of clean water looking for smaller baitfish.

Gutters or channels with deeper calm water will attract fish and hold them better than turbulent shallows which have a lot of sand in suspension. For this reason, gutters fish well on either high or low tides but sandbars and other relatively shallow sections generally only produce fish on a high tide.

Finding gutters and determining water depth on a beach is not difficult. Holes can be detected by pools of foam over darker water with less wave action than its surroundings, and gutters will sometimes run parallel with the beach or out and away into deep water in rips and undertows.

When fishing a gutter it is important to let your bait move around a little. This may involve casting in at one point and walking to another, or letting out line until the water has carried the bait the length of the gutter. Fish are easier to locate when you let the bait cover as much water as possible. Then, when the fish are located, more accurate casting will save time.

Using too much lead will inhibit the movement of the bait so it will not look as natural or catch as many fish as a rig which enables the bait to move freely with the water.

Available Beach Species & Suitable Techniques

Whiting can be caught at dawn and dusk but also in the daytime on the edges of gutters, over sandbars with enough depth and surprisingly, quite close in to the shorebreak. They often school up and can sometimes be seen through waves just before they break. Whiting feed on the bottom and will eat pipis, prawns and beach worms. Worms on a long shank hook with as little weight as possible and 3 to 4 kg line will usually catch whiting if they're there. Move the bait around if the water is calm, and when a rattling bite is felt, lift smoothly to set the hook.

Pipis can be gathered by twisting both feet into the sand at low water mark until the shells are felt underfoot.

*East coast mulloway expert Gene Dundon
with a giant fish. Beachfishing at its best.*

Making a Chain of Ganged Hooks

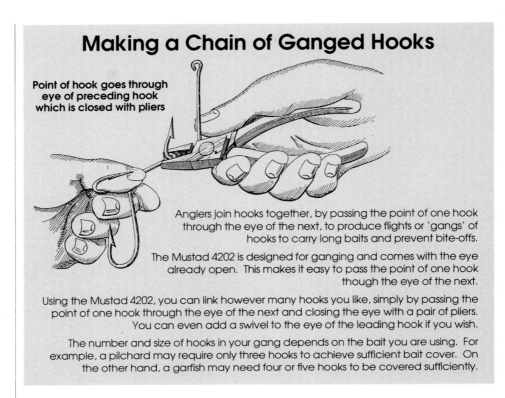

Point of hook goes through eye of preceding hook which is closed with pliers

Anglers join hooks together, by passing the point of one hook through the eye of the next, to produce flights or 'gangs' of hooks to carry long baits and prevent bite-offs.

The Mustad 4202 is designed for ganging and comes with the eye already open. This makes it easy to pass the point of one hook though the eye of the next.

Using the Mustad 4202, you can link however many hooks you like, simply by passing the point of one hook through the eye of the next and closing the eye with a pair of pliers. You can even add a swivel to the eye of the leading hook if you wish.

The number and size of hooks in your gang depends on the bait you are using. For example, a pilchard may require only three hooks to achieve sufficient bait cover. On the other hand, a garfish may need four or five hooks to be covered sufficiently.

Bream are more a low light fish with daytime captures outweighed by those at dawn, dusk and evening. They can be caught along with whiting but usually prefer deeper water. Shallow gutters or the edges of deep gutters fish best. Baits include worms, pipis, prawns, pilchard pieces or any fresh fish bait.

Once again, as little lead as possible will catch more fish, and lines from 4 to 6 kg will enable longer casts and a more mobile, attractive bait. Small baits are better for bream than large chunks and a little berley in the form of bait scraps or pilchard pieces will often attract bream into the gutter you are fishing.

Flathead are generally a daylight fish and often turn up at the tail end of a morning's bream fishing, particularly if the bait is allowed to slip out to the back of the surfline where they wait to pounce on small baitfish or prawns. The same range of baits work as on bream with the addition of larger strip baits or whole pilchards or garfish on linked hooks.

Heavy line isn't required, 4 to 6 kg line is quite enough, but a short length of heavier mono trace is a good idea to protect against the flathead's sharp, widely spaced teeth.

Tailor and salmon often patrol beach gutters at dawn and dusk, hunting for baitfish. Deep gutters with a covering of foam are good places. Unweighted baits like whole garfish or pilchard fished on three or four linked hooks are best but lures will take fish on occasion.

If casting a long way or into an onshore wind, some lead may be required, but keep it to the minimum necessary to reach the gutter where the fish are working. Often, these species can be indicated by swooping seabirds picking scraps from above a feeding school. Tailor hook themselves if you just keep winding steadily against their sharp, hard bites, but salmon may need to be allowed to play more with the bait.

Mulloway are undoubtedly the pinnacle of beachfishing targets. They mostly also require a lot of hard work and hours of patient fishing before you land one. Some anglers fish for years before catching their first big 'jew'.

Mulloway are found in deep water and more often hooked late in the afternoon or at night. Whole dead fish baits or fairly large strip baits of mullet, tailor, or blackfish are used, or if conditions are calm, small live tailor can work well too.

Heavier line is required, most anglers using from 8 to 15 kg line with a slightly heavier trace and 7/0 to 10/0 hooks honed needle sharp. The take of a big jew is often an accelerating drawing away with considerable weight behind it, and when you feel that big head shake in anger, you'll know you've hooked one of beachfishing's greatest prizes.

South Australia

South Australia can boast some of the finest surf fishing in the country. Big, black-back salmon, sharks, and giant mulloway are regularly taken from the State's beaches and there are mullet, whiting, and a host of other table varieties for fishermen with more moderate ambitions.

The best surf fishing is in the State's west, on the north-east perimeter of the Great Australian Bight. Although not easy to fish, these windswept beaches can yield huge catches of salmon and some very large mulloway.

While standard beach fishing tactics apply as elsewhere in the country, there is the notable addition that it is quite common to use large lures to catch mulloway from the beaches. This is particularly so at night, around the mouth of the Murray river, where sidecast tackle reigns supreme and the mulloway caught have weighed as much as 40 kg.

The preferred lures are usually leadhead jigs, up to 170 g in weight. These are cast out into a strong ebb tide and worked back very slowly through the roiled surf where the big fish are hunting. It helps to stop now and again and allow the lure to sink and kick up some sand intermittently.

Salmon also frequent these beaches fringing the Coorong and they respond best to pilchard or gar baits.

The beaches of the lower Yorke Peninsula frequently yield salmon to 5 kg on either lures or bait. Schools of salmon can be spotted from adjacent high ground above the beaches. You can then work out their direction of travel and hit the beach to intercept them. Cast to the edges of the school to pick up strikes without frightening or scattering the fish.

Further into the protected waters of St Vincent Gulf, the beaches slope more gently and light tackle will catch mullet, salmon trout (juvenile Australian salmon), King George and yellowfin whiting, tommy ruffs and some flathead.

Further into the protected waters of Gulf St Vincent, the beaches slope more gently and light tackle will catch mullet, salmon trout (juvenile Australian salmon), King George and yellowfin whiting, tommy ruffs and some flathead.

Mulloway in South Australia often take lures in the surf

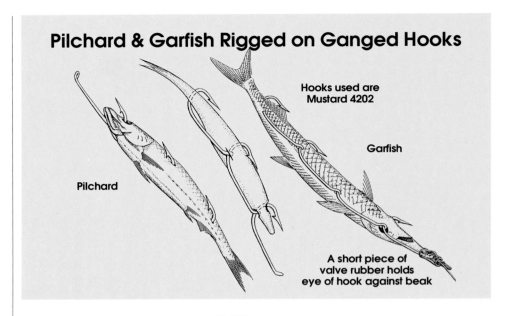

Pilchard & Garfish Rigged on Ganged Hooks

Hooks used are Mustard 4202

Garfish

Pilchard

A short piece of valve rubber holds eye of hook against beak

Western Australia

Beach fishing is very popular along the west coast, due mainly to the reliable abundance of herring, tailor and whiting. Salmon can be caught as their migrations allow, mulloway are not uncommon, and to add to the variety, there are small sharks, the odd mackerel and a handful of trevally, not to mention dart, garfish and yellow-eye mullet (called 'pilch' locally).

Seasons overlap, so there is always something to be caught. Herring are best from April to August, but can be caught in reasonable numbers all year. Tailor around 30 cm are common in the Perth area from November to May, while winter fish are few but larger. Whiting prefer hot, calm weather to come close into shore, and catches peak in early summer. 'Pilch' are a winter fish.

Proficient fishermen recognise that long casts and delicate presentation make a great difference to the number of fish caught, so long rods and light lines are the best way to go. Written advice often advocates the use of wire on tailor, but for the little metropolitan chopper tailor, linked hooks will prevent most bite-offs, enabling the use of main line down to 6 kg. Run straight down to the hooks, this rig will cast further, and draw more bites too.

Common baits are 'mulies' (blue pilchards), whitebait or blue sardines, rigged on linked hooks and trailed half a metre behind a running star or spoon sinker.

While whiting aren't very fussy, catches of herring and pilch can be dramatically increased by using fine 2 kg line down to the hook, and the judicious use of berley. A rod with a light tip will read bites better than one with a stiff or heavy tip.

Mulloway are most often an incidental catch for tailor fishermen, and usually fall to a mulie fished right at the back of the surf. Specialist mulloway anglers favour a fillet of tailor on linked 5/0 hooks, with a leader of 20 kg nylon. Such an outfit is often left set for a mulloway while the angler fishes with a lighter rod for smaller fish.

A shoulder bag can carry bait and spare rigs and also provide a place to put fish when caught. Other worthwhile equipment includes a rod belt, a knife and a tube or other holder to stick in the sand for the rod to stand up in. Night fishermen will find a headlamp more useful than a torch, and a 20 litre plastic bucket is useful for cleaning fish on the beach.

For all beach species, early morning and dusk are the prime times to fish.

STRATEGIES FOR

Islands & Inshore

Temperate Zone

The islands and inshore waters of Australia's temperate zone offer anglers a wealth of different species, most of which are good sport, and many excellent table fish as well.

The collision between the ocean and the land creates food and shelter opportunities for small fish which dart about in the white water, feeding on smaller creatures and food fragments washed back and forth by wave action.

These inshore areas act like magnets for predators, especially when the tide rises or when warm currents swing in close.

Sometimes the big fish are in residence, but waiting for bait concentrations to build up, or for some other feeding trigger like a tide change. Other times they can arrive at a spot as part of a daily patrol of likely feeding stations. Whichever, there are several things you can do to improve your chances of catching them.

Water movements tend to localise fish, and obstructions to that flow give them somewhere to feed and shelter. Referring this information to local bottom formations, you can almost pinpoint where the action will occur and concentrate your fishing efforts right on top of hungry fish.

You'll often find inshore fish suspended in midwater behind a pinnacle or ridge, or hovering near bottom depressions in the path of drifting food. Some species pick their way along shallow slopes, or browse across rubble and boulder-strewn areas. Often, fish aren't located hard up against underwater features, but some distance away. This is because it's easier for them to sit where the spent water flows and eventually carries the food.

To successfully fish inshore areas you need some idea of the underwater terrain. But how do you get this information? Short of going over the side for a first hand look, there are ways of establishing what things are like down there.

Admiralty charts show water depths as a series of contour lines, not unlike a land map. These charts are available from boat and map shops and they're a useful fishing tool as well as a legal requirement for outside boating.

An echo sounder can show you underwater landforms, how much water is under you, and even reveal fish, but its usefulness depends on being above the hot spot in the first place. To find areas where the sounder can benefit you, plan your trip with the Admiralty charts, then when you get there, 'read' the water from what you can see at the surface.

'Reading' the water means finding the most significant underwater structure in the area. It could be the slopes of a rocky headland or bay, or perhaps a reef or bombora standing off an estuary mouth. It could be an island or even a lone rock off the back of a long sweeping beach. Once you've decided which locale to focus on, then use the sounder for more precise information. This will help you set the boat's position in relation to the wind or current and to drop your bait or lure into the most likely areas.

There are various surface clues to the presence of underwater feeding places. A rock-line entering the water will probably continue at the same angle for some distance under the surface if not right to the bottom. Current humps or surface 'boils' suggest rises in the bottom, and floating foam patches can indicate an eddy or a patch of slack water over a hole. All these are likely feeding places for fish.

Currents which split down either side of an island create ideal feeding stations. Baitfish swept along by these currents are disoriented by the turbulence as the streams rejoin, and become easy prey. Big fish hole up near these ridges of rock or slow moving eddies and either wait for the bait to come to them, or charge through in feeding raids.

Berley is often the catalyst that transforms a dead situation into a hot bite, and there are good and better ways of using it. Whether you use berley at all, depends partly on the strength of the current and whether you can anchor conveniently upstream of the fish. If you can trickle a steady stream of berley into the hot zone, you can encourage fish to feed, but hard running currents can disperse berley quickly or carry the fish away from you, which is counter-productive. Even in moderate currents it's better to keep the berley stream to a constant trickle rather than release large amounts intermittently.

Offshore berleying lays down a long surface slick of mostly small particles and oily liquid. This can be done either on the drift or at anchor and is meant to intercept travelling fish and draw them up the berley trail to your boat. But if you are fishing a localised area, a workable rule is that the current shouldn't carry the berley more than a comfortable casting distance before it sinks from sight. If you are berleying shallow water in a light run, you can use a buoyant berley mix, like cereal grains soaked in tuna oil. Fast runs may call up berleys like mixes of sand and particles of fish flesh, or even the use of berley bombs.

When fishing shallow water in popular, hard fished spots, your catches will improve if you anchor some distance from where you reckon the fish to be and make longer casts than usual to reach them. This is because hard-worked fish can become uneasy when a boat is directly overhead. The ploy works, but you need to work on your casting skills, and use suitable tackle like long supple rods and light line. Choose tougher baits and pay attention to how you bait up, so the baits stay connected and withstand the stresses of casting.

Live-baiting is underrated as an inshore technique for big fish. Small-boat fishermen can benefit greatly from this tech-

Floating pilchard or garfish
on 3 x 4202 3/0 hooks

Berley bomb

Rocky
Hump

Anchoring on a rocky pinnacle can let you drift your baits and berley back into an eddy area created by current flow past the underwater structure. Berley can be distributed by means of a berley pot, or a canister dropped over the side. The latter technique helps localise the berley in a strong current.

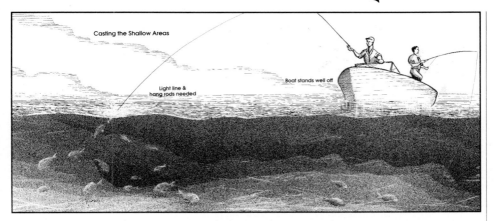

Casting the Shallow Areas

Light line &
hang rods needed

Boat stands well off

Bream often school right on top of shallow areas or in adjacent holes. By standing off and casting from some distance away you can avert the boat scaring the fish.

nique developed by offshore gamefishermen, as it will attract big mulloway, teraglin and snapper too. In waters north of Newcastle you can add cobia and big mackerel to the list. The livebaits are generally small yellowtail or slimy mackerel and despite what some folks tell you about sharks, a berley trail is well worth the trouble.

You can also troll or spin with baits, (and many fishermen do), as a moving bait will always attract more attention than a stationary one, but let's look briefly now at using lures.

Trolling can be as easy as dragging something behind a boat, but like any kind of consistently successful fishing, there's a bit more to it than that.

A good inshore lure trolling tactic is to slow-troll small minnows close to the ocean rocks or the corners of islands. Try to have the lure zip in and out of the white water where baitfish gather and big fish like tailor, salmon, bonito and kingfish make regular early morning raids.

Keep an eye out for shallowing rocks, and have a prudent regard for how close inshore you can go without being on the

Baiting with Large and Fleshy Baits

Wide gape hooks with long sharp points are chosen for baiting up with large, fleshy baits because there is less chance of obscuring the point.

Snapper are the main species sought on such baits, so the hook needs to be fairly strong because snapper have powerful jaws. For this reason, the Mustad 92552 is suggested. Several examples are shown as a guide.

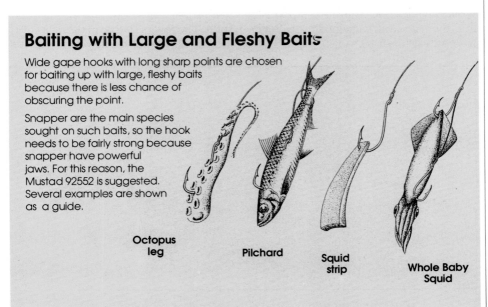

Octopus
leg

Pilchard

Squid
strip

Whole Baby
Squid

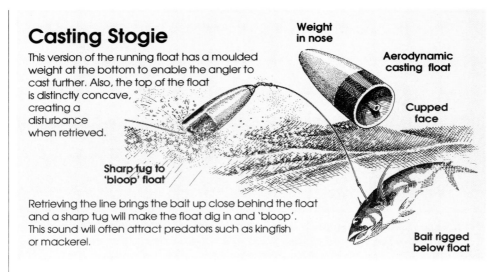

Casting Stogie

Weight in nose

This version of the running float has a moulded weight at the bottom to enable the angler to cast further. Also, the top of the float is distinctly concave, creating a disturbance when retrieved.

Aerodynamic casting float

Cupped face

Sharp tug to 'bloop' float

Retrieving the line brings the bait up close behind the float and a sharp tug will make the float dig in and 'bloop'. This sound will often attract predators such as kingfish or mackerel.

Bait rigged below float

dangerous side of a swell - that is inside it, where it could lift you up and dump your boat on the rocks.

As the morning progresses and the sun gets up a bit, you can troll or cast slim metal jigs near wheeling seabirds or schools of surface fish. Note the direction of the wind as tuna and other surface fish consistently feed up into it. Yellowfin tuna are better eating than you might suppose and Striped and Mackerel tuna are a great source of bait and berley, as well as being terrific sport. If you plan your day properly, you can gather your bait and berley while having some really torrid sportfishing, then go and concentrate on better table fish to finish off.

What could be better than that?

Tropical

To fish the islands of the tropics, and the inshore waters around them, most visitors use a trailer boat of suitable size. Car-toppers can only cover sheltered waters. To fish the islands of the north involves a boat size suitable for sea-going for the same reason it would anywhere else.

Fishermen visiting the tropics for the first time sometimes assume the waters will be blissfully calm and the distances short. The reverse is true in the majority of cases. The further north you go in Aus-

Position boat upwind and cast in front of advancing school

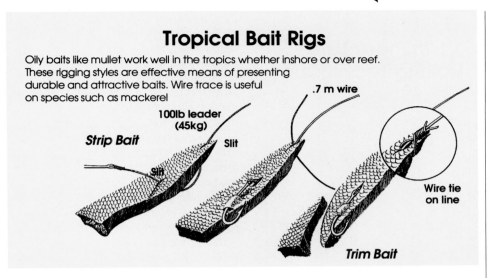

Tropical Bait Rigs

Oily baits like mullet work well in the tropics whether inshore or over reef. These rigging styles are effective means of presenting durable and attractive baits. Wire trace is useful on species such as mackerel

.7 m wire

100lb leader (45kg)

Strip Bait

Slit

Slit

Slit

Wire tie on line

Trim Bait

tralia, the more you are subject to the prevailing trade winds. This is especially so in the winter months, with the pattern being for south-easters along the coast of Queensland, with a more easterly trend at the tip of Cape York and across the top of the country. It is common in the Kimberley region for winds to blow from the shore, offering calm but deceptive inshore waters.

The sea in most tropical locations is shallower than in the southern States, with less of a regular oceanic swell and more of a fast-developing chop. Thus, conditions are more likely to be uncomfortable than dangerous. The greater tidal range often produces a wind-against-tide situation which can be especially vicious in less predictable waters such as Torres Strait and the Kimberley.

Distances are greater for Barrier Reef fishing, with 60 km each way being common for day trips. Longer trips, say north from Cairns or out to the Swains off Rockhampton, may mean 300 km each way. The inshore islands range from a few kilometres out, to a round trip of 100 km in a day. Boats need fuel capacity to match the distances.

Lightweight boat camping is a natural option for visitors. Many islands are National Parks, with camping permits on sale at various rates (commensurate with facilities) from National Parks offices in major

towns. These offices can also provide safety advice and information about insects, weather and water.

A short camping trip, covering two or three nights, allows much more efficient use of fuel (no long trips to and fro). Available fishing time is increased, because you may fish before dawn or after dark as well as through the day. Safety is also enhanced, because weather patterns follow the norm for most coastal regions. It is easier and safer to return in the calm of morning than when the sea breeze has come up in the afternoon.

On most National Parks islands, firewood is unavailable and fires have been banned in favour of small gas stoves. Conditions are often idyllic, with the worst problem coming from insects. These can be controlled in a number of ways. Burning mosquito coils in fireproof containers will deter all pests day and night, at least inside a tent. Insect repellents applied to cool cotton clothing will outperform the same repellent applied to the skin. A careful approach to the insect problem can add up to a very comfortable trip. Safety includes knowing about sea stingers in season, and about crocodiles or sharks. A prior check with local National Parks staff will afford the protection of up to date advice on these factors.

The tidal range may be much greater than you are used to, so anchoring needs

Inshore Lure Trolling Techniques

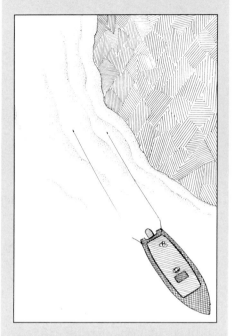

Troll close to shorelines and island corners. The path of the lures should cut through wash areas

Lures passing close to bait schools have a better chance of being taken

care. It is not unknown for a high tide to lift an anchor off the bottom. Depending on the tides, boats can be beached overnight in total safety when a rising tide next morning will float them. If anchored off an island beach, a second line ashore is needed for overnight security.

Watch for basic traps, such as having a boat stranded on a beach by a falling tide. The typical situation is for people to go ashore for lunch, leaving the boat at the water's edge. Returning an hour later, the falling tide may have left them high and dry. Boats too heavy to be manhandled stay there until the tide returns.

Tackle for these inshore islands should be versatile. A typical rod and reel combination will cast and troll with equal ease.

Many tropical fish have teeth - barracuda, mackerel, queenfish - so a short wire trace is advisable. A typical rig would be a 2 m spin rod, a reel with a capacity of at least 200 m of 6 to 10 kg line, and a range of casting and trolling lures.

Alternatively, a geared casting reel (large baitcaster) and two-handed casting rod works well with the same line size.

Gear needs to be well-maintained and tuned to cope with the runs of fast and powerful fish. Those who have already caught tuna or kingfish in the south will feel quite at home with this style of fishing.

Regardless of the tide, the very first faint light of dawn is the best time to start fishing around the islands. Tidal rips around headlands and coral slopes facing into the tidal current provide more reliable action.

Through the day, an echo sounder will locate new territory and show deep bottom formation for reef fishing. Schools of baitfish are often indicated by diving seabirds. Especially in calm conditions, approach a bait school very cautiously. The ability to cast a dense lure so it will sink quickly to whatever predators are following the bait is a standard tactic.

Other easy and successful options include slow trolling with whole pilchard baits, or drifting a pilchard on ganged hooks around bomboras and over broken rock and coral.

Trolling a Whole Fish for Mackerel

Spanish mackerel and other members of the mackerel family do not engulf the bait, but slash at the rear of the bait to immobilise it. For this reason the hook needs to be placed well back in the bait, not in the front half as is preferred for bill-fish.

Single strand wire

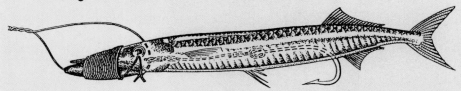

Sinker bound under chin closing mouth and tie off to close gills

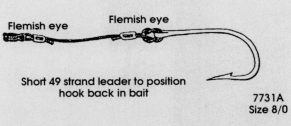

Flemish eye **Flemish eye**

Shown is a garfish rigged on single strand wire but with a short length of forty nine-strand wire, with a Flemish Eye in each end, extending back to the hook, usually a 7731A in size 8/0.

Short 49 strand leader to position hook back in bait

7731A Size 8/0

This method of baiting involves poking the short, forty-nine strand extension and hook up through the body so that the towing strand of wire can pass through the leading Flemish Eye.

A number 6 barrel sinker is then threaded onto the single strand tag, but under the chin, and tied off with dacron so that the mouth and gills are closed in the process. The tag is then extended through the sinker and secured in a loop, first by making a haywire twist, and then a series of tight barrel rolls.

While this rig takes a little time to prepare, it can be trolled for hours without breaking up.

The strategy here is to find a shoal of fish which can then be presented with more hurriedly prepared baits which will be quickly taken once the fish have been located.

This brilliantly coloured coral trout was taken offshore on a white lead-head jig

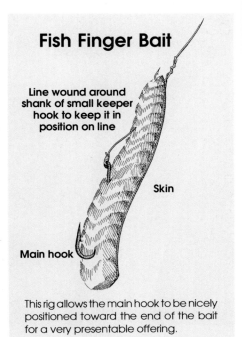

STRATEGIES FOR
Offshore

Temperate & Tropical

Fuel prices being what they are these days, offshore anglers need to consider ways of fishing which maximise their returns. By that we don't mean having to bring home an extravagant haul of fillets in order to justify a trip – species bag limits are designed to discourage that approach. These days we fish not only for food, but also for recreation and sport.

The overwhelming majority of offshore anglers fish for bottom species such as snapper, teraglin, morwong, and in the tropics, sweetlip and coral trout. An available option – not always used – is to troll lures when heading to and from the grounds. This can pick up additional table fish of kingfish or mackerel, or perhaps a juicy tuna that can be used for bottom fishing cut baits.

Developments in lure technology have resulted in trolling speeds thought impossible a few years ago, up to 20 knots with lures like the narrow high speed bibless types. Cheap and effective feather jigs provide a cost-effective option for boat speeds up to 15 knots. For slower speeds, bibbed minnows are worth considering too. These bibbed lures have a positive niche while mooching around reef complexes.

Best results on bottom fish come at specific times. In the tropics, it's best to have some tidal movement. The coral trout adage – "no 'run' – no fun" – certainly holds true. This puts the best fishing times towards the spring tides that coincide with full and new moons.

The full moon is traditionally the best time for reef dwelling jewfish and teraglin. Billfish also tend to feed more noticeably around the full moon. It's no accident that many gamefish clubs set their tournament dates around that time.

Tides may not be important with snapper as time of day. Of course, much depends on location. What applies in South Australia's Spencer Gulf isn't necessarily the case at Coffs Harbour. Snapper aggregate to feed on mussel beds and spawn in South Australian inshore waters; a different approach is necessary for reef dwelling fish off the east coast.

An early start is important with snapper. They go off the bite as daylight increases. Around dusk is also good. However, once full darkness sets in, fish can get scarce. Bottom rung food chain predators such as Sergeant Baker and Red Rock cod have very nasty spines. Handle these with extreme care, as they are often encountered while fishing for snapper. When that hap-

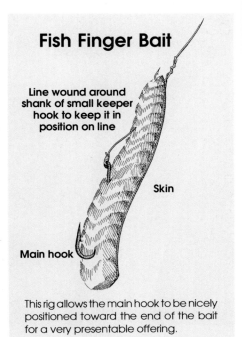

Fish Finger Bait

Line wound around shank of small keeper hook to keep it in position on line

Skin

Main hook

This rig allows the main hook to be nicely positioned toward the end of the bait for a very presentable offering.

141

Marlin taken with a bridle rigged striped tuna offshore from Bermagui, NSW

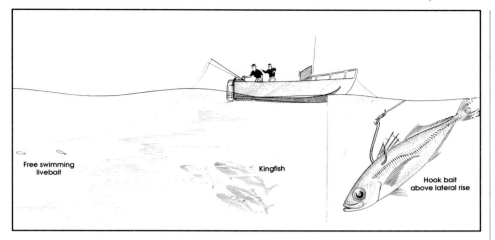

**Kingfish are naturally inquisitive and will investigate
live baits, berley trails and even the pounding of a berley bucket**

pens, take the hint and move. There aren't too many snapper about.

The aftermath of big southerly seas is a special time for snapper along the east coast. The large ground-swells associated with these sea conditions pose hazards for small boats however, especially around headlands and bomboras, so temper your eagerness to capitalise on such times with caution and commonsense.

Floating baits are infinitely more productive in such conditions than rigs anchored to the bottom with a massive sinker. If conditions do require some weight, use a ball sinker, riding directly on the hook eye. It's a universally simple and deadly rig.

Fishing trips cannot always be scheduled to coincide with periods of fish feeding activity. Quite often success depends on the ability of anglers to create their own localised food chain with the use of berley.

All fish are opportunists and will rarely knock back a free meal – especially of fresh baits, thoughtfully presented. Berley

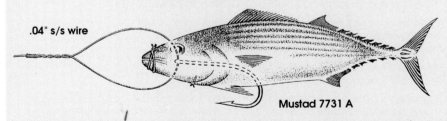

Trolling Large Baits on Game Fishing Tackle for Billfish

.04" s/s wire

Mustad 7731 A

Marlin and other billfish respond to large baits held fairly short in the outrigger so that they skip out of the water behind the boat. Shown is a bonito rigged on single strand wire (the choice is usually .040 inch diameter).

A single Mustad 7731 hook is placed inside the fish as shown, and secured on the loop made by the towing strand. The mouth and gills of rhe fish are sewn closed.

When the billfish strikes, it pulls the line out of the outrigger clip which gives it enough slack to take the bait, provided the angler feeds line quickly to the fish.

Rigging a Live Frigate Mackerel as a Troll Bait

Used to best advantage as a troll bait at slow speeds. The hook is attached to the head with a towing bridle. A second hook extending to the rear of the bait on a slack trace is desirable for better hook-ups on tuna, kingfish and wahoo.

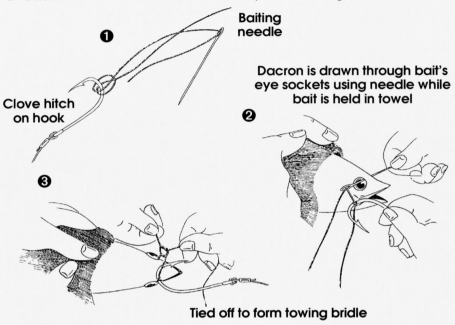

❶

Baiting needle

Clove hitch on hook

Dacron is drawn through bait's eye sockets using needle while bait is held in towel

❷

❸

Tied off to form towing bridle

Frigate mackerel will take virtually all Australian saltwater game fish. They are most productive when fished live, and the favoured strategy is to troll them behind a slow moving boat on a bridle.

To make a towing bridle, you will need a length of 24 or 36 kg dacron and a baiting needle.

❶ Attach the dacron to the hook with a clove hitch as shown.

❷ After catching a live frigate mackerel, hold it in a damp towel while the angler threads a length of dacron through its eye sockets (above the eye) with the baiting needle.

❸ The bridle is tied off, usually with a reef knot, and the frigate mackerel is ready to be trolled.

Trolling speed is dead slow while the angler holds a loop of line which trails in the water as a drop-back. When a strike occurs, the angler releases the drop-back, allowing the fish to take the bait properly before striking.

Completed frigate mackerel rig with hook attached to head

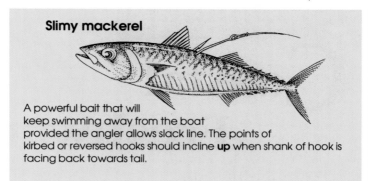

Slimy mackerel

*Slimy mackerel
live bait rig
commonly used
offshore*

A powerful bait that will
keep swimming away from the boat
provided the angler allows slack line. The points of
kirbed or reversed hooks should incline **up** when shank of hook is
facing back towards tail.

can range from chook pellets for bream, through to tuna chunks for bigger tuna, kingfish, billfish, or sharks.

Other creatures of the sea – such as mutton birds – are quick to exploit any such handouts however. So rather than be driven to distraction by the capacity of mutton birds to dive faster than a snapper lead can sink, you can keep them at bay by rigging up a suitable slow-release container, such as a medical drip bag filled with tuna oil.

The birds generally won't land on the slick, allowing the berley to get down where it can do its job.

An echo-sounder is essential equipment for the serious offshore angler. The latest generation Liquid Crystal Readout sets – called 'LCR fishfinders', rather than plain old sounders – have performance levels that effectively relegate the old paper chart units to the status of dinosaurs.

The best LCR's will tell you precisely where the bottom is; what it consists of; whether there are any fish hugging the seabed, or if they are suspending between the bottom and surface. With proper installation, they'll also do it at any speed of which a fishing boat is capable.

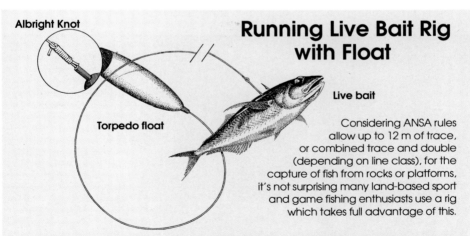

Albright Knot

Running Live Bait Rig with Float

Torpedo float

Live bait

Considering ANSA rules
allow up to 12 m of trace,
or combined trace and double
(depending on line class), for the
capture of fish from rocks or platforms,
it's not surprising many land-based sport
and game fishing enthusiasts use a rig
which takes full advantage of this.

A torpedo float rigged to run on an extended leader allows deep bait presentation where it will be most attractive to target species like kingfish and tuna, and less likely to attract the unwelcome attention of predatory birds like gannets, albatross or sea eagles. Besides that, an extended leader of heavier line which can be wound onto the reel, gives the angler a decided advantage in controlling a large fish in close to the rocks.

The Albright knot (illustrated), provides a join between the line and leader which can be wound in through the runners, and also acts as a stop to prevent the float from sliding up past the leader and onto the line.

Coastal Freshwater

Temperate Zone

Temperate coastal freshwater in angling terms generally means one thing to most folk -.bass fishing - and it's true that bass are indeed the best bet, and most worthy angling target in this climatic and geographic region.

There are however, other options and they are encountered often enough for them to be considered in any planned trip to fish these waters.

Equally native and proper in an ecological sense are the 'Tandanus' or eel-tail catfish, an excellent table fish and fair old scrapper too. Usually a bait only proposition, they can be conned into taking a lure, but only by the somewhat questionable method of dropping it into a nesting site and hooking the fish when it picks the lure up to eject it from the nest.

Freshwater herring are an ideal kid's fish and one on which the basic skills of bait presentation and water reading can be learned with ease.

They don't pull hard and no-one but a starving man would bother eating the little flesh that surrounds their many bones, but there are enough of them to satisfy any youngster's yen for a bit of fishing fun. In fact, more than a few dads have been seen to sneak some enjoyment from the rapid fire action that herring can provide.

Some theoretically fresh sections in the upper reaches of estuaries have rewarded bass anglers with some sturdy bream that exploded all over a lure fished near sunken timber.

Bass live underneath foliage like these ti-trees and lily pads

***Even small bass like this fish will hit
lures that are nearly as large as they are***

Both these and the 'stray' flathead that are taken in supposedly freshwater locations are there due to the wedging effect of saltwater that creeps further up most rivers than is realised, sitting underneath the less dense freshwater that runs un-mixed on top.

There are carp of course, regrettably, and in growing numbers, but suffice to say these pests can be caught on bread and garden worms fished unimaginatively on the bottom and aren't worth considering for food or subsequent release.

How different from the pugnacious, handsome bass with its endearing habit of belting anything that is remotely mouth sized and careless enough to stray within its strike zone.

That strike zone of bass can be as tight and as critical as landing a lure within centimetres of a chosen target and making it pass right in front of the fish's nose, or on some hot sultry nights, the strike zone can be as broad as the margins of the river and anywhere between the surface and the river bed.

Generally, for best results on bass, you need to work on close presentation of baits and lures being the key to strikes. It

also helps to mount your trip when the barometer is rising and to concentrate your effort in the first and last two hours of daylight.

Bass are a cover-related or structure-conscious kind of a fish. That means they will more often than not be found tucked in tight to some form of protection like steep rocky banks and overhanging foliage, or alongside and underneath sunken timber. They also have a penchant for cruising along the edges of weed beds, particularly in the early morning and late afternoon.

At these times they are usually foraging for shrimp, or small fish like gambusia, and are suckers for well-presented flies that suspend in the top few centimetres or so of the water. They'll also hit surface lures with gusto then. Patterns like Crazy Crawlers, Jitterbugs and various popping bugs are all good choices.

Toward the mid morning or afternoon, they are much more amenable to a live cricket or grasshopper floated under overhanging trees, or a couple of live shrimp fished under a float and slow drifted tight in alongside a weed bed or a deepwater rock face.

*Bass can be safely held with a thumb-grip
in the mouth. Barbless hooks are also easier to remove.*

Deep-running lures are a standby you can't ignore, as they will work at almost any time of day. The key to their success is something you could call the bass's 'envelope of tolerance'. If a suitably provocative lure passes within a centimetre or so of the fish when it is hungry, it will simply be seized without a second thought. But even when the fish isn't hungry, or just resting, there is a natural phenomenon at work not unlike that aspect of human behaviour when someone gets right in your face. You feel so uncomfortable about the proximity, you have no choice but to move away, or repel the intrusion.

Given that the lure is smaller than the bass, and so doesn't frighten it, the fish's most likely reaction to something repeatedly invading its private space is to attack and drive it off. This is why you'll often foul hook fish on deep divers in the middle of the day. The strike hasn't been a feeding lunge, but a territorial shoulder charge.

While bank angling can produce bass, any kind of boat at all is preferable, as it enables you to present the lures and baits right in tight to the cover where they live and still stand some chance of getting the fish back out again after it hits.

Barbless hooks make release of big breeding bass easier, and less traumatic for fish and angler alike. Just squeeze down the barbs on your lures and bait hooks with long-nosed pliers. You can also use these to release fish humanely, by gripping the hooks while the fish is still in the water and rotating the barbless point out of its mouth.

Bass are in such dire straits ecologically now, that catch and release is really the only responsible course of action for anglers with any care for the future. The fish needs uninterrupted annual access to salt water to breed and the hundreds of weirs and locks on our coastal river systems effectively hamper that natural replenishment so much that the fish's survival is in real doubt.

Bass aren't all that good to eat that you can't afford to put them back. They are, however, such a good and unique sportfish that we can't afford to lose them.

Tropical Zone

Queensland

A majority of Australia's freshwater fish species are found in the tropics, with little in the way of introduced species.

The native species include a number which occur also in salt water, such as barramundi, mangrove jack and tarpon. In a healthy tropical river it is possible to catch as many as six different kinds of native fish in a day's fishing. Lucky anglers might encounter barramundi, any of several varieties of sooty grunter, freshwater longtoms, two varieties of catfish, jungle perch, mangrove jack, rifle fish (sometimes known as archer fish) or eels.

In parts of Cape York, saratoga may be added to the list, mainly in lagoons or slow moving rivers.

The southern boundary can be taken as the Tropic of Capricorn, and so includes rivers from the Fitzroy north. The larger systems, such as the Fitzroy, Burdekin and Mitchell (Gulf country) drain huge areas through long tributaries, and these inland and tableland sections are dealt with separately as inland freshwater.

Some of the most intriguing coastal streams are the short, fast-flowing rainforest streams between the Herbert River and the Daintree River. Backed by high coastal ranges running to 1700 m in height, these are subject to summer monsoon rains originating in dense rainforest. Most of the remaining tropical streams originate in less mountainous country with lower average rainfall. The banks are less heavily timbered and the streams slower and more open.

Anglers trained on Australian bass, trout, or inland fish will be quite at home in the tropics. Whether it is a simple bait such as a worm or shrimp on a hook, or methods such as lure or fly fishing, tropical fish are versatile and available.

The most numerous of these are the various varieties of sooty grunter. An omnivore, these will eat anything from small fruit falling from rainforest trees to surface insects, small fish, shrimps and crayfish. More civilised baits such as small cubes of corned beef or cheddar cheese are also acceptable, so it's not hard to find bait in the north.

An effective method, either from a boat or from a bank, is to fish a bait under a small float (even a bottle cork will do) drifted close to a sheltering rock or snags. Hook size for sooties is easily remembered, being simply a strong 1/0.

Lures are equally diverse. It is hard to name a lure which would not attract a sooty grunter. Trout spinners and spoons, wobbling minnows, surface lures suited to Australian bass and even soft plastic twin-tail jigs all work on Sooties. If there are differences in lure choice, they relate to the nature of the country. In rainforest streams with overhanging vegetation, surface lures which can be twitched and wobbled and splashed should be worked in underneath the trees.

A favourite style of lure is one which floats high in the water but works a few centimetres beneath the surface on a steady retrieve. Such lures can be manipulated at the surface or made to resemble a struggling fish or frog. The fastest fishing comes under various berry trees, when fish will take anything as it hits the water.

Access:
You Can't Fish Without It

In almost all rivers, the use of a punt or canoe opens up the entire stream. Road

Barra are capable of spectacular aerial fights –
but they aren't the only species available

access is always available where bridges cross the water, so most streams can be fished for their full length. Alternative access through farms or cattle stations entails the landholder's permission, and a thoughtful and courteous approach usually gets results.

These days, the typical landholder will have no objection to catch and release fishing, or to those who only take enough for a family feed. Those bringing in a large portable freezer may find the landowner less agreeable - much the same as anywhere in this country. The general attitude with freshwater fish is for greater care than in the past. It's a mistake to assume that someone out in the bush won't mind at all if you take a hundred fish from his creek.

The focus on sooty grunter is useful because the general tactics applicable to them are acceptable to most other species. Tackle should be about the same as for bass or redfin in the south - a spinning rod and reel with 4 kg line will also handle the majority of other species, although you may need to use heavier tackle if barramundi or saratoga are possible. In general, there's no need for anything stronger than a short nylon trace two or three times the strength of the main line. An abrasion-resistant, co-filament trace is ideal.

Although sooty grunter and jungle perch may be found at least as far downriver as tidal freshwater, the lower stretches of the rivers are the best bet for the barramundi option. After major floods, barramundi may have been able to work well upstream unless the rivers have been blocked by barrages and weirs. It takes a really huge flood to overcome these obstacles to fish movement.

Sooties are available all year along the Queensland coast, with fishermen preferring to leave them alone during their breeding period in October/November. The best time of day to fish for them is the latter half of the afternoon.

These strategies relate specifically to freshwater extremities of tidal rivers. It is quite common for a river to contain both freshwater and salt water. Where the two meet will depend on the time of year, the extent of rainfall during the preceding wet season and the tidal movement on any given day.

Northern Territory

In the Northern Territory's Arnhem Land and Kakadu National Park, most of the fishing is for barramundi in flood plain lagoons. In this area, barramundi have retained their position as the dominant species, with saratoga as a shoreline fish mostly located around Pandanus or other cover. Sooty grunter will be found in the flowing sections of the rivers, such as the Daly.

Trolling for Barramundi

Trolling big minnows over deep snags and across rock bars is the best approach when looking for big barramundi.

In the diagram above 'X' represents where the line should enter the water, approximately 15 to 20 metres behind the boat. The perforated line depicts the lure depth and line of travel. The rod is hand held with tip laid out and back, providing a better feel so the angler can 'steer' the lure over obstructions and allow the tip to be dropped or lifted in reaction to a strike.

The ideal water depth for trolling big barra is approximately 1.8 to 3.5 metres. Boat speed and drop back are adjusted to control lure depth, so it travels within 'bumping distance' of bottom structure.

Lagoon fishing is often a trolling situation, using relatively shallow minnows such as the Nilsmasters, Rapalas and the proven Australian lures. For barramundi, fishing is at its best in autumn months, rather than winter and spring - barra become less active when water temperatures drop below 23 degrees.

Almost to the exclusion of all other fish, the barramundi is the dominant angling species. In nearly all rivers, the best freshwater fishing is in the wet season. Although there are access limitations in remote regions, all-weather roads lead to many big rivers, particularly those in Kakadu National Park, while others can be reached via the Arnhem Highway, Stuart Highway and Victoria Highway, and the MacArthur River from Borroloola.

During the wet season, water levels often rise and barramundi have the opportunity to move freely through floodplain channels and even across the floodplains themselves. For this well-adapted tropical predator, it is a time of plenty, when frogs, crustaceans, insects and small fish abound. For the angler however, a flooded, rising river is not conducive to good fishing because barramundi tend to spread out over a great deal of water.

By late March to early April, when the heavy monsoonal rainfall has stopped, the floods recede, the river levels begin to drop and fishing improves dramatically. The reason is that barramundi begin to leave the floodplains to congregate and feed where water is funnelled off them (as shown above).

Other fish move up the rivers from the salt water to join in the easy pickings at creek mouths and at the base of rapids and small waterfalls.

Straight after the wet season at these locations, barramundi are often caught easily, sometimes at a frenetic pace. Casting with swimming minnows is usually the most productive fishing method, but

Barramundi gather where inundated floodplains drain into rivers

surface lures such as poppers and fizzers can also be effective.

Late in April, and certainly by mid-May, the initial dramatic fall in river levels is over, and drainage off the floodplains has slowed to a trickle. At this time, barramundi take refuge in deeper holes, next to underwater dead trees and on or around submerged rockbars. Here, they feed according to the availability of food, water clarity and the movement of tides.

Although we are still considering freshwater sections of rivers, there can be some tidal influence. For example, an incoming spring tide will usually push muddy salt water up the river, and push the freshwater back.

Conversely, during neap tides, when tidal movement is minimal, the clear freshwater can work its way well down a river.

When you're aware that water clarity can be critical to the quality of barramundi fishing, it is easy to understand why the best fishing is usually during periods of neap tides.

Both trolling and casting are proven fish catchers during this period of falling water levels which might last until well after mid-year, depending on water temperature and when the freshwater pushing down a particular river stops completely. Trolling big minnows over deep snags and across rockbars is the best approach when looking for a big barra.

Once the freshwater runs out, in most rivers tidal range increases, water clarity reduces, siltation begins to take place and catching barramundi becomes more difficult. There are, however, exceptions to this pattern - rivers which retain their clarity even though salt water has replaced the freshwater completely. In these rivers, the quality of fishing will often improve as water temperature increases around September.

Inland Freshwater

Temperate Zone

Streams

A fundamental rule in streams is that any obstruction which provides a break in the flow may have the potential to hold fish. Stream dwelling fish utilise cover which deflects current and creates vantage positions from which to monitor food items washed downstream.

The skill of recognising fish-holding cover is an essential part of streamcraft. Some forms of cover are impossible to miss; snags and rocks are amongst the most obvious. Just as important but less easily discovered are channels.

Look Upstream for Silvers in Rising Water

Silver perch can be located in streams after heavy rain by looking for creek junctions, weirs and aquaducts where water is piped from an upstream level down to a lower stretch. This is so because these fish respond to rising water by moving upstream. Sometimes this can be put down to an expression of the spawning urge, but it often happens that fish caught in these places at such times are not in roe at all.

Generally speaking, the fish will be found a little to one side or the other of the strongest flow, and at such times, when gathered in numbers, will readily strike at small bladed spinners or the smaller kinds of wriggling deep-diving plugs.

Baits that work consistently on Silvers in such situations include worms, bardi grubs, small crayfish with the nippers removed or several small live shrimp impaled on a fine wire short shank hook.

All rivers have a main channel which generally follows the path of the water's fastest flow. They vary from a mere trickle in the case of a spring fed mountain stream to a veritable torrent when a big inland river is running a banker. Channels are most obvious along the outside of any river bend. Water moves faster through the outside of a bend, and has a scouring effect on both bank and river bed. Consequently, the water is deeper and the channel clearly defined.

Conversely, water travelling through the inside of the bend moves more slowly. This allows suspended silt to settle and accumulate over time forming the sand and mudbanks that characterise the inside bends of most rivers.

Fish of the temperate inland freshwater streams include Murray cod, these days becoming known by its aboriginal name of 'goodoo'. Golden and silver perch, Macquarie perch, and eel tail catfish are also here with trout in the mountainous headwater reaches. Redfin and carp are two less desirable residents.

Strategies for Murray cod and golden perch overlap. Both are predatory and bite best on a rising river. Lures and baits are both effective; however with increasing water quality problems in the inland rivers brought about by siltation, chemicals and irrigation, fish populations and water quality have both been degraded.

Water sufficiently clear for lure fishing is difficult to find in the far west inland rivers. How clear does the water need to be? The elbow test is a good guide. Immerse your arm to the elbow and your fingers should still be visible.

Diving lures with a strong, wide, and slow action are best for Murray cod and yellowbelly in rivers. Lure fishing options include trolling and casting to places where fish may be holding position. Spinning and baitcasting outfits and lines in the 4 to 8 kg class make for sporting encounters while retaining the firepower to land any Murray cod.

A multitude of baits will work on cod and yellowbelly. These include shrimps and crayfish, and wood and bardi grubs (which emit an odour that cod find attractive) and worms. Prohibitions now exist on the use and transportation of carp for live baits.

A standard rig for most inland bait fishing includes a French style hook (Mustad No. 540) in sizes 1/0 to 5/0 that has a ball sinker resting directly on the eye of the hook. This rig is versatile, effective and offers a considerable degree of snag proofing when compared to other alternatives. The golden rule with sinkers - 'only use the minimum weight necessary to get the job done' – applies equally to inland stream or dam fishing.

Silver and Macquarie perch have become somewhat scarce in inland rivers. Water quality problems brought about by farm runoff and cold water are major causes. Baits of worms and shrimps on 1/0 hooks are the best means of catching this elusive pair.

Catfish are likewise susceptible to deteriorating water quality. In many rivers, their niche has been taken over by European carp, a fish that should never be released when caught.

The redfin is a menace fish but it is good to eat and obliges anglers by readily responding to a wide array of angling techniques. They're a schooling fish that are at their best around the August/September period, when they gather to spawn.

This is one species on which anglers should do their utmost to rack up cricket score catches. An effective way to keep a redfin school biting is to keep one hooked fish in the water.

Most of the major inland rivers have big dams at their headwaters. Downstream reaches have become prime trout habitat because of the cold water released from the bottom of these dams. Flies, unweighed baits and small bladed spinners work well in such waters.

Wind can Determine Fish Location

One of the factors not understood too well by some lake fishermen is how the wind can determine where the fish will be.

Wind is one of the primary forces acting on large bodies of still water to induce currents and movement of food and other suspended matter.

It can also determine which parts of a lake are the warmest and coldest by means of its effect on the thermocline. The thermocline loosely defined, is a temperature break-line created by the stratifying effect common in all large bodies of enclosed water.

In the warmer months, water below a certain depth tends to be much colder than that at the surface, and this difference in temperatures can be quite marked at times, even differing by several degrees Centigrade.

Since fish show a marked dislike for moving from one temperature zone to another, this thermal 'barrier' can effectively keep fish locked up in a certain 'layer' or strata of water. What the wind does is to tilt this layering of differing water temperatures, piling all the warmer water up on one side of the lake and allowing the colder subsurface layers to slip up to the surface on the other.

Native fish tend to prefer the warmer water and so will characteristically be on the side of the lake the wind is blowing towards.

Trout and redfin on the other hand can be inclined to keep to the side from which the wind is blowing, although at night, trout will move into the windblown shoreline to feed on the gathered food items there.

Line Twist –What Causes It and How to Overcome It

Line twist is more common with threadline or spinning reels than baitcasters, but can occur with any type of reel when fishing fast water, or casting and retrieving repeatedly into moving water.It's usually caused either by the bait or lure being rigged off-line enough for the force of the water to make the bait gyrate and with each revolution, another twist is imparted to the line.

To correct this, make sure your lures are rigged with the knot centrally fixed on the leading wire loop or ring of the lure if using a clinch knot, or better still, use a small loop knot which allows the lure to track straight and not kick out to one side.

Still on lures, some bladed models cannot be retrieved against a current without imparting twist to the line, some other swimming plug type lures will only stay on track at slow speeds or when being retrieved through still water. Match the lure style and retrieve speed to the prevailing conditions and if all else fails, try rigging a small trolling keel between the lure and the mainline to assist in maintaining the lure's alignment. This makes them more troublesome to cast, but may be the only way to avoid the problem of twist.

When fishing with baits, it is vital that the bait be rigged to lie symmetrically, ie. in line with the direction of pull from the main line. Retrieving a curved or irregular shaped bait like a shrimp or yabbie hooked through the middle is just asking for the water to spin it around.

Sometimes line twist is caused by the tackle, or more to the point, the way it is used. If you are using a spinning reel and you have the drag set too lightly, you can find yourself winding in against the pressure of water or a struggling fish and not getting any line back. This is because the clutch is slipping line instead of allowing it to be gathered in by the reel's spinning rotor. What it is also doing is imparting one full twist to the line with each rotation of the bail arm. Tighten the drag enough to prevent this happening and you will minimise the risk of line twist.

Golden Perch respond to lures retrieved slowly and erratically

Redfin can be taken by trolling along lake margins or on the outside edges of points. When bait-fishing or using dense sinking lures for 'bobbing', large numbers of redfin can be caught by keeping one hooked fish in the water until another one is hooked

Most lure rigs work best with a minimum of encumbrances like swivels and clips and so on, but often a good quality swivel is necessary to minimise this problem. It is possible to buy good quality ball bearing swivels in sizes to suit all but the lightest of rigs these days. They're not cheap, but they are the very best kind of swivel for this particular job.

Impoundments

In every sense, freshwater impoundments have a lot of water mixed in with the fish. Any strategy for fishing the big dams has to come to terms with this fact and work on the process of eliminating unproductive areas, and concentrating on likely habitat.

It's not hard. Native fish such as Murray cod (goodoo), golden, silver and Macquarie perch are found around the fringe areas of a lake in water depths roughly between 2 and 6 m. The summits of submerged hills within that distance of the

surface are also worth seeking out and trying.

Their presence is often signposted by trees poking out in the middle of nowhere. However, a sounder is a better means of confirming bottom formations.

Redfin likewise occupy these lake margins but go deep to escape the heat of summer. At times they can be down around the 12 m level. At that depth, a sophisticated fish finder is definitely needed to pinpoint their position. Trout have a similar vertical movement when the summer heat hits.

Covering water is the name of the game when fishing impoundments. There is no better way to do this than trolling lures. Deep diving wobbling lures fished on spin or baitcasting tackle are popular choices.

The great sensitivity of graphite rods allows the angler to monitor the action of the lure by the way this material transmits the throb of the lure to the flicking rod tip.

Another source of feedback on lure position is when the lure regularly bumps over the bottom and snags. True, this will result in some hangups, but anglers who aren't making contact with underwater objects with their lures are often fishing where there are no fish either.

When and if you do snag a lure, don't make the situation worse by heaving on the rod. By backing up past the snagged lure, a firm pull on the line will generally free the lure. Failing that, use a lure retrieval device, like a 'Tackle back'. At today's lure prices, lure retrievers are a wise investment.

There are specific shorelines which anglers should troll. These include steep rocky banks, treelines, points and the edges of weedbeds. Some locations cry out for more attention than just a cursory troll. Probing these with bait is the way to go.

Unquestionably, live shrimps are the best all-round bait for impoundment fishing.

Shrimps are plentiful in dams during the summer months and can be gathered in traps baited with bread or soap.

They can be rigged in a number of ways, but the same 540 Mustad hook and ball sinker rig used in freshwater streams lets anglers use the deadly technique of 'bobbing' around snags and points. This involves repeatedly lifting the rod tip a few inches so that the bait has a yo-yo action just off the bottom.

The bobbing technique is also deadly on redfin. Small metal lures can also be successfully fished in the same manner when the school becomes excited. September is a prime time.

Freshwater catfish, known in various parts of their range as jewfish or even (curiously) 'dhufish', have proliferated in dams.

The most productive technique is to fish for them around dusk on gently sloping mudbanks. Soft baits such as worms and peeled crayfish tail provide excellent results. Care is needed when handling this fish. The leading edges of its pectoral and dorsal fins have sharp spines which can inflict painful wounds.

There are a number of specific techniques for trout in temperate impoundments. These include fishing mudeyes under a bubble float. Trolling mudeyes behind ford fenders and other attracting devices in the summer months, can be used in conjunction with downriggers to reach suitably cool water layers.

Casting and retrieving 'spoon' lures from rocky points is a successful method when trout are in the surface layers.

Arguably, the majority of trout caught in temperate zone dams are taken in September/October by anglers trolling over gently sloping shorelines. Best lures are such proven favourites as the Tasmanian Devil, McGrath minnows and the Jensen Killroys.

Native fish can be difficult to find and catch in dams. Techniques which work in rivers don't necessarily produce in impoundments. Atmospheric and water conditions provide the key. Best fishing is between late spring and early summer.

Finding Fish in the Middle of the Day

In the heat of the day, you can still continue to catch fish by looking for places where there are likely to be significant contrasts in light intensity or water temperature.

This means the deep dark corners of undercut banks or shady areas under overhanging trees are worth investigating at such times. So are creek mouths and junctions of rivers where there may be a definite rise or fall in temperature where the joins flow.

It can also pay at such creek junctions to work the edges between clear and discoloured water as the dirty water is often more comfortable for the fish, filtering out much of the strongest light at midday.

Tarpon this big are a rarity but even the small models have tremendous speed and strength for their size.

Tropical Zone

The most overlooked region of tropical fishing is the inland freshwater. It offers fishing ranging from the exploratory in pristine streams to newly stocked water storages. The popular focus on rainforest streams and the coastal floodplains of the Northern Territory often ignores the rewards of inland angling.

Queensland

The size and number of major catchments offers a variety of prospects to travellers. These can be roughly divided into three or more categories, including:

❶ **Inland tributaries** – major river systems such as the Fitzroy, Burdekin and Mitchell have thousands of kilometres of tributary rivers, which are often hundreds of kilometres in length.

❷ **Tableland plateaus** – primarily the Atherton Tableland, inland from Cairns,

plus some of the headwater country above coastal gorges on rivers like the Herbert. These are generally smaller streams.

❸ **Impoundment fishing** – a number of large storages have now been successfully stocked with sooty grunter, barramundi, saratoga and other species. The best established of these is Tinaroo (inland from Cairns) but a number of others are coming increasingly into play.

They include Koombooloomba (Tully Falls Dam), Copperlode, Burdekin Falls Dam, and Eungella (inland from Mackay). Although stocked, not all of these are available for fishing by the public. Copperlode, for example, is the Cairns water supply dam, and as such is restricted.

Koombooloomba is known to contain sooty grunter of about the same size as those of Tinaroo (impoundment sooties grow to record sizes) but access is not easy without a boat. Inquiries should always be

Above: Saratoga will strike willingly at lures presented close to cover where they may be waiting in ambush or cruising.
Right: Classic saratoga habitat – pandanus trees with fringing cover of lily pads.

Sooty grunter are the mainstay of many tropical inland streams.

made as the requirements are always subject to change.

The inland tributaries of the Fitzroy River (such as the Dawson, Isaac and McKenzie) offer two interesting variants on other tropical fishing. They contain yellowbelly (golden perch) in eastern watershed system, as well as saratoga and other natives, especially the large 'sleepy cod'. Dams and barrages on coastal rivers have largely blocked the inland movement of barramundi which were often present well upstream in pioneering days. This is generally undulating cattle country interspersed with coal mining towns, and a great deal of access is through the courtesy of local landholders.

The Burdekin tributaries further north contain neither yellowbelly nor saratoga, but are home to several species of sooty grunter, including the small-mouthed grunter. Catfish, eels, freshwater rifle fish and sleepy cod cover most of the list.

Prior to the building of barrages, weirs and dams, barramundi used to work upriver as far as the Bowen Junction and above Dalbeg. With the removal of barramundi from the river system, catfish took over the middle sections. Well inland, there are still some good sooty regions (including small-mouth grunter) in tributaries such as the Bowen, Belyando, Suttor, Cap and Star Rivers, and Keelbottom Creek.

The Mitchell River headwaters run well inland to the tablelands north-west of Cairns and include good sooty country. Lower down, where the rate of flow is slower, the Gulf drainage rivers offer some of our most reliable saratoga fishing - mostly ignored through the presence of barramundi closer to the sea. A surprising amount of inland fishing is available in the Northern Territory, at places like Bottletree Waterhole, Mataranka and Broadmere.

Tableland Plateaus

The Atherton Tableland is the tropical equivalent of the New England or Monaro Tablelands of NSW. Some prime small waterways, including Herbert river tributaries like the Millstream and tributaries of the Mitchell, offer quiet exploring for sooty grunter under pristine conditions. Results are often spectacular in numbers.

This fishery is not widely exploited by anyone except locals, and is notable for the relief it offers from the high temperature and humidity of the coast. The Tablelands are degrees cooler and the air is drier, there are no problems with crocodiles (apart from a few of the harmless freshwater variety) and people pressure is lower.

Impoundment Fishing

Impoundment fishing in the north always involves Tinaroo, the agricultural lake between Atherton and Mareeba. Prospects include barramundi, saratoga, huge sooty grunter, sleepy cod, rifle fish and silver perch.

Although barramundi have grown well in this fertile water, they have proven hard to catch. In autumn, winter and spring, water temperatures in Tinaroo are generally too low for good barramundi fishing. Barramundi need water temperatures at or above 23 degrees celsius to prompt feeding behaviour conducive to capture.

Only a handful of saratoga were initially released, and these appear not to have increased greatly. Silver perch fattened quickly but as in many other impoundments, have not been a top proposition. Sleepy cod are a fine table fish but are not rated highly in angling terms, and rifle fish, though abundant, are only pan size.

The big success story then is the sooty grunter, which are regularly caught in weights of 2 kilos or more. They are never as numerous as the same species in the rivers, but they fight well - much more strongly than most other native species in still water. Many are caught on sinking, rattling lures amongst the trunks of standing trees - drowned timber is thick around the margins of the dam.

Apart from its fertility, which results from the run off of surrounding rich farmlands, Tinaroo has benefited from the proximity of the Walkamin Research Station, an agricultural facility which includes a Fisheries sector. Other dams will come on stream shortly.

Eungella is already well established as a freshwater fishery; the Burdekin Falls Dam offers future potential and a huge area of water; and the Tully Falls Dam may expand during the late 1990s.

The Northern Territory

The Top End is well known for its abundance of inland waterways or lagoons, some large enough to accommodate dozens of small boats without anglers getting in each other's way. With some exceptions, fishing in these lagoons is restricted to the dry season because of lack of wet season access.

Typically, a Top End lagoon is a landlocked freshwater stretch of river. Most rivers flow from their headwaters to the sea during the wet season, then progressively break up into a series of lagoons during the dry season. Some lagoons are not part of a river course, and can even be located some distance from the nearest river. These lagoons might only be linked to a river during a major flood. It means that barramundi, which begin life at the river mouths and spend their early years in the lagoons, can be trapped in the freshwater for longer than they intended to stay. In these instances, anglers have the opportunity to catch fish much bigger than normally encountered in lagoons.

Barramundi inhabit most lagoons in the Top End. However, they decrease in numbers the further inland one travels, and the quality of fishing varies greatly.

At the beginning of the dry season, the water is still warm and fish are quite active. As in the rivers, they can be located where floodplain swamps drain into the lagoons. But they can also be caught wherever there is shelter. Submerged dead trees and rockbars are always worth trying, as are weed beds and around patches of lilies.

During the middle of the year, water temperatures in the lagoons are low and barramundi tend to be much less active. Good catches can still be taken, but generally only early in the morning and from late in the afternoon until dark.

Without doubt, the best lagoon fishing for barramundi is during the hotter, humid months preceding the wet season. September is usually the month when the barramundi become active. From then until the first significant rainstorms, la-

Young Matt Chan caught this saratoga on a small surface popper.

goon barramundi are likely to feed at any time of day. Typically, a feeding period will last for an hour or two. Trolling lures, or casting lures and flies will take fish. Use a good depth-sounder to outline structures and shelter points, and to show fish, as this will definitely improve the catch.

Barramundi can readily be caught at night during the late dry season. This is very exciting angling because the fish tend to move out into the open, sometimes even schooling. The pace can be hectic, and the noise from chopping barramundi remarkable. Surface lures such as poppers and fizzers are ideal in these conditions, but large, dark, swimming minnows also work well.

One technique for locating a patch of feeding barra at night is to troll both a popper and a minnow very slowly, using an electric outboard motor. The speed should be slow enough to work the popper effectively. This speed would be too slow for the minnow to be effective in daylight hours. Minnows therefore should be worked by jigging the rod steadily. During a full moon, trolling shallow run-

ning minnows at normal speeds can also catch fish.

Special mention should be made here of sinking-rattling lures which, in recent years, have increased in popularity with barramundi anglers. Both during daylight hours and at night, these lures sometimes catch fish when all else fails. They are either cast and jigged slowly to the boat, or simply lowered into a snag and jigged, or they can be trolled. They attract fish by both noise and sight and can be worked at any depth.

The saratoga is another popular angling quarry in the lagoons. Like the barramundi, it takes lures and flies, and has a similar tendency to jump clear of the water when hooked. It is invariably located near the surface, usually in the midst of a patch of lily pads or in the shade of an overhanging pandanus tree. Surface poppers work well, and weedless popping or "blooping" surface flies are very effective in the lilies. The saratoga is not generally regarded as a good eating fish and is prone to stress, so it should be handled carefully before being released.

163

Northern Territory Wetlands

During the wet season low-lying country is inundated and when this water begins to flow back into the rivers, fish congregate at these drainage points.

In fact, care should be taken with all fish destined for release. In particular, do not lift fish by their gill-covers. Take full advantage of a large landing net, even to the point of weighing the fish in a net. In the Top End, the use of barbless hooks is also becoming popular as a sporting conservation measure. Simply squeeze the barbs in with a pair of pliers. This facilitates the speedy removal of hooks from fish, and can save a great deal of discomfort when removing hooks from fish – or people.

Particularly in respect of barramundi, there will be no noticeable increase in fish lost through the use of barbless hooks. In fact, the hook-up rate can be better with barbless hooks because penetration is easier.

Further inland, tropical freshwater will provide members of the grunter family. Most anglers refer to these fish as sooty grunter or black bream. They are prevalent in rock pools such as those found in escarpment country. Grunter take small lures but are more easily caught on bait. Red meat is a favourite.

Other angling species encountered at inland freshwater locations include oxeye herring or tarpon, sleepy cod, archer fish and catfish.

Repetitive Casting – Why it Works &When

One of the tricks experienced fishermen learn very quickly is that barra are a lazy fish most if the time, not neccessarily rushing out and hitting a lure just because it swims within reach.

Often, a barra can be goaded into striking a lure if you are persistent enough to work away on a likely snag or holding position long enough to wear their resistance down.

The reasons it works are basically recognisable within generally understood principles of fish behaviour, but there are so many variables that each specific situation requires its own set of solutions before you can be certain that there is not a fish in residence.

Granted that you have learned to recognise the kinds of places that barra like to camp, patience and persistence are the keys to success.

Just why a fish will ignore the lure twenty or thirty times then suddenly rush out and grab it can vary from a steady rise in water temperature as the day wears on, to subtle differences in the path or retrieve speed and general behaviour of the lure. Or it can simply be a mounting aggravation with this little 'invader' that persists in violating the fish's private space. Sometimes, you'll feel a hint of a strike, or a subtle touch during a retrieve, or even a fairly solid whack that doesn't properly connect or result in a hookup. This is very often the sort of evidence that novice anglers miss, not being tuned to the feel of the lure and not being really sure whether the lure bumped a branch, pulled through some weed or what. It's these low-key signals however that encourage the experienced angler to persevere and intensify his efforts, often securing a hookup when a beginner might have given up and moved onto another snag or corner.

If you get a bump on the way in on one retrieve and not on another put in exactly the same place, it's unlikely to be a branch as dead trees don't move around much. It's much more likely to have been a fish. If it's a snag, you'll feel the bump in the same place at the same depth and you should be able to get it three or four times in a row. If it's weed, or mud, you'll generally bring up some evidence of either, attached to the lure.

Often, a sudden change in pace or retrieve style can trigger a following or swirling fish to lose control and really whack the lure. The thing is, you have to try to visualise what the lure is doing down there and work it as if there was a fish after it each time.

*Barramundi this size continue to attract
anglers to the Northern Territory.*

STRATEGIES FOR

Alpine Freshwater

Streams

Some New England and Victorian highlands contain native fish like cod and Macquarie perch, but most of the angling species you'll find in Australian alpine freshwater streams are trout. That's no burden though, as strategies which work for trout are effective on other alpine fish too.

Strategy for alpine stream angling can be summed up in one word - presentation, but like most simplifications, hides a wealth of complexity. Under the simple umbrella of 'presentation' there are many related factors.

To begin, most streams confront you with a body of water moving pretty much in one direction. That single factor is responsible for many of the angling problems and opportunities encountered in fishing alpine rivers.

Stream flow over vegetation and boulders provides oxygenated water for the fish to breathe, while simultaneously delivering a good deal of food to it. Thus, in all but the deepest and slowest pools, the fish will face more or less into the current. Those which don't are either sleeping, hiding, or cruising. When you can't see fish, the tactics differ somewhat from when the fish is spotted and is in plain view. Each can be dealt with however, so let's consider strategies for when you can't see the fish, then look at some for when you can.

Fishing to unseen fish is a lot less dull and boring if you consider where the fish are likely to be. The clues to fish location are visible even when the fish aren't. Each pool and bend or run has its own set of natural 'furniture' which can help you deduce where the fish might be.

Trees, banks and bottom contours determine where water is directed and where the shade falls at different times of the day. Fish generally take up positions out of direct sunlight, where they can hold station with very little effort, yet intercept any food brought to them by the current. They also cruise under overhangs of rock, foliage or bank undercuts.

Look for logs lying at an angle to the bank, or clumps of reeds or grasses that form little islands around and between

Even quite large fish can take up position in seemingly insignificant places. This 1.5 kg brown trout came from a narrow gutter barely wide enough for the fish to turn around in. The critical factor here was that there was enough water depth and flow to provide a feeding station.

Alpine Stream

The trout closest to the bottom of the page has taken up residence in a depression scoured out by water flow deflected off the large boulder. It has little real 'cover' other than the light-diffused effect of water depth and the camouflage of rippled water surface.

The other fish is lying in the shelter of bank-side foliage which enables it to utilise a shallower depression than the first fish.

Both fish are in the optimum available positions for cover, rest and food supply. Best presentation on both cases is to approach from downstream, cast up past the fish, and rely on the fish making an instinctive grab at the passing lure, bait or fly. For best results, cast a little to one side of the fish to avoid 'lining' and frightening it.

which water is funnelled. The heads of pools are good places to explore with spinners or flies, as fish often sit in the holes gouged out by water tumbling from the pool above. In long runs, cast up past boulders or alongside overhanging blackberry bushes. If you see the bow wave of a pursuing fish closing in behind the lure, don't stop or speed up – do both – the change in speed often prompts a following fish to hit instead of turning away.

Broad shallow pools with a long flat glide to the tail can be fished effectively by casting cross-stream. Allow the bait or lure to swing down through the tail of the pool as this can pick up fish sitting in small depressions just ahead of the tail-end shallows.

Floating baits such as crickets, grasshoppers, or even Christmas beetles, can be drifted downstream and worms are effective too, especially after rain. Worms should be tumbled naturally along the bottom, using split shot only if the current is too strong to present the bait otherwise.

Fish respond best when the offering is put where they are, not half a pool away. It works even better when it's presented right where they can't ignore it, in a way they can't resist. That's the essence of presentation - pulling something they can't resist right past their noses. It works much better than 'chucking and chancing it'.

Presentation is easier to understand but more difficult to achieve when approaching fish you've already sighted on a stream. Fish are relatively blind to anything directly behind them, so it's easier to approach them from downstream. Provided you move quietly and your presence is masked by steep banks or bankside foliage, you can get within a rod's length of such fish without them knowing you're there. Try to avoid heavy footfalls or being silhouetted against the skyline or contrasting backgrounds.

When releasing fish, hold them upright in the water, with minimal hand pressure – allowing the current to revive them before letting them go.

If you see a fish lying motionless and facing downstream or across stream, it could be asleep, but more probably, it has already seen you and in response to the threat, has "frozen". This is a common predator/prey response pattern. Lack of movement can be an effective form of flight itself, especially for species reliant on camouflage, like trout.

A scared fish can be approached again an hour or so later - but rather than just slip away without gaining anything from the pool, recognise that the damage is done and move quietly past or through the pool - but watch where the fish goes, as chances are it will scoot off to a secure bolt hole nearby.

Often, if you draw a mental line between where it froze and where it ran to, you can sometimes spot the lie it was occupying when you scared it. At least, having made a careful examination of the pool, you can locate feeding lies and with that information, plan a better approach later.

Cruising fish move in roughly an elliptical circuit or 'beat'. They present one of the most challenging angling situations you can face, but also one of the most exciting and rewarding.

The problem is, you have to be close enough to the fish to cast, yet right in its line of sight at some part of its beat. To avoid it seeing you, your skills of concealment have to be pretty good, but you can learn from the trout you just scared in the last pool. If you freeze, you'll be harder for the fish to see.

When the fish completes its beat toward you and turns to swim away again, you can move quickly, set yourself and deliver a cast while the fish has its back to you. The cast should be slightly ahead and to one side of the fish and although difficult, can be very satisfying when it works.

You hold your breath, watch the fish, and when it veers over to inhale your fly, it's one of fishing's best highs!

The first time you sneak up on a fish, you'll probably surprise yourself. Surprise quickly gives way to fascination though as you watch the fish go about its business without a care in the world. Such events will at first be more the result of accident than design, but that doesn't matter. Each encounter will give you insights into little quirks and variations of trout behaviour and you won't forget them - adrenalin will burn them into your brain.

Spotting fish is an acquired skill, and there are some very helpful tools and techniques, all of which stand or fall on the foundation stone of approach. The first, most important thing to learn is to move quietly and unobtrusively through (or preferably) alongside a pool. To that, add a wide-brimmed hat to shade your eyes, good polarising sunglasses to cut glare and heighten contrast, and dull clothes and rod fittings to avoid scaring fish.

Snakes can be a problem in summer, but usually only for the careless or fool-hardy. Wearing adequate footwear and sensible clothing which includes loose-fitting, long-legged trousers is a must, and waders are even better protection. There is no substitute for using your eyes though.

Most good trout water runs through somebody's private property. Usually they're working farms with real costs and overheads and farmers don't appreciate having fences or gates damaged, or fires lit, or stock let in or out of places they're not supposed to be. So don't light fires, or negotiate fences and gates without due care, and leave gates as you find them. That means if you find a locked one, don't open it at all.

Treat the farmer's land like the private property it is. If the land were yours and somebody wanted to come onto the place, you'd want to know about it beforehand. Exercise good manners and good sense, and seek permission before you enter anyone's property.

Lakes

Angling strategies for trout and salmon in alpine impoundments vary. Best techniques depend on the time of year or even the time of day.

Trolling is one of the most effective methods of capturing trout in alpine lakes. The best times for trolling are between April and early November, the colder months when trout are near the surface and feeding in shallow water.

Trolling is often referred to as 'flat-lining' because the lures don't go down very deep. Most lures such as Tassie Devils, Rapalas, spoons, and other general swimming plugs run at about 1 to 2 m down. Even the best deep-diving trout plug, the McGrath diver, only runs down to about 3 m.

Lakes often provide more food than streams, resulting in faster growth rates and fatter fish. This rainbow from Ben Chifley dam near Bathurst was full of small carp

So, conventional trolling is best in the cooler months when the fish are feeding up in this depth range. Troll slowly, say at 1 to 2 knots and if there's not much response from the fish, try a longer drop back to the lure. Anywhere between 3 m and 30 m may be necessary.

During the marginal months of November and March, when the water is a bit warmer,. many anglers use a system of attractors, which are flashing metal blades connected to wire harnesses. These are variously called 'cowbells', 'ford fenders', 'dodgers' and 'dodger chains' - you get the idea, they're big and flashy and they make a lot of underwater 'noise' and attract the attention of trout that are tending to hold at depths where normal lures can't call them up.

Because they're heavy, they also get down a bit further to begin with as well, so they serve quite well for a middle depth trolling device. They can be used to troll lures at 1 to 1.5 knots, or to troll baits like mudeyes or worms, at a slower speed, say less than 1 knot.

In the really warm months, the way to get lures and baits down to the cold-loving trout and salmon is to use downriggers. Downriggers allow you to troll a lure or bait at a precise controllable depth. A downrigger is a simple winch unit which lowers a very heavy weight called a 'bomb' to a predetermined depth.

The line is clipped to the bomb in such a way that when a fish strikes the lure or bait, the line comes free and the angler can fight the fish unencumbered by any of the downrigging apparatus. This alone makes the system superior to anything like flashers or lead core line which remain part of the rig during the fight and get in the way.

Generally, any bait or lure can be trolled behind a downrigger bomb. Trolling speeds can vary between 1 and 3 knots and varying the speed may help produce results. The distance the lure or bait is dropped back behind the bomb should be anywhere between 5 and 50 m depending on fish timidity.

Good downrigging lures include Tassie lures, Rapala CD series and floaters, Jen-

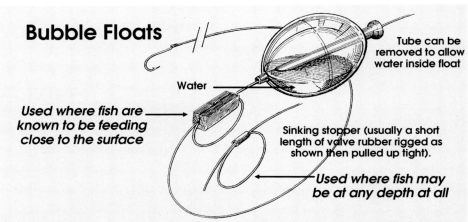

Bubble Floats

Tube can be removed to allow water inside float

Water

Used where fish are known to be feeding close to the surface

Sinking stopper (usually a short length of valve rubber rigged as shown then pulled up tight).

Used where fish may be at any depth at all

Bubble floats are hollow and may be partially filled with water to give added weight for casting. They come in two types, spherical and egg-shaped. The latter are the more versatile and popular, and generally rigged as running floats. The bottom stopper may be of cork, foam or hypalon, all of which float – or it may be of rubber which will sink slowly provided the line is slack. With low density bottom stoppers, no top stopper is required.

When split shot is used to sink a bait below a bubble float, then a top stopper is needed to prevent the bait sinking all the way to the bottom. Rigged this way however, the fish feels the weight of the float and can drop the bait. That is why this rig is seldom used.

Sometimes, a small running ball sinker is placed on the line above the bubble float when fishing a windward shore. The strategy is to anchor the float so it doesn't drift into the bank, yet still retain the free running characteristics of the rig.

sen Killroys, Pegron Tiger Minnows, Flutterspoons (on a long drop-back), small J-Plugs, Rebel's Crawfish and the Producer's Crawdaddy.

Lurecasting from the shore is best during autumn and spring, and in the early morning and evening. The traditional heavy trout spoons have been replaced in modern angling with minnows from Rapala, Daiwa, and Bill Norman, and lighter lures like the Landa Lukki.

During the day, the angler should concentrate on the deeper water off points, and use deep diving floaters or sinking minnows. When fishing bays and flats areas when the light levels are lower, shift to shallower running lures.

In winter, it pays to target the mouths of creeks and rivers because trout will congregate here as they run up to spawn.

Flyfishing alpine lakes falls into two categories. The first, and usually the best, is to work the shallows and margins in the months between September and November. Use nymphs or wet-fly patterns like Mrs Simpsons or Hamill's Killers on a floating line in the early morning and later afternoon to evening.

On bright, blue-sky days, the angler equipped with polarising sunglasses can spot trout working in the shallows and cast to specific fish with nymphs or dry flies.

During summer, there are often big trout to be had by fly-fishing the margins at night. The fish are encouraged by the darkness and cooling water to enter these food rich areas and successful flies include black Muddler Minnows, Craig's Night-times and similar dark patterns.

Baitfishing accounts for good fish both from the shore and from boats. A mudeye under a bubble float or mudeye waggler is very effective. Worms can also be fished under a float or on the bottom with a running sinker rig.

A good guide is to fish in known fish feeding zones like drop-offs near shallow areas, deep channels like old river beds running across otherwise flat country, and anywhere around trees or other submerged cover like rocks.

Rigging a Mudeye for Trolling

Mudeyes make excellent troll baits, particularly behind flashing spoons, cowbells or other attractors. It is paramount to rig the bait properly though, as it may spin or bunch on the hook.

The method shown here is used successfully by Fred Jobson of Cobram in Victoria. The hook is a Mustad 7692 which accommodates this bait well. Size 6 is recommended.

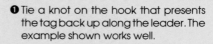

❶ Tie a knot on the hook that presents the tag back up along the leader. The example shown works well.

❷ Cut the mudeye's bottom jaws away and put the point of the hook in its mouth.

❸ Work the bait around the curve of the hook and down the shank.

❹ The point of the hook should emerge at the rear of the bait in the centre of the three spikes. The eye of the hook should have been drawn inside the mouth of the bait where the tag will prevent it bunching on the hook. Trolling speed needs to be very slow.

CHAPTER

5

MAPS & REGIONAL GUIDES

Tweed Heads to South West Rocks

Tweed Heads offers good estuary fishing, particularly from the seawalls in the river, while outside there is good rock and surf fishing as well as fishing for snapper and other reef fish. In calm weather seaworthy boats venture out over the Tweed River bar. Near Cook Island, just to the south, is a good location for bottom fishing and light-tackle gamefishing.

Below Fingal Head the basalt rocks of the Devil's Causeway descend in giant steps to high flat rocks which present good rock fishing and spinning. This is a hotspot for tailor, kingfish, bonito, tuna, Spanish mackerel, and trevally. Further south, Kingscliff has good rock and beach fishing around Cudgera Head while Cudgen Creek offers bream, flathead and whiting.

Hastings Point offers rock beach and estuary fishing and there is surf and estuary fishing at Pottsville and Mooball Beach. Brunswick Heads has surf, rock, seawall and estuary fishing. It is a summer hotspot for whiting and flathead.

Byron Bay to Woolgoolga: Byron Bay has excellent surf and rock fishing. Cape Byron, below the lighthouse, gives scope for rockfishing and spinning. Facing north to the Julian Rocks there is a boulder-bed to the west and deep water to the east. To the south, Seven Mile Beach has good surf and rock fishing as far as Lennox Head. Ballina has good estuary and river fishing. Seawall, surf and rockfishing is close at hand and Evans Head to the south has good surf and rockfishing.

Iluka and Yamba are respectively north and south of the Clarence River entrance. Both offer excellent seawall and estuary fishing, surf and rockfishing to the north and good surf fishing south toward Angourie and Brooms Head. There is good inshore angling as well as surf and rockfishing for tailor, bream, mulloway and whiting at Angourie and Sandon River, down to Minnie Waters and Wooli. Minnie Waters is famed for its plentiful pipis and beach worms. Below there, Red Rock offers rock, beach and estuary fishing and Woolgoolga beach is used to launch small boats for trips to the Solitary group of islands.

Coffs Harbour to South West Rocks: Coffs Harbour has good fishing from its harbour walls and adjacent rocks and beaches. There is also excellent offshore fishing around Split Solitary and South Solitary islands for flathead and all desirable reef species as well as kingfish, tailor, Spanish mackerel, cobia and mulloway.

Bonville Reserve south of Sawtell offers creek, surf and rockfishing. Further south, Urunga has estuary, rock and beach fishing, good outside snapper grounds, and lure-eating bream upstream in the South Arm of the Bellinger River. Valla Beach is good for estuary and surf fishing.

Nambucca Heads offers estuary fishing in the Nambucca River, a productive seawall and good reef fishing outside. Macksville has estuary fishing, Scotts Head and Grassy Head have good rock fishing and Stuart's Point on the Macleay's blind northern arm is good for estuary species.

Just south of the Macleay, and reached by road from Kempsey, South West Rocks offers excellent rock, beach and estuary fishing and access to stunning inshore fishing from Grassy Head in the north to Smoky Cape and Fish Rock in the south.

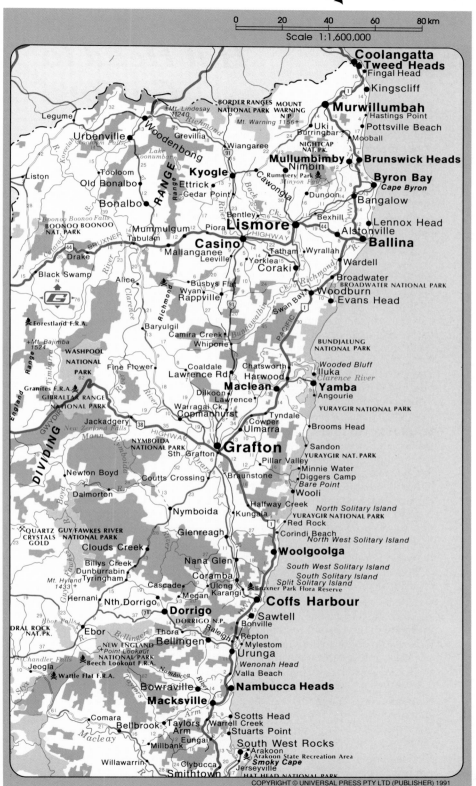

0   20   40   60   80 km

Scale 1:1,600,000

Coolangatta
Tweed Heads
Fingal Head

Kingscliff

BORDER RANGES MOUNT
NATIONAL PARK WARNING
N P
Mt. Warning 1156+

Murwillumbah
Hastings Point

+Mt Lindesay
1240

Legume

Urbenville

Woodenbong

Grevillia

Wiangaree

Uki
Burringbar

NIGHTCAP
NAT. PK.

Mooball

Pottsville Beach

Mullumbimby
Nimbin

Brunswick Heads

Liston

Tooloom

Kyogle

Rummery Park

Cawongla

Byron Bay
Cape Byron

Old Bonalbo
Ettrick
Cedar Point

Dunoon

Bangalow

Bonalbo

Bentley
Piora

Bexhill

Lennox Head

BOONOO BOONOO
NAT. PARK

Mummulgum
Tabulam

Lismore

Alstonville
Ballina

Drake

Casino

Mallanganee
Leeville

Tatham
Yorklea
Coraki

Wyrallah

Wardell

Black Swamp

Alice

Busbys Flat
Wyan
Rappville

Broadwater
BROADWATER NATIONAL PARK
Woodburn
Evans Head

Forestland F.R.A.

Baryulgil

Camira Creek
Whiporie

BUNDJALUNG
NATIONAL PARK

+Mt. Bajimba
1524

WASHPOOL
NATIONAL
PARK

Fine Flower

Coaldale
Lawrence Rd

Chatsworth
Harwood

Wooded Bluff
Iluka
Clarence River

Granites F.R.A.
GIBRALTAR RANGE
NATIONAL PARK

Dilkoon
Lawrence

Maclean

Yamba
Angourie

Jackadgery

New Zealand Falls

Warragai Ck.
Copmanhurst

Tyndale
Cowper
Ulmarra

YURAYGIR NATIONAL PARK

Brooms Head

DIVIDING

NYMBOIDA
NATIONAL PARK

Sth. Grafton

Grafton

Sandon
YURAYGIR NAT. PARK

Newton Boyd

Coutts Crossing

Pillar Valley
Braunstone

Minnie Water
Diggers Camp
Bare Point

Dalmorton

Wooli

Nymboida

Kungala

Halfway Creek

North Solitary Island
YURAYGIR NATIONAL PARK

QUARTZ
CRYSTALS
GOLD

GUY FAWKES RIVER
NATIONAL PARK

Glenreagh

Red Rock
Corindi Beach
North West Solitary Island

Clouds Creek

Nana Glen

Woolgoolga

Billys Creek
Dunburrabin
Tyringham

Coramba

Mt. Hyland
1433+

Cascade

Ulong
Megan Karangi

South West Solitary Island
South Solitary Island
Split Solitary Island
Bruxner Park Flora Reserve

Hernani

Nth. Dorrigo

Dorrigo

DORRIGO N.P.

Coffs Harbour

Sawtell
Bonville

DRAL ROCK
NAT. PK.

Ebor

NEW ENGLAND
NATIONAL PARK

Thora
Bellingen

Repton
Mylestom
Urunga

Chandler Falls

Jeogla

Point Lookout
Beech Lookout F.R.A.
Wattle Flat F.R.A.

Wenonah Head
Valla Beach

Bowraville

Nambucca Heads

Macksville

Comara

Bellbrook

Taylors
Arm

Warrell Creek

Scotts Head
Stuarts Point

Millbank

Eungai

South West Rocks
Arakoon State Recreation Area

Willawarrin

Clybucca
Smithtown

Jerseyville

Smoky Cape

HAT HEAD NATIONAL PARK

Hat Head to Gosford

Hat Head has excellent rockfishing for snapper, drummer, tailor and mulloway, and is famed for its landbased captures of Spanish mackerel and cobia. In summer, boat fishermen catch small black marlin on trolled lures and on livebaits.

Crescent Head to Seal Rocks: Crescent Head and Point Plomer offer good beach and rockfishing. Port Macquarie offers the gamefisherman a fairly safe river bar and good offshore grounds, while the holiday angler can find most estuary species in the Hastings River, and superb beach and estuary fishing south at Laurieton.

Crowdy Head has snapper and drummer available to rock fishermen who are geared to fish the cliff tops and there is good snapper and trevally fishing within a short offshore run to Mermaid Reef. Harrington provides bream, tailor, flathead and whiting from its seawall and estuary reaches and kingfish and mulloway from a spot known as the Gantry.

Taree sits on the Manning River which offers good estuary fishing and bass and mullet in its upper reaches. To the south, Old Bar has good surf and rockfishing. The twin towns of Tuncurry and Forster straddle the entrance to Wallis Lake and the estuary fishing is as good as you'll get when it fires. There's good surf and rockfishing, but the rock spots are difficult and can be dangerous. Seal Rocks to the south is a quaint fishing village with superb inshore reef fishing and good fishing for snapper, mulloway and kingfish from the rocks. These rocks, however, can be risky.

Myall Lakes to Lake Macquarie: Tea Gardens and Myall Lakes are good for estuary species, and Hawks Nest provides access to excellent beach fishing right up to Seal Rocks. Nelson Bay is the main town servicing Port Stephens and the estuary fishing here is very good in season. Tomaree and Fingal headlands are renowned landbased gamefishing venues and the cluster of islands immediately offshore are great fish producers. Reef fishing is good too, favourite sites being the 'V' reef and Gunsight reef, wide of Cabbage Tree Island. Port Stephens provides multiple options for dedicated or casual fishermen.

Between Port Stephens and Newcastle, Stockton Bight offers good beach fishing, and Stockton Breakwall yields many estuary and rock species with occasional visits from speedsters like kingfish and tuna.

Newcastle Harbour is always worth a look as is Lake Macquarie. The entrance at Swansea has a spurwall where kingfish bite on a rising tide, and upstream of the liftspan road bridge, fishing for flathead, tailor and bream is excellent. There are luderick in the weedy channels and whiting over the sandflats, and at night, some big mulloway have been taken on baits of live mullet, yellowtail or small bottle squid. Owners of small boats are advised to treat the lake with respect if the wind gets up.

Central Coast: Tuggerah, Toukley and Budgewoi are all excellent estuary spots, with the famed 'run' at the entrance to Tuggerah Lake providing some impressive mulloway captures over the years. Gosford offers excellent estuary fishing.

NB: Angling is prohibited within the Bouddi Marine Sanctuary which extends from Gerrin Point to Third Point and eastward to just inside the Maitland Bombora.

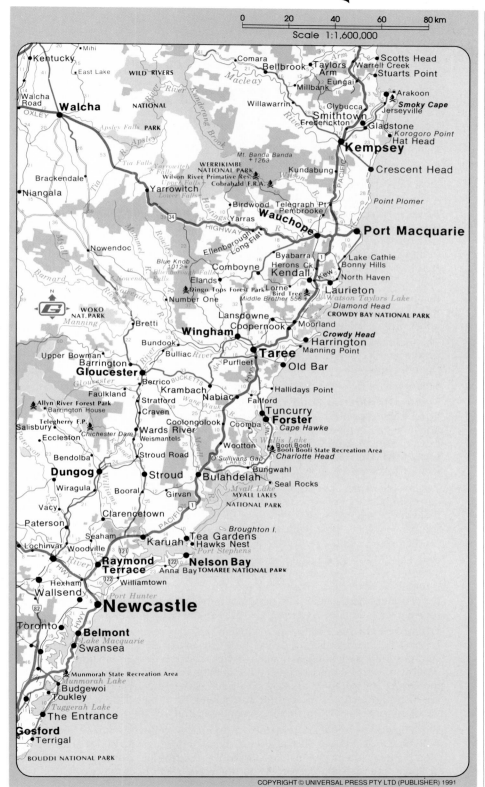

0   20   40   60   80 km

Scale 1:1,600,000

• Mihi
Kentucky •
• Comara
Bellbrook •   Taylors •   Warrell Creek   • Scotts Head
East Lake •   WILD RIVERS   Arm   • Stuarts Point
Macleay   Eungai •
Willawarrin •   Millbank •   • Arakoon
Walcha •   NATIONAL   Clybucca   Smoky Cape
Road   Smithtown •   Jerseyville
Walcha   Frederickton •   • Gladstone
OXLEY   Apsley Falls   PARK   • Korogoro Point
                    KEMPSEY   • Hat Head
Tia Falls   Yarrowitch   Mt. Banda Banda   Kundabung •
Falls   +1263
Brackendale •   WERRIKIMBE   • Crescent Head
    NATIONAL PARK   Wilson •
Niangala •   Yarrowitch •   Wilson River Primitive Res.
    Upper Falls   Cobrabald F.R.A.
    Lower Falls   • Point Plomer
    • Birdwood   Telegraph Pt •
    Yarras •   Pembrooke
HIGHWAY   Wauchope
    Ellenborough   Long Flat   • Port Macquarie
Nowendoc •   18
    Byabarra •   • Lake Cathie
Blue Knob   Herons Ck. •   Bonny Hills
1012+   Comboyne •   Kendall   Kew •
    Elands •   • North Haven
Number One •   Dingo Tops Forest Park   Lorne •   • Laurieton
    Middle Brother 556+   Bird Tree •
WOKO   Watson Taylors Lake
NAT. PARK   • Diamond Head
    Bretti •   Lansdowne •   CROWDY BAY NATIONAL PARK
Manning   Coopernook •   Moorland •
    Wingham   • Crowdy Head
Upper Bowman •   Bundook •   Harrington
Barrington •   Bulliac •   Manning Point
    Gloucester   Purfleet •   TAREE
Faulkland •   Berrico •   • Old Bar
Allyn River Forest Park   Krambach •   • Hallidays Point
Barrington House   Stratford •   Nabiac •   Failford •
Telegherry F.P.   Craven •   Tuncurry
Salisbury •   Coolongolook •   Coomba •   Forster
Eccleston •   Chichester Dam   Weismantels •   • Cape Hawke
    Wards River   Wallis Lake
Bendolba •   Stroud Road   Wootton •   Booti Booti
    O'Sullivans Gap   Booti Booti State Recreation Area
Dungog   Stroud   Bulahdelah   • Charlotte Head
Wiragula •   Booral •   LAKES   • Bungwahl
Vacy •   Girvan •   Myall Lake   • Seal Rocks
Paterson •   Clarencetown   MYALL LAKES
    PACIFIC   NATIONAL PARK
    Seaham •   • Broughton I.
Lochinvar •   Woodville •   Karuah   Tea Gardens
    • Hawks Nest
    Raymond   Nelson Bay
    Terrace   Anna Bay   TOMAREE NATIONAL PARK
Hexham •   Williamtown •
Wallsend •
    Port Hunter
    Newcastle
Toronto •   Belmont
    Lake Macquarie
    Swansea
    Munmorah State Recreation Area
    Munmorah Lake
    Budgewoi •
    Toukley •
    Tuggerah Lake
    • The Entrance
Gosford
    • Terrigal
BOUDDI NATIONAL PARK

Broken Bay to Port Hacking

Despite the fishing pressure exerted by a massive number of urban anglers, the Sydney metropolitan area still has consistently good angling. At times the fishing is excellent, although it does vary according to season and conditions.

Pittwater carries small to medium sized fish. Whiting, flathead, bream, tailor and school mulloway are the major species.

Broken Bay: The mouth of Broken Bay and up towards Flint and Steel Point, contains a lot of surface fish. Tailor, salmon, bonito and kingfish regularly feed along current lines on a rising tide. The area also holds large mulloway during summer, particularly spots such as Lion Island, Box Head, Barrenjoey Head and Flint and Steel Point. Live bait is essential for these fish.

Just past Flint and Steel Point is the entrance to Cowan Creek. During winter this area is home to hairtail, and bays such as Waratah, Jerusalem, Akuna and Yeomans all hold these toothy and tasty fish.

The main body of the Hawkesbury River from Juno Point up to Bar Point produces a lot of good estuary fish. Mulloway, flathead, bream, whiting, flounder and blue-swimmer crabs all feature in this area.

This is one of the most productive regions in Sydney.

Sydney Harbour to Botany Bay: In Sydney Harbour east of the Bridge, good catches of both bottom and surface fish are taken. Kingfish, bonito and tailor are commonly trolled in the lower reaches. Bream, flathead and trevally are the main bottom fish captures along with quite a few school mulloway. Upstream from the Harbour Bridge, bream, flathead and leatherjacket are the main captures.

Botany Bay is an open and fairly featureless piece of water that holds a surprising number of good fish. Bream, trevally, tailor and flathead are the main species, along with a few other bits and pieces. The eastern side of the bay produces best, with the shipping channel edges and reef areas holding quality fish.

Port Hacking: An attractive fishing area, although it has suffered from siltation over the past few years, Port Hacking does have Sydney's best population of whiting, plus some very large flathead. The deep areas on the channel edges are the place to look for the flathead. Whiting are mostly found over sand flats. As a sidelight, the Lilli Pilli area holds lots of squid.

Offshore Fishing: Sydney metropolitan area has several distinct forms. Deep-water headlands produce surface fish on trolled minnows and also snapper, tailor and kingfish on pilchard rigs. The deeper reefs offshore hold mulloway, snapper and kingfish with the famous 'Peak' off Maroubra and the 'Wreck' of Marley in the Royal National Park being great producers of kingfish and snapper in autumn and winter. Drifting offshore grounds yields snapper, morwong, flathead, nannygai and trevally.

Gamefishing is excellent off Sydney, with marlin, yellowfin tuna, wahoo, dolphin fish and sharks all available. Trolling or drifting with berley are the most popular and productive forms of fishing. During late autumn, drifting, or anchoring over the deep reefs and berleying with pilchards produces big yellowfin tuna.

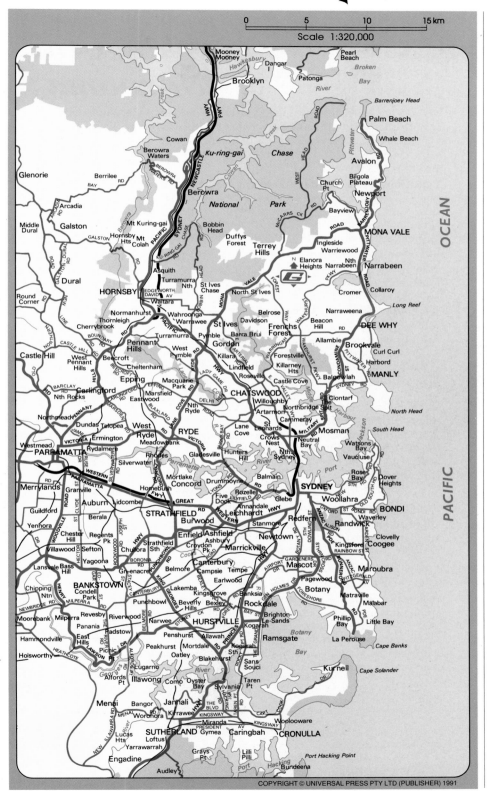

Scale 1:320,000

0   5   10   15 km

Sydney to Narooma

For a major capital city, Sydney has exceptionally good fishing in its four major waterways - Broken Bay, Sydney Harbour, Botany Bay and Port Hacking - and the Hawkesbury, Parramatta, Georges and Hacking Rivers which feed them. For detailed information refer to pevious map - Broken Bay to Port Hacking.

Lake Illawarra to Kiama: South of Sydney, Lake Illawarra offers surf, rock and estuary fishing. There are prawns west of the Windang road bridge and up to Griffin Bay, and green weed for blackfish can be gathered along this shore. Shellharbour offers rockfishing at nearby Bass Point - the 'Church Ground' mark straight off Shellharbour, has snapper, kingfish, mulloway and occasional tuna and marlin. Off Bass Point, 'The Humps' produce kingfish and snapper.

Minnamurra provides estuary fishing for bream, flathead, whiting, mullet and silver trevally on a rising tide. The Blowhole at Kiama has a good rock platform for spinning or livebaiting and Gerringong offers beach and rock species.

Shoalhaven to Jervis Bay: Shoalhaven Heads offers flathead and mulloway as well as bream, luderick, tailor and whiting in the river, and offshore from Nowra, 'The Banks' is a premier gamefishing and reef fishing hotspot. Large boat access is usually from Shoalhaven Heads. Small boats use the natural ramp at Currarong but exercise caution - while the ramp is sheltered from the south, any strong northerly wind makes launching and retrieving difficult. Jervis Bay has beautifully clean water and prolific fish life. Snapper, kingfish, tailor, salmon, and bream, flathead and whiting are the mainstays, but the region is also renowned for landbased gamefishing. Several marlin, kingfish, yellowfin and other smaller tuna have been landed from the rocks here.

Sussex Inlet is a broad, shallow estuary lake with plentiful flathead, bream, whiting and luderick. Small 'chopper' tailor take trolled lures in the channel.

Ulladulla to Narooma: Ulladulla is home to the commercial fishing fleet which mostly chases tuna and salmon. There is jetty fishing in the harbour and rock and beach fishing north and south of town.

Pretty Beach (Kioloa) has snapper, bream, tailor, luderick, drummer and salmon - and kingfish and tuna on live baits.

Batemans Bay has good estuary fishing in the lower Clyde river. Bream spinning is productive along the steep cliffs above the road bridge. Most ACT fishermen pass through Batemans Bay on their way to Narooma, where the offshore grounds of Montague Island provide excellent reef and gamefishing. Wagonga Inlet runs through Narooma and yields superb flathead, bream, whiting and luderick fishing.

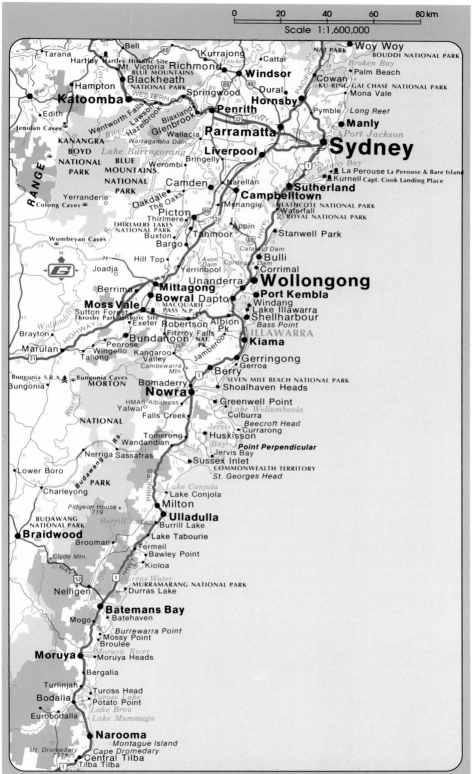

Scale 1:1,600,000

| 0 | 20 | 40 | 60 | 80 km |

Far South Coast &Tablelands

Bermagui has many estuary fishing opportunities in its nearby lakes and classic gamefishing offshore on the '4', '6' and '12' mile reefs which produce most gamefish in season, snapper year round and big kingfish in winter. Drift-fishing in summer anywhere within sight of the shoreline will produce flathead, especially near Camel Rock.

Tathra is reached by turning off the highway at Bega, and has a famed wooden jetty from which many captures of large tuna and sharks have been made, but it is chiefly fished by weekend and holiday family groups for much smaller fare.

The twin towns of Merimbula and Pambula offer rock, beach and estuary fishing and good inshore boat fishing prospects. Launching ramps are at the road bridge at Merimbula and off the Eden road into the Broadwater at Pambula.

Eden and Twofold Bay offer good estuary and rockfishing with snapper, morwong and kingfish offshore. Further south, Green Cape offers legendary rockfishing for game species.

Freshwater and Inland: Moving inland, the country climbs rapidly into tablelands and trout country. The stretch between Bombala and Nimmitabel on the Snowy Mountains Highway gives access to the Maclaughlin, Delegate, Undowa and Snowy Rivers and Cambalong Creek. Towards Cooma, the Kybean - Countegany road runs past the Numeralla, and Kybean Rivers.

The Maclaughlin is crossed west of Nimmitabel on the Dalgety - Berridale road. Look for Bobundra and Curry Flat Creek, which offer excellent fly fishing.

Lake Jindabyne, south-west of Cooma is reached on the Alpine Way. Lake Eucumbene is on the Snowy Mountains Highway, which leads through Adaminaby, Kiandra, past Tantangara, Talbingo and Blowering dams to Tumut. All the lakes here offer excellent trolling, bait fishing, spinning, or fly fishing for trout, with cod, yellowbelly and redfin in Blowering. Khancoban dam and the Swampy Plains River can be reached via Jindabyne or through Kiandra and Cabramurra.

Both the Thredbo River which runs into Jindabyne and the Eucumbene River which runs into Lake Eucumbene, are excellent trout waters. The Tumut River has excellent trout fishing and there are native fish in the Murrumbidgee at Gundagai.

Canberra and the ACT offer trout fishing in local streams, and native fish in the Murrumbidgee River and Lake Ginninderra. There are also redfin in Lake George.

The streams around Goulburn such as the Lachlan and Wollondilly offer trout fishing, and there are trout and native fish in Burrinjuck Dam.

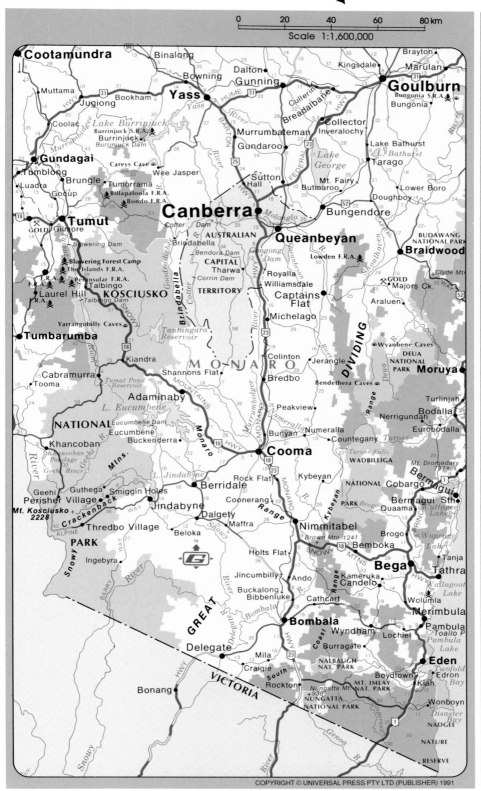

Albury to West Wyalong

There are two major bodies of water of interest to fishermen in the lower part of this region. Lake Mulwala in the west between Corowa and Yarrawonga and Lake Hume to the immediate east of Albury. Both lakes have good populations of native species such as cod and yellowbelly.

Murray River: The interconnecting stretch of the Murray River carries good cod water to the north, the Murrumbidgee River yields cod, yellowbelly, and silver perch, with some redfin as well.

Wagga is a good jumping off point for fishing trips to the Riverina, because it is so central to the many kilometres of westward flowing rivers carrying native fish and is within striking distance of all major highland impoundments as well.

Murrumbidgee Irrigation Area: An important aspect of water conditions within the Murrumbidgee Irrigation Area is that the water drawn from the high ground impoundments is always cold as it comes from the bottom of the lakes. This is not suitable for native fish and often puts them off the bite. Ideal conditions in this area are when heavy rainfall raises the general water temperatures in the rivers and stabilises the content of the dams. The discolouration of the water at these times is a trade off, requiring more reliance on baits than lures until it clears.

Recent developments with downriggers and sophisticated echo sounders have extended the effective fishing season here into those times when the cold water species like trout and redfin go deep to escape the heat of summer.

A growing understanding of the effects fluctuating water levels and water temperatures have on native species have likewise led to techniques such as concentrating fishing effort in the middle of the day on rivers and within the margins of impoundments down to depths of about 6 m.

Towns like Griffith, Ardlethan, Temora and West Wyalong have only scanty water resources with minor rivers and creeks, some of which are dry most of the time while others only fish well during and immediately after times of extensive flooding.

Talk to local tackle shop owners and National Parks staff at the various impoundments and they will provide you with up-to-date fishing reports.

Spring and autumn are reliable times for inland fish because water levels and temperatures tend to stabilise. Aside from occasional irrigation drawdown most times of rising water levels will be the result of moderate rains and prompt greater fish activity.

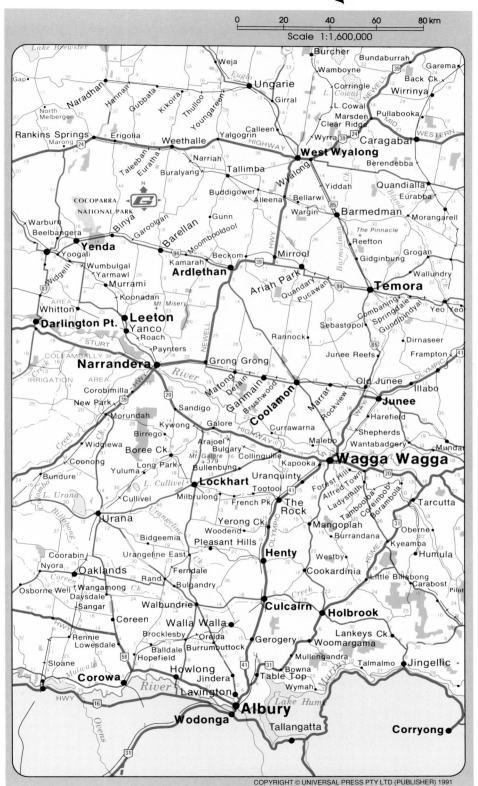

Scale 1:1,600,000

0   20   40   60   80 km

NSW

Goulburn to Dubbo

There are three major impoundments in this region - Wyangala Dam just east of Cowra, Lake Burrendong between Mudgee and Wellington and Lake Windamere on the Lithgow - Mudgee road north-west of Rylstone and Kandos.

All these contain cod and yellowbelly, with good populations of trout in Wyangala and Burrendong. Redfin are a problem in Burrendong.

Besides these there are three smaller dams, Oberon Dam has excellent rainbow and brown trout (and so far no redfin). Ben Chifley Dam has both kinds of trout, some yellowbelly and a few good cod, but is falling under the curse of redfin lately. Lake Lyall, a relatively new impoundment created as part of the hydro-electric facility of Wallerawang near Lithgow, has excellent, if tough rainbow fishing, some browns and so far no redfin.

Trout Fishing Areas: The region is very well endowed with trout streams, ranging from the Lachlan, Crookwell, Boorowa, and Abercrombie Rivers between Goulburn and Cowra, to the Fish, Campbells, Duckmaloi, Macquarie and Turon Rivers in the Bathurst, Oberon, and Sofala area.

To the east is the steep rugged country which forms the watershed of Warragamba Dam. The country is almost impassable and the dam itself is off limits to fishing, but the many rivers which flow into it have accessible sections in which fishing is legal, although difficult at times. These include rivers like the Tuglow, Kowmung, Cox's and lower Wollondilly Rivers.

Ben Chifley, Lake Lyall, Burrendong, Wyangala and Windamere are open to boating traffic, but Oberon Dam is not - and severe penalties apply to the use of boats on this lake of whatever type - except curiously, for the local sailing club which operates from the western shores of the dam, just below the Oberon golf club!

Ben Chifley responds well to trolling small minnows (3 cm to 5 cm) especially over drop-offs where the old river bed deepens the dam in sections.

Oberon produces when flyfished from the side facing the prevailing winds. Easterlies are best, and early morning and late evenings better still.

Lake Lyall is a good place to use downriggers or lead-core line to get lures down deep as the trout in here stratify, sometimes as far down as 15 - 20 m. The basin near the dam wall is best mid-week and early morning before the water-skiers get going.

All of the best trout water in these central tablelands runs through private property and it is strongly advocated that entry should only be sought after approaching the relevant land-owners and gaining their permission. Trespassing pressure has reached the point where even long-standing arrangements with land-owners are now in doubt because of unauthorised entry, hooliganism and damage to property by those careless or short-sighted enough not to appreciate this area which offers some of the best trout fishing in the southern hemisphere.

Genuine anglers will find very few problems however if they seek and obtain approved access.

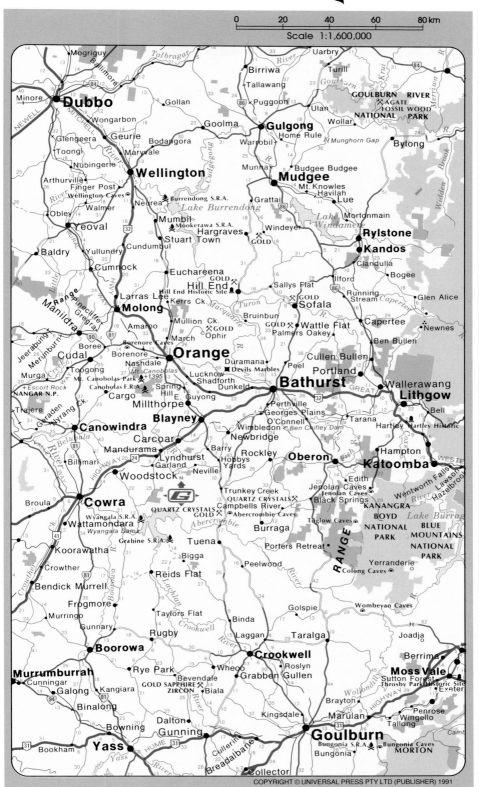

0   20   40   60   80 km

Scale 1:1,600,000

Mogriguy
Ballimore
Minore
Dubbo
NEWELL
MITCHELL
Wongarbon
Glengeera
Geurie
Bodangora
Toongi
Maryvale
Nubingerie
Wellington
Arthurville
Finger Post
Wellington Caves
Neurea
Obley
Walmer
Yeoval
Mumbil
Mookerawa S.R.A.
Baldry
Yullundry
Cundumbul
Cumnock
Euchareena
Hargraves
Stuart Town
Larras Lee
Hill End
Hill End Historic Site
Kerrs Ck.
Molong
Amaroo
Mullion Ck.
March
Ophir
Boree
Orange
Jeeraburg
Merlinburn
Cudal
Borenore Caves
Borenore
Nashdale
Duramana
Murga
Togong
Mt. Canobolas
Canobolas F.R.A.
Cargo
Millthorpe
Trajere
NANGAR N.P.
Escort Rock
Canobolas Park
Spring
Hill
E. Guyong
Dunkeld
Blayney
Perthville
Georges Plains
Canowindra
Carcoar
Wimbledon
O'Connell
Mandurama
Barry
Newbridge
Billimari
Lyndhurst
Garland
Neville
Rockley
Hobbys
Yards
Oberon
Woodstock
Trunkey Creek
Broula
QUARTZ CRYSTALS
Campbells River
Black Springs
Cowra
Wyangala S.R.A.
GOLD
Abercrombie Caves
Wattamondara
Wyangala Dam
Grabine S.R.A.
Burraga
Tuena
Koorawatha
Crowther
Bigga
Peelwood
Porters Retreat
Bendick Murrell
Reids Flat
Frogmore
Golspie
Murringo
Gunnary
Taylors Flat
Rugby
Binda
Boorowa
Laggan
Taralga
Crookwell
Murrumburrah
Rye Park
Wheeo
Roslyn
Cunningar
Galong
Kangiara
GOLD SAPPHIRE
ZIRCON
Bevendale
Grabben Gullen
Biala
Binalong
Brayton
Bowning
Dalton
Kingsdale
Yass
Bookham
Gunning
Cullerin
Breadalbane
Collector

Talbragar
River
Birriwa
Tallawang
Puggoony
Goolma
Gulgong
Home Rule
Warrobil
Munna
Budgee Budgee
Mudgee
Mt. Knowles
Havilah
Grattai
Lue
Windeyer
GOLD
Sallys Flat
Sofala
Bruinbun
Wattle Flat
GOLD
Palmers Oakey
Peel
Cullen Bullen
Portland
Bathurst
Devils Marbles
Lucknow
Shadforth
Tarana
Ben Chifley Dam
Edith
Jenolan Caves
Abercrombie Caves
Tuglow Caves
Yerranderie
Colong Caves
Wombeyan Caves
Joadja

Uarbry
Turill
GOULBURN RIVER
AGATE
FOSSIL WOOD
NATIONAL PARK
Ulan
Wollar
Bylong
Munghorn Gap
Lake Windamere
Rylstone
Kandos
Clandulla
Ilford
Bogee
Running Stream
Glen Alice
Capertee
Newnes
Ben Bullen
Wallerawang
GREAT
Lithgow
Bell
Hartley
Hartley Historic
Hampton
Katoomba
Lawson
Hazelbrook
Wentworth Falls
KANANGRA
BOYD
NATIONAL
PARK
BLUE
MOUNTAINS
NATIONAL
PARK
RANGE
Lake Burrag
Berrima
Moss Vale
Sutton Forest
Throsby Park Historic Site
Exeter
Penrose
Wingello
Tallong
Marulan
Goulburn
Bungonia S.R.A.
Bungonia Caves
MORTON
Bungonia

Quirindi to Tenterfield

The western sector of this region offers excellent stream fishing for native species such as yellowbelly and cod and there is good trout fishing in the highland streams of the New England tablelands around Armidale, Guyra and Glen Innes.

Major impoundments are Keepit, north-west of Tamworth, Split Rock Dam between Barraba and Manilla and Copeton Dam just south of Inverell.

All these contain good stocks of cod and yellowbelly - Split Rock and Keepit also have carp and there are redfin in Split Rock. Copeton contains good sized cod and yellowbelly, as well as catfish and trout.

In Keepit, it's a good idea to bounce crayfish or shrimp baits right in amongst the snags or to troll deep running lures along the old river bed. You can use a sounder to pick out the channel edges or if the water is low enough, you can trace the old water course by the weaving rows of tree tops poking up out of the water.

Split Rock responds to trolling deep lures along the lake margins in depths between 3 - 6 m and especially working points and inside corners of bays and inlets.

Copeton often has yellowbelly situated over warm shallows with a muddy bottom, but they like some structure such as fallen trees, rock piles and boulders.

Using a sounder, you can often see fish, both cod and yellowbelly, holding station in deep water. These sometimes respond better to bait, particularly if the water is very cold.

The Namoi, Mooki, Peel and Manilla Rivers have native fish and the Beardy, Severn, Mole and Styx have trout.

Tamworth to the Queensland Border: If you have some time on your hands, the huge carp in the Peel River right in the heart of Tamworth's township will oblige you with a tussle on baits of worms or shrimp. They also take small black flies however, and have smashed up the gear of more than one over-confident angler who thought they were easy game.

Tenterfield Creek in its gorge sections is hard walking but excellent for cod and yellowbelly, and the Gwydir and Severn also have good native fish.

In the eastern half of this region, there are good bass waters right to the coast for the whole distance between Nowendoc in the south right to the Queensland border.

The bass in this area are usually quite large and fit as the rivers here fall swiftly for some distance and keep the fish working fairly hard for their supper. Fortunately, there are periods of high food availability too, resulting in good growth rates and strong, vigorous fish.

These bass respond well to trolled lures and repetitive, accurate casting to cover, such as fallen trees, overhanging foliage or river banks, and midstream snags, boulders and narrows.

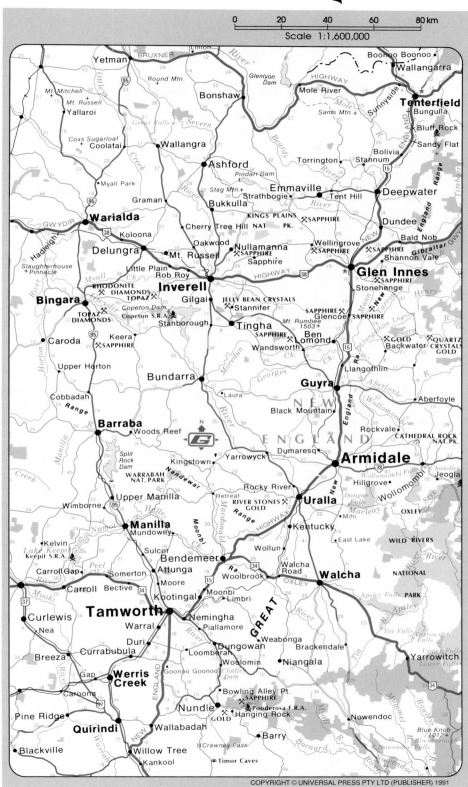

0   20   40   60   80 km
Scale 1:1,600,000

191

Mallacoota to Lakes Entrance

Mallacoota: Located 24 km from Genoa on the Princes Highway, Mallacoota offers lake-side moorings and a sheltered boat ramp. Offshore access depends on the bar, but bottom fish and pelagics are plentiful.

Inside, exceptional flathead are caught in the bottom lake. Mulloway are caught in the narrow channel (The Narrows), between the bottom and top lakes. Above Gipsy Point, the estuaries of the Wallagaraugh and Genoa Rivers produce estuary perch and an excellent spring run of bream.

Tamboon Inlet: Access is from Cann River to Furnell's Landing by car, then by boat to the inlet. Lake-side camping is permitted but there are no facilities. Bream fishing is excellent, prawns are plentiful in late summer and autumn, and salmon provide top sport at the entrance on the rising tide.

Bemm River: The Bemm River township on Sydenham Inlet is a bream fisherman's mecca; access is from the Princes Highway. Bank access is poor and shallow draft boats are required. Bream are prolific throughout with the option of estuary perch in the river upstream from the inlet.

Marlo: Sixteen km from Orbost on the Princes Highway, Marlo is situated on the combined estuary of the Brodribb and Snowy Rivers.

The inlet offers sheltered fishing with an adequate boat ramp. Estuary perch, luderick and bream top the list within the inlet. Offshore fishing is excellent with abundant reef fish and pelagics.

Lakes Entrance: The township of Lakes Entrance is on the Princes Highway at the entrance to the Gippsland Lakes. All facilities for fishermen are present. Offshore access is usually possible but the bar can be dangerous.

Inside the entrance, anglers catch tailor, salmon and luderick at Bullock Island. The township wharves produce bream, luderick and flathead while the Kalimna jetty is always worth trying.

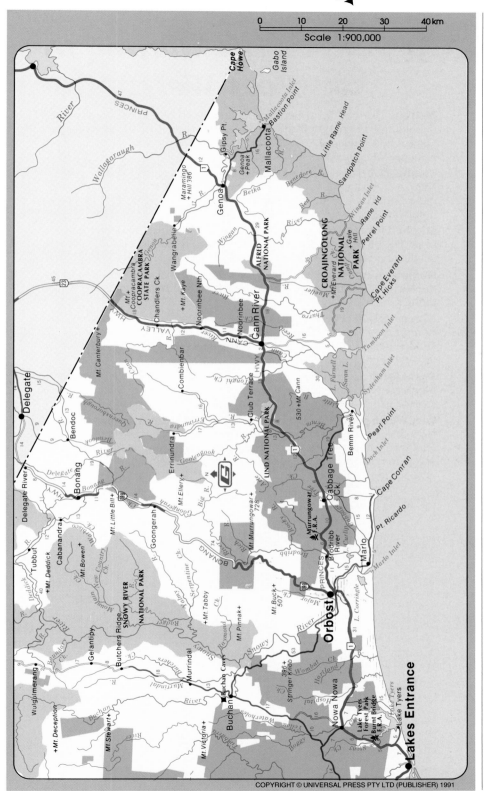

Scale 1:900,000

0   10   20   30   40 km

Metung to Port Welshpool

Metung: Catering for fishermen, Metung on Bancroft Bay is just a few minutes from Swan Reach on the Princes Highway. Here, suitably equipped anglers take bream, luderick, trevally and flathead. The deep water off Shaving Point produces several big mulloway each year.

Tambo River: Bank access extends from above the highway down to Lake King, with boat ramps at Johnsonville and Swan Reach. The Tambo is the most popular river in the Gippsland Lakes system and bream are the dominant species.

Mitchell River: Bank access is from Paynesville Road, and boat access is from 'The Bluff' above Paynesville. The Mitchell produces excellent bream fishing and bait can be pumped from extensive silt beds at the mouth.

Nicholson River: Least fished of the major rivers of the Gippsland Lakes, the Nicholson is the most picturesque; boat and bank access are limited though.

Ninety Mile Beach: Ninety Mile Beach extends from Corner Basin to Cape Conran. Access points are at Lakes Entrance, and via Sale to Seaspray and Golden Beach. With good water close in, catches of salmon and tailor are the rule.

Port Albert: Six km from Alberton on the South Gippsland Highway, Port Albert provides outstanding whiting and snapper fishing. Offshore access is some 8 to 10 km from an excellent boat ramp in the town.

Port Welshpool: Just off the South Gippsland Highway, Port Welshpool has a fine jetty popular with anglers. The boat ramp gives access to Corner Inlet where target species include flathead, whiting and snapper. Offshore access to Bass Strait and Seal Islands is about 10 km from the ramp.

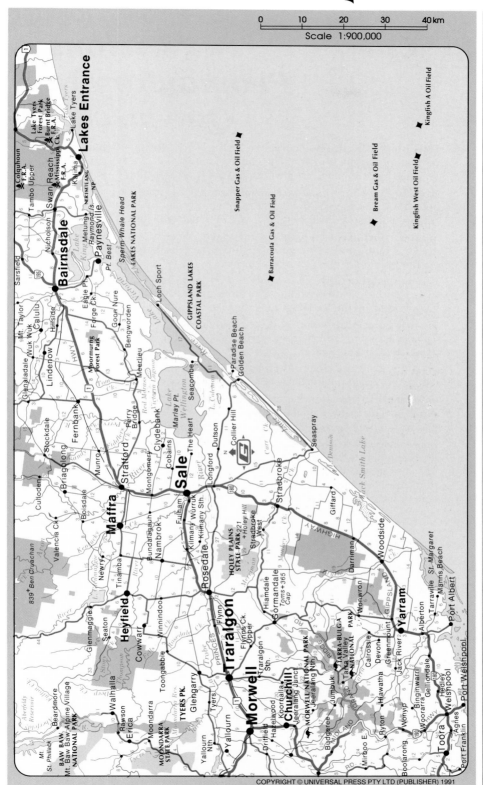
0   10   20   30   40 km

Scale 1:900,000

Kingfish A Oil Field ◤

Snapper Gas & Oil Field ◤

Bream Gas & Oil Field ◤

Barracouta Gas & Oil Field ◤

Kingfish West Oil Field ◤

Lakes Entrance

Lake Tyers
Forest Park
Burnt Bridge
Lake Tyers F.R.A.
Lake Tyers

Colquhoun F.R.A.
Tambo Upper
Swan Reach
Mississippi Ck.
Nicholson
Kalima

NEERMILANG N.P.
Raymond's
Metung
King Nure
Paynesville
Eagle Pt.

Bairnsdale

Sarsfield
195

Mt. Taylor
Glenaladale
Wuk Wuk
Calulu
Lindenow
Hillside
Forge Ck.
Bengworden
Goon Nure

Sperm Whale Head
Pt. Best
LAKES NATIONAL PARK

Loch Sport

GIPPSLAND LAKES
COASTAL PARK

Culloden
Stockdale
Fernbank
Moormurng
Forest Park

Briagolong
Boisdale
Munro
Perry Bridge
Stratford
Clydebank
Cobains
The Heart
Marlay Pt.
Seacombe
Dutson

Paradise Beach
Golden Beach

Maffra
Sale

Valencia Ck.
839 ⁺Ben Cruachan
Tinamba
Newry
Bundalaguah
Nambrok
Kilmany
Kilmany Sth.
Fulham
Wurruk
Longford
Collier Hill

Stradbroke
Stradbroke West

Seaspray

Heyfield

Cowwarr
Seaton
Glenmaggie
Winnindoo

Rosedale
Flynn
HOLEY PLAINS
STATE PARK
Flynns Ck. Upper
Traralgon Sth.

Hiamdale
Gormandale
Giffard
Darriman
Woodside

Traralgon

Waihalla
Rawson
Erica
Moondarra
Toongabbie
Glengarry

Tyers
Flynn

Koornalla
Hazelwood
Driffield

Morwell
Churchill

Jeeralang Junc.
MORWELL NATIONAL PARK
Jeeralang Nth.
Budgeree
Jumbuk
Mirboo E.

TARRA-BULGA
Tarra Valley
NATIONAL PARK
Won wron

Calrossie
Devon
Greenmount

Tarraville
St. Margaret
Manns Beach
Port Albert

Yarram
Alberton
Jack River

Mt. St. Phillack
BAW BAW
Mt. Baw Baw Alpine Village
NATIONAL PARK
Beardmore
Aberfeldy Reservoir

MOONDARRA
STATE PARK

TYERS PK.

Yallourn Nth.
Yallourn
Yinnar

Hiawatha
Ryton
Binginwarri
Wonyip
Woorarra
Hedley
Gelliondale
Welshpool

Boolarong
Manns Beach
Agnes
Toora
Port Welshpool
Port Franklin

Wilsons Promontory to Queenscliff

Wilsons Promontory: A declared Marine Park, Wilsons Promontory is more popular with bushwalkers than anglers. Road access is to Tidal River which is more suited to family outings than serious fishing.

Inverloch: At Inverloch, near Wonthaggi, an adequate boat ramp gives access to both the sheltered waters of Andersons Inlet and Bass Strait. Anglers also fish from the jetty near the entrance and adjacent beach.

Westernport Bay: Though severely tidal, Westernport Bay produces quality whiting and snapper fishing throughout the warmer months of the year.

Boat ramps are at Cowes, San Remo and Corinella in the east, and Tooradin in the north. However, preferred boat ramps are at Hastings, Stony Point, and Flinders on the Mornington Peninsula.

Mornington Peninsula: Land based anglers fish Flinders jetty, and the Cowes jetty on Phillip Island. The rocks facing Bass Strait are also productive, but take care.

Boat ramps are at Sorrento, Mornington, Frankston, Carrum and Mordialloc on the Mornington Peninsula.

Queenscliff: This town handles boat traffic at Port Phillip Heads where prime species include whiting, snapper, flathead, squid and kingfish. The pier is also popular and the lighthouse rocks fish well at low tide.

Experienced club fishermen work the often dangerous area known as 'the Rip' for kingfish, with large lures and either whole squid or garfish baits. The current is so strong here that boats can work their baits at considerable troll speeds and actually lose ground backwards! This is no place for small craft or inexperienced skippers.

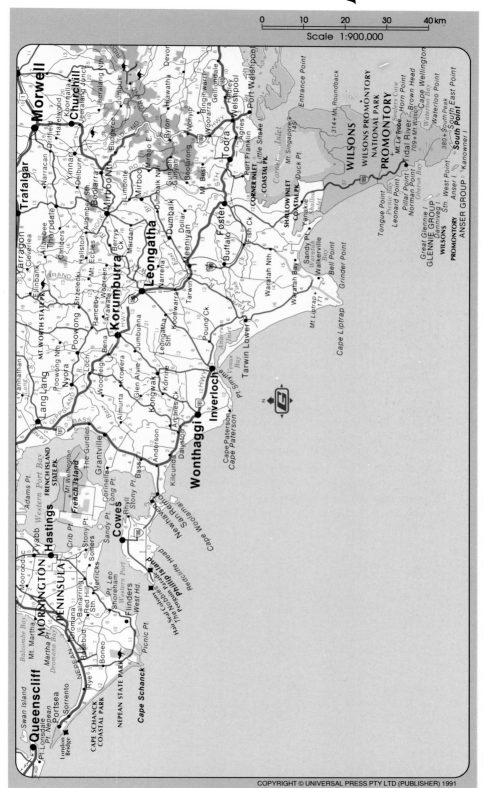

Scale 1:900,000

0   10   20   30   40 km

VIC *Port Phillip Bay to Apollo Bay*

Port Phillip Bay: Although heavily fished, Port Phillip Bay produces good whiting, flathead and snapper throughout the warmer months of the year while St Kilda handles Metropolitan boat traffic. You may also launch at Williamstown, Altona and Werribee South.

Corio Bay is serviced by ramps at Kirk Point, Avalon, St Helens, Limeburners Point and Clifton Springs. Bellarine Peninsula is serviced by ramps at Point Richards, Indented Head and St Leonards.

Barwon Heads: Twenty two km from Geelong, Barwon Heads is serviced by boat ramps at the Sheepwash, and at Guthridge Street, Ocean Grove.

The Barwon estuary fishes best during the first two hours of the incoming tide. Casual anglers catch salmon, mullet and silver trevally while serious anglers take bream, luderick and mulloway.

Boat fishermen enjoy permanent access to Bass Strait where they catch barracouta and sharks. Adjacent surf beaches fish well at evening.

Torquay: Twenty four km from Geelong, Torquay offers beach fishing for whiting and snapper in Zeally Bay. The boat ramp is often covered with sand, but anglers who manage to launch take good catches of whiting.

Anglesea: The Anglesea River, 30 km from Geelong, is popular with bream fishermen. Point Roadknight boat ramp is sheltered from prevailing winds but seldom used by locals who prefer to launch from the beach.

Lorne: Around 60 kilometres from Geelong, Lorne provides good rock and beach fishing close to the town. The pier is usually crowded on weekends, and good catches of mullet, salmon, barracouta and garfish are taken. Lorne boat ramp is adequate in calm seas but treacherous with a swell running.

Casual anglers take mullet and small trevally from the Erskine River nearby, while serious anglers take bream and estuary perch.

Apollo Bay: Around 110 km south-west of Geelong, the Barham River estuary at Apollo Bay produces bream and estuary perch with pan-size trout upstream.

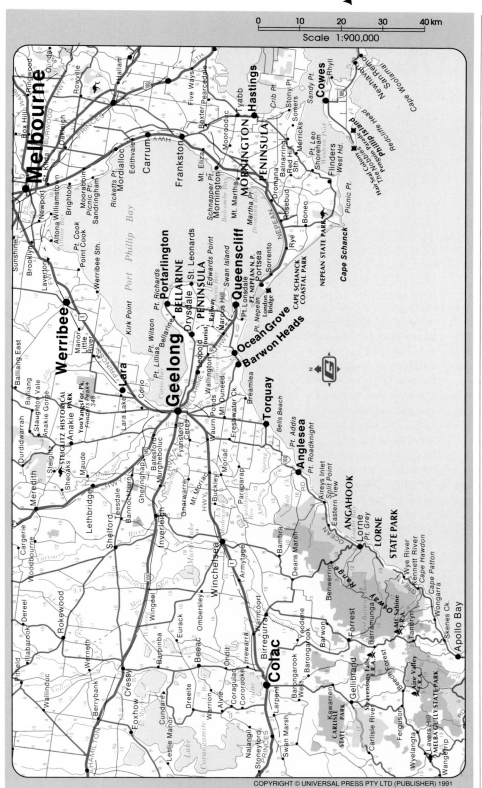

0 10 20 30 40 km

Scale 1:900,000

Cape Otway to Portland

The fishing here ranges from freshwater lakes and rivers to estuary, surf, rock, bay and offshore locations each with good stocks of catchable fish. Major towns where anglers can base themselves are Camperdown, Warrnambool, Port Fairy and Portland.

Lakes: Lakes Purrumbete and Bullen Merri hold substantial stocks of rainbow trout and chinook salmon. Caravan parks and good launching facilities are available at both lakes.

Purrumbete requires a boat for best results, and deep trolling with downriggers or paravanes is the best method in summer. In cold months, a mudeye fished under a bubble float in the shallows is effective and again best results are obtained from a boat.

Lake Bullen Merri is ideal for both landbased and boat anglers. There is road access for most of its shoreline. During autumn and winter, lure casting, as well as shore-fishing with baits on the bottom or under a float, provide great sport. Other productive lakes in the area include Elingamite (boat required), and Winslow (shore).

Rivers: The trout rivers in this area are rarely fished hard as they can be difficult to get to, but the Gellibrand and Aire in the Otways are two of the very best, with good stocks of large wild brown trout.

The upper and lower reaches of the Merri, the Hopkins above Allansford, and Mt Emu Creek all have good brown trout fishing and are amenable to lure, fly or baitfishing. They are also easier to gain access to.

Estuaries: By far the best estuaries in the region are the lower Hopkins River at Warrnambool and the Curdies, near Peterborough. Expect to catch bream, estuary perch and mullet. Other species available are mulloway, garfish, whiting and flathead. The Aire River estuary produces bream, mullet and brown trout, which don't seen to mind the brackish water. Access is from Horden Vale, clearly marked on the Great Ocean Road.

Surf and Rockfishing: Most rockfishing is around Peterborough and Cape Otway for small snapper in summer. Since the coastline here is very dangerous, it is not recommended for the inexperienced.

Surf fishing is a different matter. The area has good, safe, surf fishing beaches with the main prize of salmon, but incidental captures also of trevally, snapper, gummy shark and whiting. Best beaches are Lewis Beach, Logan Beach, Killarney, The Basin, East Beach, Yambuk and Narrawong.

Offshore and Bay-fishing: Lady Bay (Warrnambool), Port Fairy Bay, and Portland Bay are sheltered from westerly winds and fish best early morning or late evening during summer. Expect small snapper if moored over light reef, or whiting, mullet, barracouta and trevally over various kinds of sea bottom.

Offshore, the predominant species is barracouta, but during winter, there is always a chance of Southern bluefin tuna or salmon, sweep, snook and snapper, and for the shark fans, blue sharks, makos and thresher sharks.

Preferred launching sites for large offshore craft are at Portland, Port Fairy and Warrnambool in that order. Lady Julia Percy Island is an excellent gamefish area but its distance from Port Fairy precludes it as an option on all but the calmest days.

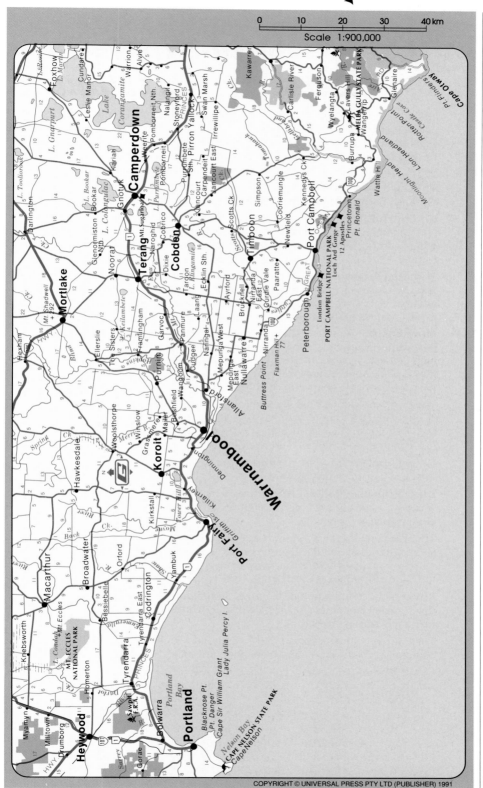

0   10   20   30   40 km

Scale 1:900,000

VIC

Mid-Northern Inland

The mid-north of Victoria is characterised by warm weather, big rivers and native fish species. The centre-pieces of the region are the Murray River, Lake Mulwala, the Goulburn River and to a lesser extent, the Ovens and Broken Rivers.

Murray cod are dominant, although good numbers of golden perch and silver perch can be found. Redfin are also numerous, especially in the Waranga Basin, the Murray, and many of the irrigation channels of the area.

Goulburn River: The Goulburn River around Shepparton offers Murray cod and silver perch in the hot months. Best local baits are Bardi grubs which can be bought in Shepparton tackle shops, while shrimp can be caught.

Waranga Reservoir: Large redfin will take lures or bait are the attraction here. While a boat is handy, you can effectively fish the Stuart-Murray canal which runs between the Goulburn weir and the Waranga Basin. Best time is summer, when the channels run strong and clear.

Murray River: Serious angling requires a boat, however many fish are still taken from shore by casting baits out and downstream to snags. The best baits are Bardi grubs, although yabbies, shrimp and scrub worms will take fish as well. Anglers must fish right in and around snags in these waters to have a reasonable chance of catching cod.

There are excellent access tracks all along the Murray from Yarrawonga to Tocumwal. Please note that it is now illegal to catch and kill cod in the section between Yarrawonga and Cobram, so here, you should direct your fishing efforts to other fish and release any cod accidentally caught.

During April and May the river usually clears enough to lure fish. Trolling the locally made 'Stumpjumper' lures or big Flatfish from a boat is best.

Lake Mulwala: Mulwala is recognised as the best Murray cod water in Australia. Boat angling is good and there are plenty of landbased locations which are also productive.

The area between the Shoreline Caravan Park and Northern Bight has many shore-fishing places. Bardi grubs on a Paternoster rig are best. The secret with trolling lures here is to slowly work over the old river channel, or to troll along the edges of the tree line at the western end toward Yarrawonga.

Recommended lures are Boomerangs, Stumpjumpers, various Bagley deep divers, and Hammerheads. Vertical fishing with Bardi grubs or yabbies is extremely successful here.

There are numerous caravan parks and holiday units around the lake and launching at Mulwala, Yarrawonga, Bathumi, Major's Lane and Bundalong.

Other Rivers: The Ovens River here is in its lower reaches and is badly silted from Wangaratta to its junction with the Murray. Redfin are abundant, but cod are not plentiful at all.

The Broken River is the best trout water in the region and the best water is above Benalla. Downstream from Benalla there are Murray cod, golden perch and river blackfish, but again, the area is dominated by redfin. The Edward River, where it flows into the Murray, is worth trying for cod.

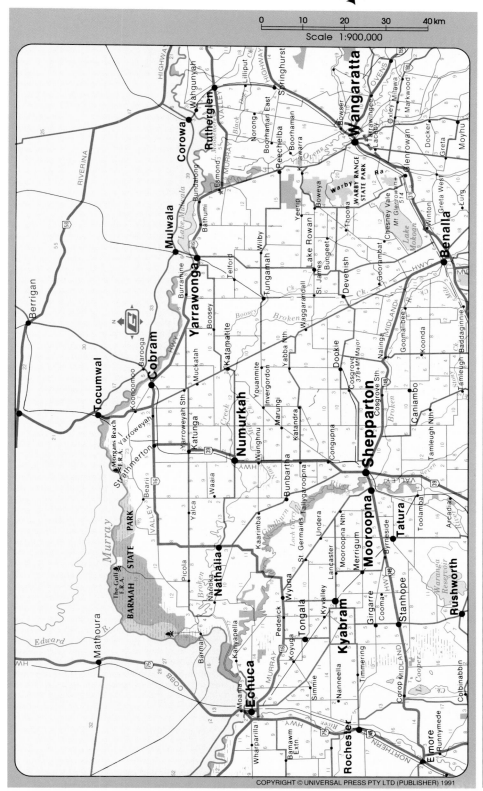

Scale 1:900,000

0   10   20   30   40 km

Highland Waters

Victoria's highland fishing centres on two major impoundments - Eildon and Dartmouth. But there are many other minor and major rivers and a number of smaller reservoirs, namely Nillahcootie, Lake Buffalo, Lake William Hovell, Rocky Valley Dam and Lake Omeo.

There are Murray cod and other native species in this region, but brown and rainbow trout predominate. Alpine National Park plus the State Parks of Eildon, Wabonga and Mt Samaria are located here.

Dartmouth Dam: Accommodation, hire boats, fishing guides, supplies and petrol are available in the Dartmouth Corporation township. Dartmouth is famous for brown and rainbow trout as well as good Macquarie perch. A boat is virtually a necessity and the ramp near Eight Mile Creek provides launching access.

Best fishing is in spring when trout will readily take Tassie devils, or baits such as worms or mudeyes trolled behind 'cowbell' flashing attractors. Bait is effective in spring and early summer. Set mudeyes or worms under a bubble float, 5 m down for trout and 20 m down for perch. In November, there is a closed season for perch when they travel up to spawn.

In summer, troll deep, using heavy ford fender flashers, paravanes or downriggers. The open area from the dam wall across to the arms is popular for deep trolling. Lure casting late on summer evenings works well around the shore. In winter, fish well up the Dart or Mitta arms, as trout move up there to spawn. Landbased angling is available in the regulatory dam behind the town, as well as in the Mitta Mitta river, between the dam and the Mitta Mitta township.

Lake Eildon: Eildon is Victoria's most popular trout lake. Land based access is good in the Bonnie Doon, Delatite and Howqua arms where trout are taken all year round. The Goulburn and Big River arms have reputations for big fish but must be approached by boat. Trolling is productive in these area. Best lures are Tassie devils, McGrath divers, Rebel Crawdads, Rapala CD3 and CD5's and Landa lures. May and June are noted months for big fish in these two arms.

The northern area of Eildon fishes best in spring. Fly-fish the upper sections of Bonnie Doon and baitfish at Howqua. Bait bobbing with small yabbies around snags produces big redfin in summer, while small fish gather around the jetties and pontoons. Eildon has caravan parks, motels, and hire boats available.

Smaller Lakes: Lake William Hovell is a very scenic lake with a reasonable stock of medium sized brown trout. Bank access is limited and boats are allowed, but there is a 10 hp limit on outboard motors. Rocky Valley Reservoir is high in the alps and freezes in winter, but in the summer it yields numerous small brown trout. Boats and shore anglers are both well catered for. Lake Nillahcootie has redfin, Buffalo Lake is deep, containing numbers of brown and rainbow trout. Pretty Valley Dam is one of Australia's highest and boasts some large brown trout.

The Rivers: There are numerous trout streams in this area, notably, the Kiewa, the Mitta Mitta below the dam and the King. Other good trout waters are the Buffalo, Buckland, Howqua, Goulburn, Snowy Creek and the Cobungra. In the wide lower reaches, lurecasting is the best method, but in higher water, flies and unweighted baits come into their own.

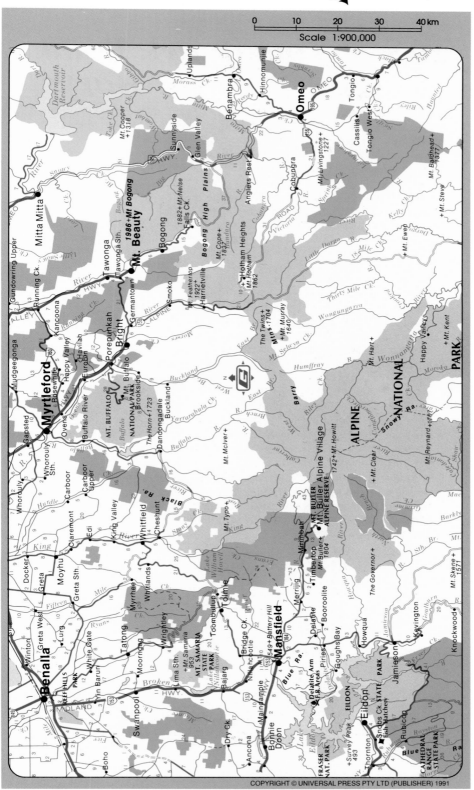

0   10   20   30   40 km
Scale 1:900,000

Dartmouth Reservoir
Mitta Mitta
Omeo
OMEO
Benambra
Hinnomunjie
Uplands
Sunnyside
Glen Valley
Anglers Rest
Cobungra
Mt Livingstone 1227
Cassilis
Tongio West
Tongio
Mt Baldhead 1377
Mt Steve
Mt Cooper 1318
Gundowring Upper
Running Ck
Kancoona
Mudgeegonga
Gapsted
Myrtleford
Roseville
Happy Valley
Havilah
Eurobin
Whorouly Sth
Whorouly
Carboor
Carboor Upper
Hurdle
Docker
Moyhu
Claremont
Edi
King Valley
Whitfield
Cheshunt
Benalla
Winton
Greta West
Greta
Greta Sth
Lurg
White Gate
Tatong
Myrrhee
Whitlands
Wrightley
Moorngag
REEFHILLS PARK
Tyn Barun
Swanpool
Maindample
Bonnie Doon
Ancona
Boho
Dry Ck
Tawonga
Tawonga Sth
Mt. Beauty
1986 Mt Bogong
Bogong
Bogong High Plains
1882 Mt Nelse
Falls Ck
Harrietville
Mt Cope 1837
Hotham Heights
Mt Hotham 1862
Smoko
Germantown
Porepunkah
Bright
Buffalo River
MT. BUFFALO NATIONAL PARK
Brookside
The Horn 1723
Dandongadale
Buckland
Feathertop 1922
The Twins 1704
Mt Murray 1640
Mt Selwyn
Mt Harr
Mt Reynard 1709
Happy Valley
Mt Kent
Mt Ewen
Mt McIver
Mt Typo
ALPINE NATIONAL PARK
Mt Clear
Mt Howitt 1742
Mt Buller Alpine Village
MT BULLER 1804
ALPINE RESERVE
Timbertop
Merrijig
Merribah
Mt Samaria 953
MT. SAMARIA STATE PARK
Lima Sth
Nillahcootie
Toombullup
Tolmie
Mansfield
Battery Hill 549
Delatite
Booroolite
Goughs Bay
Howqua
The Governor
Mt Skene 1571
Kevington
Jamieson
Knockwood
EILDON STATE PARK
Eildon
Delatite Arm
F.B. Areas
Thornton
Rubicon
Sncbs Ck STATE Fish Hatchery
Survey Peak 493
FRASER NAT. PARK
CATHEDRAL RANGE STATE PARK
Blue Ra.

TAS *Tomahawk Point to St Marys*

Ringarooma Bay to Eddystone Point: Ringarooma Bay and Boobyalla Beach yield large flathead, salmon, and snapper, and occasional kingfish. The north-eastern tip of Tasmania, from Cape Portland to Eddystone Point has similar species plus barracouta in season. This is big boat country however as the swells and weather can be rough and sometimes dangerous.

Ansons Bay to St Helens: The coastline from Ansons Bay to St Helens offers bream and salmon fishing in the surf. St Helens provides access to some of Tasmania's best offshore fishing. The weather is warm in summer and usually fairly stable making it a good port, but the bar at the entrance to Georges Bay requires care and experience. The launching ramp inside the bay isn't the only one, there is another outside as well, but this is subject to any easterly weather. Georges Bay itself provides salmon, flathead, trevally and bream, and is one of the few places in Tasmania with reliable supplies of luderick.

Outside, trolling or spinning are effective techniques, as is floating a bait down a berley trail of small chopped pieces of fish. There are flathead grounds outside the bar, and on the rocky bottom, morwong, cod, and in deeper areas, large striped trumpeter can be caught. The striped trumpeter at this size is an excellent table fish and is a highly prized catch among local fishermen. Trolling lures close to shore will produce pike, salmon, snook, 'couta, and in summer, small kingfish.

St Helens is Tasmania's marlin and yellowfin tuna capital. Each year the small gamefishing fleet lands marlin up to 200 kg and yellowfin to 100 kg. These are taken on trolled lures anywhere between the entrance and the Continental Shelf.

St Marys & Environs: St Marys is a quiet peaceful place with friendly people and good general supplies. Just west of town there is good trout fishing in the South Esk and Break 'O' Day Rivers. The Break 'O' Day in particular has big fish in the weedy margins and good evening rise fishing in the long slow glides.

Scale 1:500,000

0   5   10   15   20 km

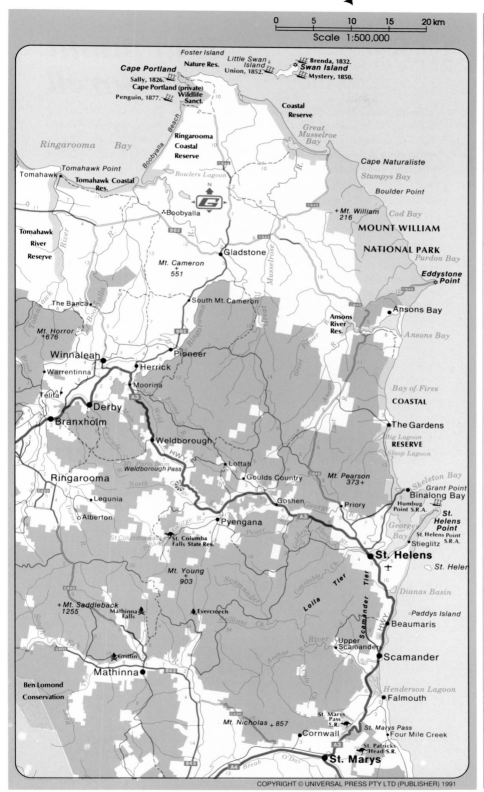

Foster Island
Cape Portland
Nature Res.
Little Swan Island
Union, 1852.
Brenda, 1832.
Swan Island
Mystery, 1850.
Sally, 1826.
Cape Portland (private) Wildlife Sanct.
Penguin, 1877.
Coastal Reserve

Ringarooma Bay

Boobyalla Beach

Ringarooma Coastal Reserve

Bowlers Lagoon

Tomahawk Point
Tomahawk
Tomahawk Coastal Res.

Great Musselroe Bay

Cape Naturaliste
Stumpys Bay
Boulder Point
Mt. William 216
Cod Bay

MOUNT WILLIAM
NATIONAL PARK

Tomahawk River Reserve

Boobyalla

Gladstone

Mt. Cameron 551

South Mt. Cameron

Purdon Bay
Eddystone Point

The Banca

Mt. Horror +676

Ansons River Res.

Ansons Bay

Ansons Bay

Winnaleah
Warrentinna
Telita
Derby
Branxholm

Pioneer
Herrick
Moorina

Bay of Fires
COASTAL

The Gardens

Weldborough

Big Lagoon
RESERVE
Sloop Lagoon

Ringarooma
Legunia
Alberton

Paris Dam
Weldborough Pass

Lottah

Goulds Country

Mt. Pearson 373 +

Skeleton Bay
Grant Point
Binalong Bay
Humbug Point S.R.A.
St. Helens Point S.R.A.

Goshen
Priory

St. Columba Falls
St. Columba Falls State Res.

Pyengana

St. Helens Point
Stieglitz

Georges Bay

St. Helens

St. Helen

Mt. Young 903

Mt. Saddleback 1255
Mathinna Falls
Evercreech

Loila Tier
Scamander Tier

Dianas Basin

Paddys Island
Beaumaris

Griffin
Mathinna

Upper Scamander

Scamander

Ben Lomond Conservation

Henderson Lagoon
Falmouth

Mt. Nicholas + 857
St. Marys Pass S.R.
Cornwall
St. Marys Pass
Four Mile Creek
St. Patricks Head S.R.

St. Marys

Triabunna to Sorell

Triabunna and its nearby towns of Louisville and Orford provide access and logistical support for fishing trips in Prosser Bay, Spring Bay and Mercury Passage.

These waters offer tiger flathead, sand flathead, school sharks, salmon, tuna, and large numbers of barracouta and squid when they are running.

The reef areas provide spasmodic catches of striped trumpeter and regular hauls of morwong, cod and gurnard.

Offshore, Maria Island offers striped tuna especially on its seaward side with 'couta, and salmon on lures or bait and tiger flathead on the drift.

Sorell has good general estuary fishing in Pittwater.

Tasmanian recreational anglers often make use of the fact they are allowed to use set-nets called 'grab-alls' and even to set up scallop dredges on their boats. This takes a bit of getting used to when such practises are so frowned upon in other states.

Hobart to Port Arthur

The south-eastern corner of Tasmania has many fish-rich areas, easily reached from Hobart. Even the Derwent River has salmon, pike, trevally and flathead, but local advice is against eating fish from here due to the Derwent's polluted condition.

Beyond the Derwent, the waters are generally clear and clean and access is from launching ramps at Dodges Ferry, Cremorne, and South Arm. There is also boat hire at Dodges Ferry.

The main species are flathead, salmon, cod, squid, gurnard and flounder. Whiting are large and plentiful in Storm Bay. The usual method is to drift with handlines or short stiff boat rods. Rigs are usually Paternosters with one or two baits set above the sinker. Sometimes wire trace is needed if 'couta are about as these fish can bite terminal rigs off.

Bruny Island has camping and caravan parks and launching facilities for small boats. Fish include morwong, tiger flathead, warehou and trevally. To reach Bruny Island, drive south from Hobart to Kettering and take the vehicular ferry.

Scale 1:500,000
0   5   10   15   20 km

Whitefoord
Tunnack
797 + Mt. Ponsonby
Woodsdale
Spinning Gum
+ Mt. Hobbs 823
Levendale
Prosser
Brown Mtn. 792
Buckland
TASMAN
Buckland Military Training Area
594
+ Bluestone Tier 404
Triabunna
+ Mt. Murray 317
Cape Bougainville
Okehampton Lords Bluff
Spring
Double Creek
Louisville
Orford
Pt. Home Lookout
Shelly Beach Apollo, 1827
Cape Boullanger
Darlington
Spring Beach
Stapleton Point
Three Thumbs 549
Emerald Bay
Maria
709 + Mt. Maria
Rheban
Return Point
Booming Bay
Sand
Island
Pt. Lesueur
Oyster Shoal Bay
Riedle Bay
Cape des Tombeaux
Pt. Mauge
Cockle Bay
Pebbly Point
Cape Maurouard
Barren Head
Cape Bernier
Cape Peron
Orielton
Pawleena
Nugent
Wattle Hill
Penna
Sorell
235 + Mt. Elizabeth
Pitt
Midway Point
Forcett
Water Hobart Airport
Lewisham
Kellevie
Ragged Tier 404
Bream Creek
Copping
Zephyr, 1852.
Point du Ressac
Marion Bay
ARTHUR

COPYRIGHT © UNIVERSAL PRESS PTY LTD (PUBLISHER) 1991

Risdon Cove
Meehan Range S.R.A.
Lindisfarne
Cambridge
Gordon Hill
Bellerive
Howrah
Hobart
River
Mt. Nelson
Rokeby
Batchelors Grave
Shot Tower
Kingston
Opossum Bay
Blackmans Bay
South Arm
Tinderbox
Kellys Pt.
Dennes Pt.
C. de la Sortie
Killora
Barnes Bay
The Yellow Bluff
North Bruny
Trumpeter Bay
Trumpeter Point
Great Bay
Variety Bay
Island
Church Hill 178
Bruny I. Neck Game Res.
Cape Queen Elizabeth
Water Hobart Airport
Lewisham
ARTHUR
Copping
Zephyr, 1852.
Sandy Point
Dodges Ferry
Seven Mile Beach
Parks Bch.
Carlton
Primrose Sands
Primrose Point
Dunalley
Tasman Monument
Blackman Bay
North Bay
Cape Paul Lamanon
Visscher Island
Cape Frederick Hendrick
Kelly Island
Humper Bluff
Mt. Forestier +319
FORESTIER
High Yellow Bluff
Lauderdale
Frederick Henry
Sandford
Cremorne
163 + Mt. Augustus
Green Head
Sloping Is
Lime Bay Nature Res.
Smooth Is.
Dunbabin Point
Victoria, 1850.
Chronicle Pt.
Murdunna
PENINSULA
Cape Surville
The Sisters
+591
Deep Glen Bay
Clifton Beach
North West Head
Coal Mines
Mt. Stewart +130
Norfolk
Cape Deslacs
Gwandalan
Saltwater River
Deer Point
Res.
Bay
Tessellated Pavement
Eaglehawk Neck
Blowhole
Bay
South Arm
C. Contrariety
Nature Res.
Betsey Island
Hope, 1827.
Governor Sorell, 1827.
Outer North Head
344 + Mt. Communication
Premaydena
Koonya
Eaglehawk Bay
Halfway Bluff
Penzance
Taranna
Tasmanian Devil Wildlife Park
Tasman Arch
O'Hara Bluff
One Tree Point
Auk Point
Lory Point
Amelia, 1833.
Wedge Island
Low Point
Storm Wedge Bay
Two Island Bay
Bay
Nubeena
TASMAN
Oakwood
PENINSULA
HWY
Thumbs Point
Highcroft
Australian, 1834.
Curio Bay
Stormlea
Mt. Arthur
Palmers Hill Lookout
Port Arthur
Isle of the Dead
Port Arthur
Arthur
Cape Pillar State Reserve
Fortescue Bay
The Lanterns
Cape Hauy
Munro Bight
Cape Raoul State Reserve
Ship Stern Bluff
+ Mt. Raoul 462
Remarkable Cave
West Arthur Head
Black Head
Cathedral Rock
Raoul Bay
Maingon Bay
Cape Pillar
Cape Raoul
Contest, 1831.
Tasman Island

209

COPYRIGHT © UNIVERSAL PRESS PTY LTD (PUBLISHER) 1991

Cressy to Campbell Town

Cressy is about 30 km south of Launceston and aspiring trout fishermen are well advised to call in on Noel and Lois Jetson at the Cressy Post Office. The Jetsons can give you up-to-date reports on the fishing in the whole Midland Plains district as well as the Central Highlands. You can also obtain tackle and guiding services from Noel who is a world renowned fishing guide.

Best local waters for trout are Brumby's Creek, Lake River, Macquarie River and the South Esk River.

Brumby's Creek is actually a series of weir pools and it fishes best when the power station at Poatina is running, which releases water, raising the level in Brumby's and encouraging the trout to feed around the flooded margins. Fly-fishermen can experience heart-stopping fishing, using polaroid sunglasses to locate fish visually. Red Tag dry flies and nymphs such as browns, blacks or one of Rob Sloane's Fur Flies will produce fish. This is exacting fishing, requiring accurate casts, and careful stealthy movements, but the fish are big, fat and vigorous, and beautiful to eat.

In spring and summer, there are occasional huge hatches of red and black spinners on the Macquarie River which can provide hectic and spectacular dry fly fishing.

Lake Pedder & Lake Gordon

Lake Pedder has been flooded for some time now, and has more or less stabilised into a difficult but rewarding fishery for large brown trout. Most of the fish caught are smaller than when the lake was first filling, but there are still occasional monsters about.

Bait fishing is prohibited in Pedder, but flyfishing works around shallow margin areas and creek drainage points as does lure fishing. A popular and productive method of lurefishing is to use 'fishcakes', cigar-shaped floating lures which use propellers to create surface disturbance as they are trolled or retrieved. These are most often used at night. Trolling is also effective with Wigstons Tassie Devils.

Lake Gordon is a huge impoundment with severely limited access. Only large seaworthy craft can be regarded as safe in any weather here as the lake can whip up ferociously in big winds. Also, because its margins are intensely wooded with drowned timber, it is quite possible to become disoriented and lost in the arms of Lake Gordon, so care must be taken to accurately monitor your position. It is not an unreasonable measure to use a compass and map to help find your way about in this vast water. Trolling Tassie Devils is the main technique used.

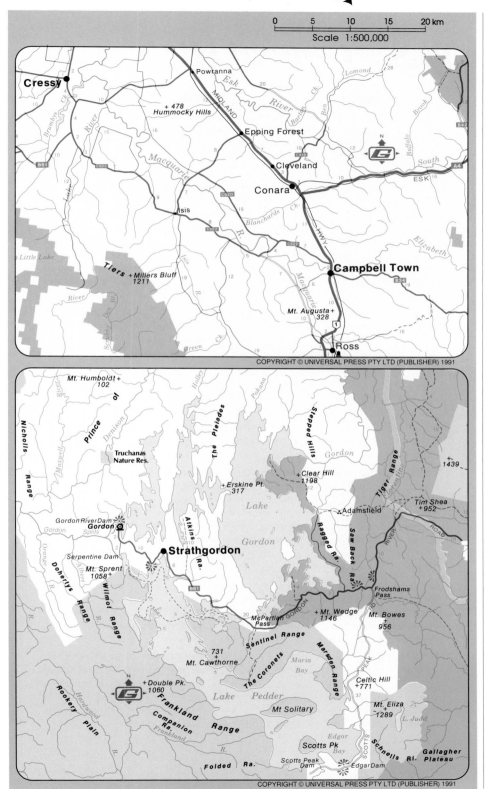

Scale 1:500,000

0   5   10   15   20 km

Cressy
Powranna
Esk
Lomond
28
+478
Hummocky Hills
MIDLAND
River
Ben
Brook
B42
Epping Forest
South
ESK
A4
Cleveland
Conara
C520
Isis
C522
Blanchards
Ck.
C522
Elizabeth
Tiers +Millers Bluff
1211
Campbell Town
B34
River
Mt. Augusta +
328
1
Green   Ck.
Ross

Mt. Humboldt +
102
Nicholls   Range
Prince   of   Denison
Truchanas
Nature Res.
The Pleiades
Stepped Hills
Gordon
Tiger Range
+1439
+Clear Hill
1198
+Erskine Pt.
317
Lake
Adamsfield
Tim Shea
+952
Gordon River Dam
Gordon
Atkins Ra.
Strathgordon
Gordon
Ragged Ra.
Saw Back Ra.
Serpentine Dam
Mt: Sprent
1058+
B61
Frodshams
Pass
Doherty's Range
Wilmot Range
McPartlan
Pass
+Mt. Wedge
1146
Mt. Bowes
+956
Sentinel Range
731
+
Mt. Cawthorne
The Coronets
Maria
Bay
Marsden Range
Celtic Hill
+771
+Double Pk.
1060
Frankland   Range
Lake   Pedder
Mt Solitary
Mt. Eliza
+1289
L. Judd
Rookery   Plain
Companion Ra.
Frankland R.
Scotts Pk
Scotts Peak
Dam
Edgar
Bay
Schnells R.
Gallagher
Plateau
Folded   Ra.
Edgar Dam

TAS   *Central Highlands*

This is the centre of Tasmania's trout fishing in more ways than one. Not only is it more or less the geographic centre of the island State, it contains a wealth of natural lakes, man-made impoundments and small isolated tarns and pondages - most of which contain trout and some of which offer trout fishing that staggers overseas anglers used to more heavily fished and less vigorous natural fisheries.

Tasmania's Lakes: The principal lakes are Great Lake, Arthurs Lake, Lake Echo and the adjoining pair of Lakes Sorell and Crescent. There are also several other smaller lakes which offer excellent fishing for fly and lure fishermen and indeed some of the fly-only waters having fishing that has to be experienced to be believed. It's not all roses however - nothing in real life fishing is. The greatest impediment to fishing these highland lakes is the fluky and often inclement weather. You rarely get the chance to fish without strong winds and when you do, the trout are so touchy in the crystal clear water that you need to take considerable pains in your approach and technique.

It's worth noting that one of the reasons Tasmania has such great trout fishing is the enlightened and thoroughly professional approach of its State Fisheries Department. Among their regulations which only irk the idle or thoughtless, are restrictions on bait fishing in some lakes and lure fishing in others.

You can flyfish in all Tasmanian waters but bait fishing is not permitted in the following places: Lake Pedder, Sorell, Little Pine Lagoon, Tods Corner in the Great Lake, and most of Brumbys Creek.

Lures are not permitted in the following: Little Pine Lagoon, Penstock, Calverts Lagoon, Bruiser's Lagoon near Great Lake and the canal between Little Pine and the River Ouse.

Trout Fishing Regulations: Generally the Tasmanian trout season opens on the first Saturday closest to the 1st of August each year except for Dee Lagoon, Lagoon of Islands and Lake Rowallan which do not open until the Saturday nearest October 1st. Most waters close on 28 April, with an extended season for the following until 1 June: Great Lake except for Canal Bay, Lake Mackintosh, Lake Rosebery, Dee Lagoon, Lake Rowallan, and Lagoon of Islands. Check with Tasmanian State Fisheries each year however, as these regulations may alter.

Licences at the time of publication were $35.00 per season for adults, $10.00 for juveniles (14 to 17), and $20.00 for pensioners. A 14 day licence is $20.00 regardless of age. Given the active and intelligent involvement of the Fisheries Department in maintaining and improving this excellent fishery, the fees are quite justifiable and reasonable.

Because the weather is subject to rapid change, capable of snowing, even in high summer, take sufficient clothing for any eventuality and make provision for poor roads with suitable tyres, snow chains, or by using vehicles with four wheel drive. Take particular care on the narrow dirt roads in wet weather, especially when sharing the road with large timber trucks which are disinclined to move off the crown of the road.

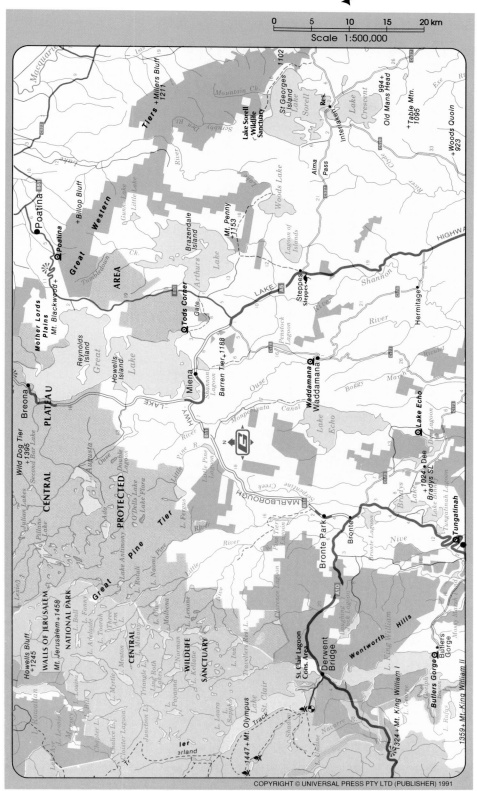

0   5   10   15   20 km

Scale 1:500,000

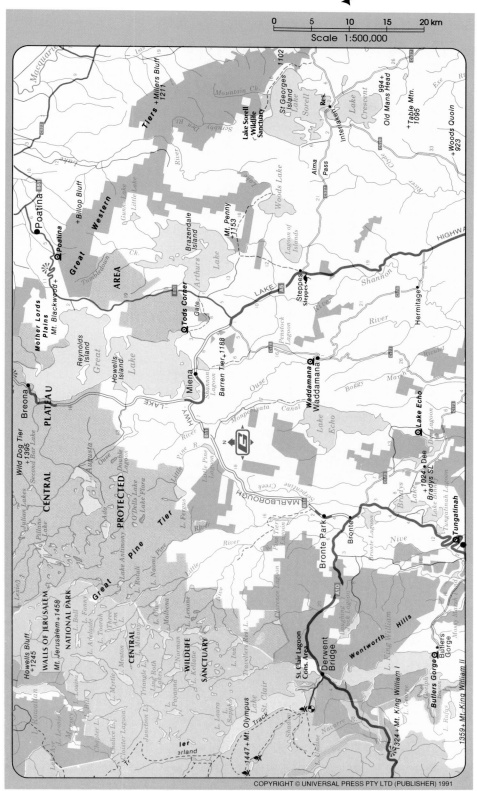

George Town to Launceston

This map brings us back to the coast again but still covers some excellent trout water. Good waters are: Brumby's Creek between Cressy and Hadspen, the South Esk at Longford, the Liffey between Liffey Falls and Carrick, Quamby Brook, The Meander, and the North Esk near White Hills.

The trout of Tasmania's northern central rivers are not generally large, but they are to be found in some of the State's prettiest country, reminiscent of the English countryside.

River blackfish, tench, redfin and eels are also caught from the Meander, and just north of here at Birralee, is Brushy Lagoon which yields both brown and Rainbow trout on mudeyes or flies.

The saltwater side of the central north is centred on the Tamar River, a large estuary which runs from the city of Launceston to the sea at George Town.

Reasonable catches of snapper are taken from the Tamar, in fact one specimen over 13 kg was landed near Deviot.

Cod are a problem, occasionally stealing baits meant for snapper, but there are also other species in the Tamar, including flathead, salmon, mullet and occasionally juvenile tailor. Sea run trout have also been caught here on rising tides using spinners and these fish are usually large, healthy specimens which give a good account of themselves.

Port Sorell has a shingle boat ramp good in all weathers, and this provides access to good flathead, salmon and mullet fishing. The same species are available to the east of the Tamar entrance where there is reasonable beach fishing, even though there is little in the way of gutters and channels.

Tam 'O' Shanter Bay, Noland Bay and West Sandy Point offer good rockfishing for parrot fish, leatherjacket, 'couta, pike and salmon.

Overall beach and rockfishing is not as good as the northeastern corner. However, there is still reasonably reliable fishing for flathead, mullet, small salmon and occasional snapper from the rocks.

To the west of the Tamar entrance toward Stanley, the major species are 'couta, pike and black-back salmon.

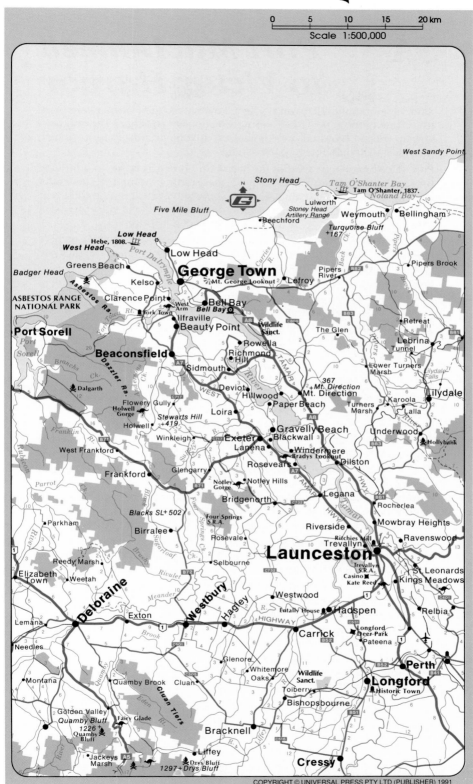

0   5   10   15   20 km

Scale 1:500,000

West Sandy Point

Stony Head

Tam O'Shanter Bay

Tam O'Shanter, 1837.

Noland Bay

Five Mile Bluff

Lulworth

Stoney Head
Artillery Range

Weymouth

Bellingham

Beechford

Turquoise Bluff
+167

Low Head

Hebe, 1808.

West Head

Port Dalrymple

Low Head

Pipers Brook

Badger Head

Greens Beach

Kelso

George Town

Mt. George Lookout

Lefroy

Pipers
River

Pipers Brook

ASBESTOS RANGE
NATIONAL PARK

Clarence Point

West
Arm

York Town

Bell Bay

Bell Bay

Wildlife
Sanct.

Retreat

The Glen

Lebrina

Tunnel

Port Sorell

Ilfraville

Beauty Point

Rowella

Richmond
Hill

Lower Turners
Marsh

Lilydale
Falls

Beaconsfield

Dazzler Ra.

Sidmouth

Deviot

Hillwood

Mt. Direction

Lilydale

Dalgarth

Flowery Gully

Holwell
Gorge

Stewarts Hill
+419

Paper Beach

Karoola

Lalla

Loira

367
+Mt. Direction

Turners
Marsh

Holwell

Winkleigh

Exeter

Lanena

Gravelly Beach

Blackwall

Underwood

Hollybank

West Frankford

Glengarry

Rosevears

Windermere
Bradys Lookout

Dilston

Frankford

Notley
Gorge

Notley Hills

Legana

Rocherlea

Parkham

Bridgenorth

Blacks SL+502

Four Springs
S.R.A.

Riverside

Mowbray Heights

Ravenswood

Birralee

Rosevale

Ritchies Mill
Trevallyn

Launceston

Reedy Marsh

Selbourne

Trevallyn
S.R.A.

St. Leonards

Kings Meadows

Elizabeth
Town

Weetah

Meander

Casino
Kate Reed

Deloraine

Westbury

Hagley

Westwood

Entally House

Hadspen

Relbia

Lemana

Exton

HIGHWAY

Carrick

Longford
Deer Park

Pateena

Needles

Glenore

Whitemore
Oaks

Wildlife
Sanct.

Perth

Montana

Quamby Brook

Cluan

Cluan Tiers

Toiberina

Longford
Historic Town

Golden Valley

Quamby Bluff

Fairy Glade

Bishopsbourne

1226
Quamby
Bluff

Bracknell

Jackeys
Marsh

Liffey

1297 +Drys Bluff

Cressy

SA   *Port MacDonnell to Victor Harbor*

Stretching from the Victorian border all the way to the Fleurieu Peninsula, this is one of the State's most exposed sections of coastline. The Southern Ocean creates hundreds of kilometres of rolling surf, some of which provides Australia's finest beach fishing.

Port MacDonnell, just west of the Victorian border, is home to a thriving professional fleet and can also be the starting point for successful gamefishing sorties. Bluefin tuna arrive between April and June each year and there are plenty of blue sharks and mako sharks offshore. Reef fishermen score snapper, whiting and big sweep inshore.

Robe and Beachport are picturesque little fishing settlements which revolve around the lobster fishing industry, but each provides good offshore recreational fishing for the same species as Port MacDonnell.

From Kingston to the Murray mouth at Goolwa, flat beaches with turbulent surf dominate the coastline. Mulloway of varying sizes, salmon, flathead and small sharks are among regular catches from these beaches.

The Coorong: Four wheel drive vehicles are required for access, and in order to get onto the beach, fishermen must cross the Coorong, one of the largest enclosed marine waterways in the country. There are several popular access points, including the 42 Mile, and the Tea Tree crossings near the township of Salt Creek.

The Coorong is an intriguing expanse of rolling sandhills, placid water and teeming wildlife. This makes it a nature reserve of great significance. Accordingly, camping permits are required by those wanting to stay overnight and four wheel drive activities are strictly controlled. Contact the South Australian Tourism offices for details.

A small boat will open up must of the Coorong and enable the pursuit of bream, mullet, salmon trout, and school mulloway. It is the mouth of the Murray river however which creates fever pitch excitement when big mulloway are on the prowl. Fish of up to 40 kg have been taken in this area, with average specimens during the run being around 20 kg.

The Goolwa surf beach is only lightly fished because it is relatively featureless. Its main claim to fame is that it is home to Goolwa cockles ('pipis' in New South Wales). These are one of South Australia's favourite whiting baits and are so numerous they support a thriving local industry.

Victor Harbor is a beautiful seaside resort with good offshore fishing, particularly during summer when the outer reefs yield big snapper, snook, oversized slimy mackerel, trevally and small to medium sized mako sharks. Big salmon are also found around the offshore islands.

Gulf St Vincent: The Gulf effectively blocks most of the Southern Ocean swell once you move west of Cape Jervis, at one time the State's most famous big snapper location. These days however, snapper catches are well down and anglers must diversify if they want good fishing. Cape Jervis has one of the State's few good all-tide launching ramps and as such is a popular launching spot for trips to Kangaroo Island.

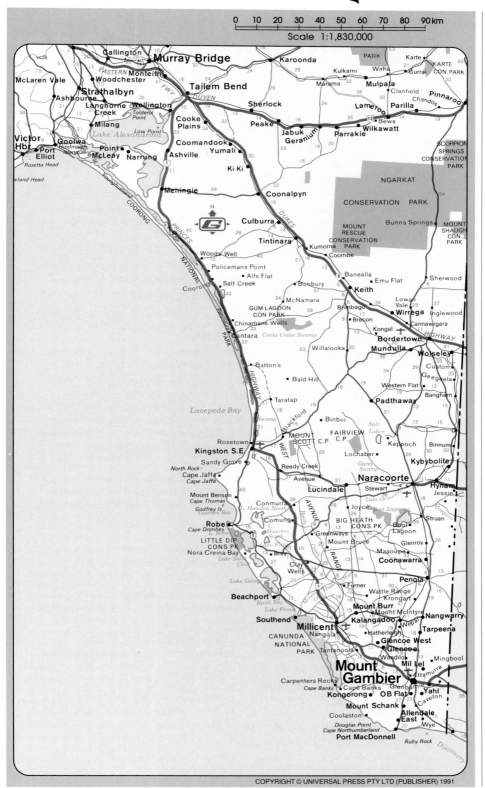

0 10 20 30 40 50 60 70 80 90km

Scale 1:1,830,000

Callington 10
Murray Bridge 32 Karoonda PARK Karte 53 40
51 23 13 EASTERN Monteith 24 Kulkami Wirha 21 Gurrai KARTE
McLaren Vale 75 Woodchester 24 29 Marama 32 Mulpata 20 Clanfield CON. PARK 32
Strathalbyn 18 Tailem Bend Sherlock 24 Lameroo Parilla Pinnaroo
Ashbourne 21 QUYEN 19 14 12 Bews Chandos 19
Langhorne 13 Wellington 21 Cooke 22 Peake Jabuk Wilkawatt
Creek Milang Toldenol Plains 34 Geranium Parrakie SCORPION
Point Low Point 18 SPRINGS
Victor Goolwa Lake Alexandrina Coomandook Yumali 29 18 CONSERVATION
Hbr. Port Hindmarsh Point Narrung Ashville 30 PARK
Elliot Island McLeay Ki Ki 22
Rosetta Head 21
Meningie 48 NGARKAT
wland Head Coonalpyn 94
CONSERVATION PARK
Culburra Bunns Springs MOUNT
45 26 MOUNT SHAUGH
Tintinara RESCUE CON
Woods Well 14 Kumorna CONSERVATION PARK
12 Coombe PARK
Policemans Point Banealla Sherwood
Alfs Flat Emu Flat 6
Salt Creek 42 Bunbury Keith 6
24 McNamara 38 Lowan 23 27
GUM LAGOON Brimbago Vale Wirrega Inglewood
CON PARK 9 Brecon Cannawigara
Chinamans Wells Kongal Bordertown HIGHWAY
Cantara 22 Coola Coola Swamp 13 Mundulla Wolseley
63 Willalooka 22 Custon 35
Batton's Geegeela
Bald Hill Western Flat 29 25
Bangham
Taratap 18 19 Padthaway 15
Lacepede Bay Binbin Salt 13 15
Swamp FAIRVIEW Lakes
Blackford MOUNT C.P. Keppoch Binnum
Rosetown SCOTT C.P. Lochaber 30 30
Kingston S.E. WEST Kybybolite
Sandy Grove 16 Reedy Creek Gareys
North Rock Swamp Hynam
Cape Jaffa Avenue 21 Naracoorte 11 41
Cape Jaffa 40 Lucindale Stewart Jessie
Mount Benson Joyce Lake Ormerod 18
Cape Thomas 39 AVENUE 26 Bool Lagoon Mesqunta
Godfrey Is. Conmurra BIG HEATH Struan 35
Guichen Bay L. Hawdon North CONS. PK Bool
Robe Comung Lagoon Glenroy 26
Cape Dombey Hawdon Greenways Mount Bruce Maaoupe
LITTLE DIP South Coonawarra
CONS. PK Bray 33
Nora Creina Bay Lake Salt 27 Clay 31 Penola
Lake George Wells 20 Furner 30
Beachport Rivoli Bay Wattle Range 16
Lake Frome Krongart 16
Mount Burr Mount McIntyre
Southend Kalangadoo Nangwarry
Millicent 19 Tarpeena
CANUNDA Nangula Hatherleigh 18
NATIONAL Glencoe West
PARK Tantanoola Glencoe Mingbool
Wandilo
Mil Lel
Mount Attamurra
Carpenters Rocks Gambier Glenburnie
Cape Banks Cape Banks Yahl
Kongorong OB Flat Caveton 36
Mount Schank
Coolaston Allendale
Douglas Point East
Cape Northumberland Wye
Port MacDonnell Ruby Rock Discovery

Kangaroo Island to Whyalla

Kangaroo Island offers good fishing on its eastern shore which can be reached by small boat from Cape Jervis. This gives access to the towns of Kingscote, American River and Penneshaw. The island's south and west coasts can only be safely fished from large seaworthy boats in good weather. Gamefishermen occasionally find Southern bluefin tuna, yellowtail kingfish and big sharks.

Whiting fishing is excellent in Antechamber Bay, American River and Kingscote. Surf fishing along the island's south coast can provide salmon, mullet and mulloway. There are bream in most of the rivers and Kingscote jetty yields tommy ruffs, snook, silver trevally and whiting.

Rapid Bay is popular during spring and summer. Tommy ruffs are staple fare from the jetty, as are garfish, trevally, snook, silver drummer and squid. Yellowtail kingfish are regular but few are hooked and fewer landed.

Headlands and coves punctuate the coastline between Rapid Bay and Myponga Beach. Squid are prolific, while offshore anglers catch whiting, gar, snook and snapper on the reefs. Good locations include Second Valley, Wirrina Cove, Normanville and Carrickalinga.

Metropolitan Adelaide: King George whiting are found at Moana, Sellicks Beach, Hallett Cove and Seacliff, with better quality fish showing up between March and September. Brighton, Glenelg, West Beach, Semaphore and Outer Harbour also consistently produce whiting and attract thousands of fishermen annually. Of all the launching facilities in the area, North Haven is the best. North of Adelaide, tidal beaches and mangrove flats predominate. While angling isn't brilliant, blue swimmer crabs are taken in large numbers each summer from beaches at Port Parham, Port Gawler and Thompsons.

Yorke Peninsula and Spencer Gulf: Yorke Peninsula is bounded by Gulf St Vincent on its eastern shore and Spencer Gulf on its west. Ardrossan, Stansbury, Port Giles and Edithburgh attract thousands of jetty anglers on weekends and during peak holiday periods. The offshore fishing is good, with whiting, snook, gar and snapper.

Ardrossan has a first rate boat ramp and it is a short trip to the sunken barge which is one of the Fishery Department's Fish Aggregation Devices. This yields large snapper and is recommended when the weather is right.

Large catches of tommy ruffs are made from the Edithburgh and Port Giles jetties, as are squid, gar and some snapper. Stenhouse Bay jetty further south, is also good.

The Peninsula's lower beaches produce mullet, salmon and school mulloway between March and May. Browns Beach is the most popular of these, with salmon to 5 kg caught quite regularly.

Point Turton, Port Victoria, Balgowan, Port Hughes, Wallaroo and Port Broughton are all good for King George whiting. Port Hughes also provides plenty of big snapper at Christmas time. Port Pirie and Port Germein both provide whiting and the snapper are found offshore.

Whyalla is famous for its giant snapper, both from the rocks and offshore, and there are plenty of whiting, gar, squid and tommy ruffs as well. Cowell is situated on Franklin Harbour – whiting, mullet, tommy ruffs and squid are inside the harbour while big snapper and snook are outside the heads.

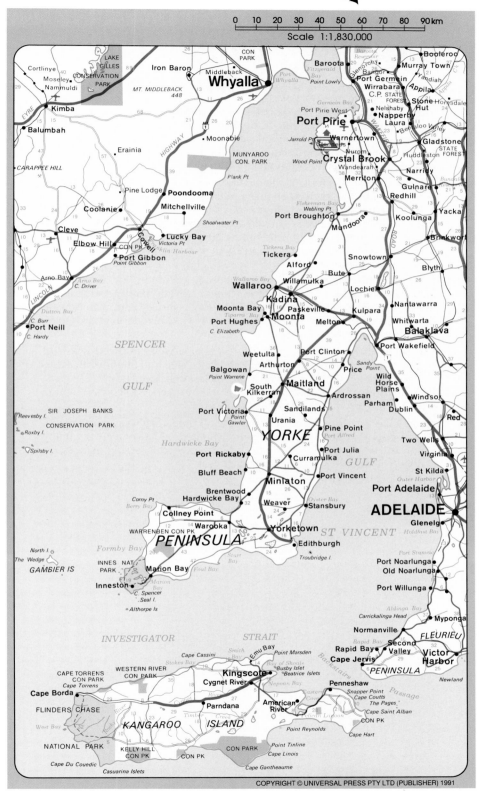

0 10 20 30 40 50 60 70 80 90km

Scale 1:1,830,000

SA

Tumby Bay to Streaky Bay

The lower section of Eyre Peninsula is not only one of the state's best for visiting anglers, it is also one of the most beautiful. Tumby Bay provides easy access to the Sir Joseph Banks group of islands, which yield snapper, big King George whiting and a variety of other desirable table varieties. It is here that game fishermen do battle with giant white pointer sharks.

Port Lincoln at the foot of the Peninsula is kind to both amateur and commercial fishermen alike, being a reliable place for land-based anglers to try their luck. As well as being home base to one of the country's largest professional fishing fleets, Lincoln attracts thousands of angling visitors each season. It has several jetties and a large sheltered bay while Lincoln Cove Marina has accommodation and boat moorings and there is an all-tide ramp at Billy Light's Point.

Nearby Coffin Bay shares Port Lincoln's attraction for vacationing fisherfolk, its sheltered waters rich in whiting, trevally, flathead and salmon trout. Almonta Beach, part of the Coffin Bay National Park, can turn on double figure salmon at times, and so can both Convention and Greenly Beaches a little further north.

The sleepy fishing township of Elliston is also well endowed with surf beaches for the long rod brigade. Both Locks Well and Sheringa Beaches are great for big salmon, albeit on a slightly less consistent basis these days. Pressure from professional netters has certainly taken its toll on the salmon schools - a worrying factor for the whole area.

Streaky Bay provides the perfect jumping off point for a west coast angling vacation, as it is close to top notch surf fishing, productive inshore whiting action and boasts a long jetty for the land-based specialist. Big snapper are caught from the jetty in late spring each year.

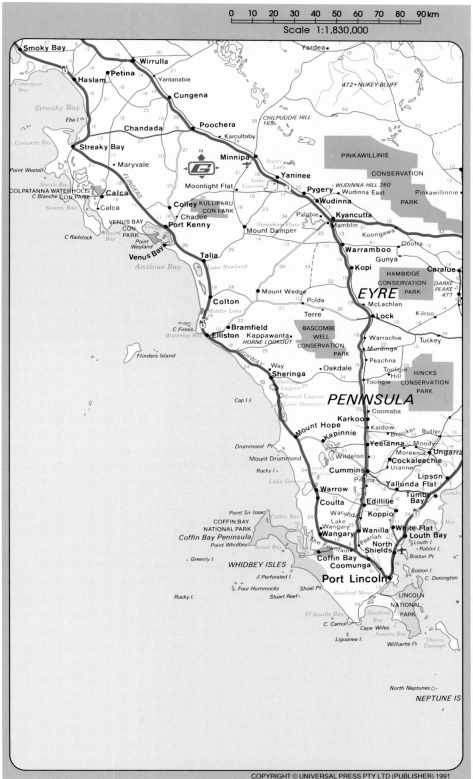

0   10   20   30   40   50   60   70   80   90 km

Scale 1:1,830,000

Smoky Bay
Wirrulla
Haslam • Petina
Yantanabie
Cungena
Cascoigne Bay
Streaky Bay
Eba I.
Chandada
Corvisart Bay
Streaky Bay
• Maryvale
Point Westall
Seale Bay
COLPATANNA WATERHOLE
C Blanche CON PARK
Calca
•Calca
Searcy Bay
VENUS BAY
CON.
PARK
C Radstock
Baird Bay
Point Weyland
Venus Bay
Anxious Bay
Lake Newland
Moonlight Flat
Colley KULLIPARU
CON PARK
Chadee
Port Kenny
Mount Damper
Talia
Mount Wedge
Colton
Middle Lake
C Finnis
Waterloo Bay
Bramfield
Elliston
Kappawanta•
HORNE LOOKOUT
Flinders Island
Way
Sheringa
Sheringa Lagoon
Cap I.
Round Lagoon
Lake Hamilton

Yardea•
472 • NUKEY BLUFF
CHILPUDDIE HILL
165•
Karcultaby
Minnipa
Agars Lake
Lake Yaninee
Yaninee
Pygery
Wudinna
Palabie•
Kyancutta
Samphire Flats
Mamblin
Koongawa
Warramboo
Gootra
Gunya
Kopi
Polda
Terre
McLachlan
Lock
BASCOMBE
WELL
CONSERVATION
PARK
Oakdale
Toolgie Hill
Tooligie

PINKAWILLINIE
CONSERVATION
WUDINNA HILL 260
Wudinna East
Pinkawillinnie
PARK
HAMBIDGE
CONSERVATION PARK
DARKE PEAKE
477
Caralue
Kilroo
Warrachie
Murdinga
Peachna
HINCKS
CONSERVATION
PARK
Coomaba

EYRE

PENINSULA

Tuckey

Drummond Pt
Mount Drummond
Rocky I.
Lake Greenly
Point Sir Isaac
COFFIN BAY
NATIONAL PARK
Coffin Bay Peninsula
Point Whidbey
• Greenly I.
WHIDBEY ISLES
Rocky I.
Mount Hope
Kapinnie
Wideloo
Cummins
Warrow
Coulta
Warunda
Lake
Wangary
Wangary
Coffin Bay
Coomunga
Perforated I.
Four Hummocks
Shoal Pt
Stuart Reef
D'Anville Bay
C. Carnot
Liguanea I.

Karkoo
Kaldow
Brooker
Butler
Yeelanna
Moody
Moreenia
Cockaleechie
Uranno
Pillana
Lipson
Yallunda Flat
Edillilie
Koppio
Tumby Bay
White Flat
Louth Bay
Louth I.
• Rabbit I.
Boston Pt.
North Shields
Boston I.
C. Donington
Port Lincoln
LINCOLN
NATIONAL
PARK
Sleaford Mere
Sleaford Bay
Cape Wiles
Jussieu Bay
Williams I.
Thorny Passage

Wanilla

Ungarra

North Neptunes ◇•
NEPTUNE IS

Streaky Bay to Fowlers Bay

Because of its remoteness from the bulk of the state's population, this region is lightly fished by recreational anglers. For this reason it is consistently productive, particularly for big whiting, salmon and mulloway.

Streaky Bay is a great whiting spot, regularly producing bag limit catches of fish way above average size. It also yields gar, snook, snapper and large tommy ruffs, as well as salmon from Back Beach to the south. Big-game fishermen can also target the Great White shark offshore from this point.

Ceduna, a fishing town and bulk grain loading terminal, is the last major settlement before the WA border. Whiting are the mainstay of the inshore fishery, along with gar, snook and seasonal snapper. This is a perfect small boat area with excellent launching facilities.

For game fishermen, Ceduna is an ideal base port. Some of the world's biggest white sharks (including the current all tackle world record) have come from these waters and there are southern bluefin tuna for those with the boats and equipment to travel wide.

Jetty anglers are well catered for at Ceduna. The long bulk loading jetty at nearby Thevenard is great for snook on summer evenings and consistently yields heavy bags of tommy ruffs. The shorter, but equally productive Ceduna town jetty is great for squid, snook, tommies and mullet.

The surf beaches west of Ceduna are awe-inspiring places to fish. You need to take food, water, fuel and bait in with you if intending to spend any time exploring up towards the head of the Bight, but experienced surf anglers find big salmon in droves here, as well as sharks and some truly giant mulloway.

Fowlers Bay is the gateway to some of Australia's greatest surf beaches. Pounded incessantly by the swells of the Great Australian Bight, these beaches turn on mulloway to 40 kg, salmon to double figures and whaler sharks of unnerving proportions. This area is remote and generally inhospitable, so those who plan extended visits must be totally prepared.

The first and most easily accessible of these beaches is Scott's and although it is under more pressure than those further west, it still yields plenty of impressive jew each year. You really need a four-wheel-drive vehicle to explore the endless miles of golden sand, as inshore gutters are constantly changing. The rewards of all this, however, can be great.

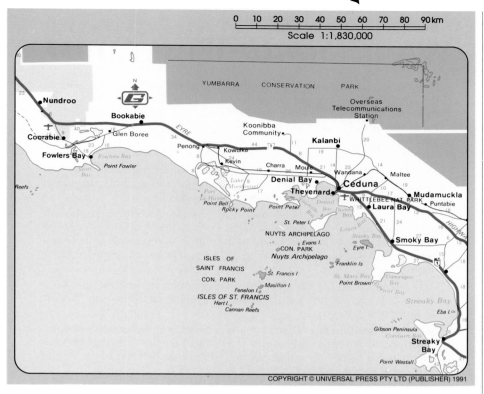

0 10 20 30 40 50 60 70 80 90km

Scale 1:1,830,000

YUMBARRA   CONSERVATION   PARK

Overseas
Telecommunications
Station

•Nundroo

Bookabie•

Koonibba
Community•

Kalanbi

23

EYRE

Coorabie •

Glen Boree

Penong•

Kowulka

Fowlers Bay

Fowlers Bay

Kevin•

Point Fowler

Charra

Moule

Wandana

Maltee

Denial Bay •

Reefs

Lake
Macdonnel

Theyenard•

Ceduna

Mudamuckla

Port
Le Hunte

WHITTLEBEE NAT PARK

• Puntabie

Point Bell

Rocky Point

Point Peter

Laura Bay

Denial
Bay

Dreary
Bay

HIGHWAY

St. Peter I.

NUYTS ARCHIPELAGO

Lirum Bay

Smoky Bay

Evans I.

CON. PARK

Snuks Bay

Nuyts Archipelago

Eyre I.

ISLES   OF

Franklin Is

SAINT FRANCIS

St. Francis I

St. Mary Bay

Gaseigne
Bay

CON. PARK

Masillon I.

Point Brown

Coorani Bay

Fenelon I.

ISLES OF ST. FRANCIS

Streaky Bay

Hart I.

Cannan Reefs

Eba I.

Gibson Peninsula

Corvisart Bay

Streaky
Bay

Point Westall

Herring, salmon and skippy (silver trevally) are the big three for anglers in the south-west corner and along the south coast. Tailor are not usually prolific, although occasionally some very large fish are caught, and whiting can be good, but are not widespread. Offshore bottom fishing is excellent, and West Australian jewfish, snapper, samson fish, blue groper, queen snapper (blue morwong) and breaksea cod are all available.

The jetty at Esperance is a popular spot for herring and big skippy. The best time, both for fish and weather, is late summer and autumn. Hopetoun offers excellent beach fishing, as does Bremer Bay.

Albany is salmon fishing headquarters in February and March, as the fish begin their run around the south-west corner. Resident salmon can be caught all year, but the beginning of autumn is exceptional. Skippy and herring are commonplace. The King and Kalgan Rivers are good for black bream.

Denmark's Wilson Inlet is great for small snapper, herring, skippy, King George whiting and tarwhine. Beach fishing all along this stretch of coast is excellent.

The Walpole-Nornalup estuary area is a small-boat fisherman's delight. Black bream are abundant in the Deep and Frankland Rivers, and the estuary holds plenty of herring, skippy, whiting, garfish and so on. Berley is useful in the estuary, and ultralight tackle is all that is required.

Augusta – Cape Naturaliste – Geographe Bay: Augusta, at the southern tip of the Cape-to-Cape stretch, is similar in many ways to Walpole. Black bream are good in the Blackwood River, and here you're within a short drive of trout country. All the estuary species are available and mulloway have also made a name for themselves in the area.

The coast up to Cape Naturaliste is best known for excellent herring and skippy fishing from the rocks and reef, although there are some beautiful beaches as well. Salmon invade the area in March and April, and Yallingup Beach and Canal Rocks are two of the premier locations.

Sugarloaf Rock is quite a climb and doesn't allow much fishing space, but is notable for its samson fish, salmon and occasional West Australian jewfish. A cliff gaff is essential.

Geographe Bay offers relatively protected water and good fishing for herring, whiting and pike. Boat launching is from Dunsborough or Busselton, where the jetty is also a popular venue.

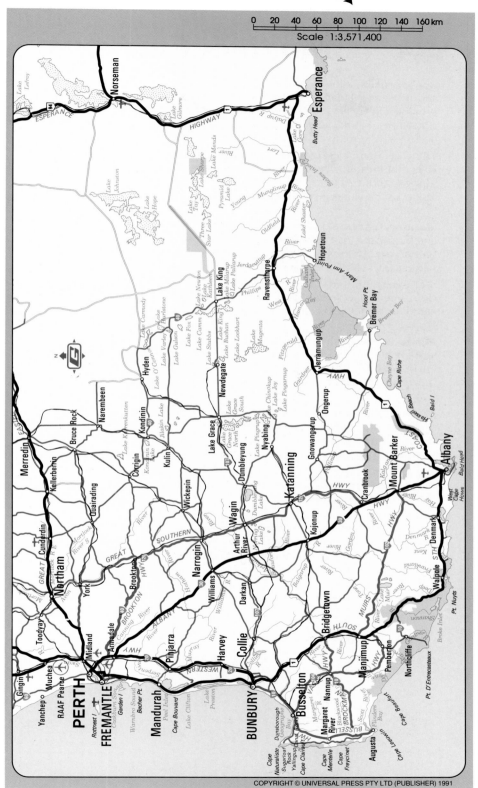

0 20 40 60 80 100 120 140 160 km

Scale 1:3,571,400

Bunbury is about the southern limit for the summer run of 'chopper' tailor, and fishes particularly well for small fish at The Cut and Myalup Beach. Whiting fish well in the estuary in autumn, and salmon and mulloway are a good bet in The Cut at the same time. Small-boat fishermen usually do best.

The coast north to Mandurah is a string of fine beaches, including White Hills and Preston. There is only one notable reef inclusion, being Tim's Thicket, about 20 km south of Mandurah. Tim's is famous for its salmon around April, although the area fishes well for tailor in summer and herring in winter.

Mandurah Area: Mandurah is excellent for small-boat fishing, with great crabbing in the inlet in summer, and plenty of skippy just offshore for most of the year. Tailor swarm to the beaches just north of town in summer, particularly at Madora, Silver Sands and San Remo.

Warnbro Sound and Cockburn Sound provide all manner of small fish from the numerous jetties and breakwaters, and plenty of herring, skippy and squid for boat anglers. Snapper are caught in winter from both shore and boat.

Perth: The Swan River offers brilliant fishing, particularly with the aid of a small boat. Flathead and flounder are abundant in the lower reaches, tailor chase whitebait through summer and autumn, and mulloway and black bream are at their peak in winter and spring.

Northern metropolitan beaches are noted for their herring and tailor, particularly in summer and autumn, and the pick of them would include Swanbourne Drain, City Beach, Floreat Beach and Brighton Road. City Beach has rock groynes for those without proper beach tackle.

Rottnest Island: Rottnest is a mecca for herring and salmon fishermen in autumn, and reef fishing at its western end also produces skippy, yellowtail kingfish and some nice tailor. Offshore fishing for jewfish, snapper, samson fish and other bottom species is a year-round proposition.

North of Perth, shore fishing is mostly for tailor and herring from beaches adjoining reefs which are commonplace. Yanchep, Pipidinny, Burns Beach and Quinns Rocks are all reliable and within easy reach of Perth. The coast is quite similar virtually all the way to Geraldton, with beaches separated by reefs, and a broken line of reef only a couple of kilometres offshore.

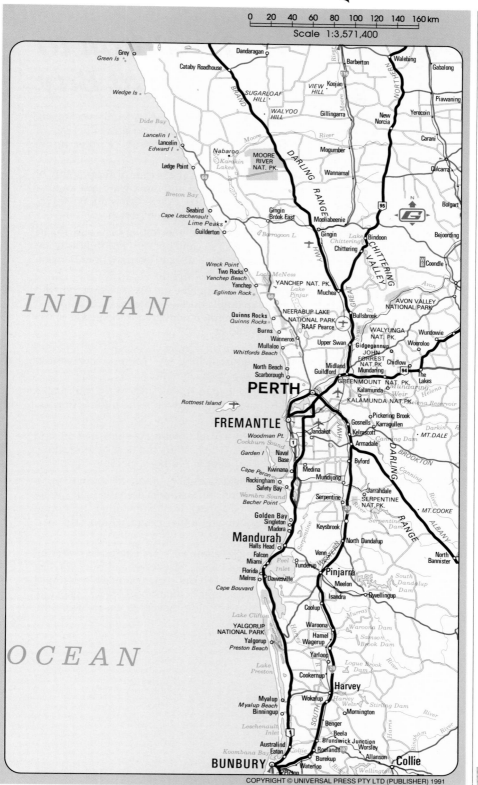

0 20 40 60 80 100 120 140 160 km

Scale 1:3,571,400

Green Is   Grey
Green Is

Dandaragan   Barberton   Walebing   Gabalong

Cataby Roadhouse   VIEW Koojan   Piawaning
Wedge Is   SUGARLOAF HILL   HILL

WALYOO HILL   Gillingarra   New Norcia   Yerecoin

Dide Bay   Moore   River   Carani

Lancelin I   Mogumber   Calcarra
Lancelin   Nabaroo   MOORE
Edward I   Karrakin Lakes   RIVER NAT. PK.

Ledge Point   Wannamal   Bolgart
                60   DARLING   Bejoording

Breton Bay   Gingin Brook East   Bindoon
                        Mooliabeenie   95   Coondle

Seabird   Gingin   Lake Chittering
Cape Leschenault   Chittering   CHITTERING VALLEY
Lime Peaks   Barragoon L.   Avon
Guilderton

Wreck Point   Loch McNess   AVON VALLEY NATIONAL PARK
Two Rocks   YANCHEP NAT. PK.
Yanchep Beach   Lake Pinjar   Muchea
Yanchep   Eglinton Rock   GREAT

INDIAN   Quinns Rocks   NEERABUP LAKE NATIONAL PARK   Bullsbrook   WALYUNGA NAT. PK.   Wundowie
        Quinns Rocks   RAAF Pearce   Wooroloo
        Burns   Upper Swan   Gidgegannup
        Wanneroo   JOHN FORREST NAT. PK.   Chidlow
        Mullaloo   Midland   Mundaring   94   The Lakes
        Whitfords Beach   Guildford   Mundaring
        North Beach   GREENMOUNT NAT. PK.   Mundaring Weir   Helena
        Scarborough   Kalamunda   Helena Reservoir

PERTH   KALAMUNDA NAT. PK.

        FREMANTLE   Pickering Brook   Darkin
                Gosnells Karragullen   MT.DALE
        Woodman Pt.   Jandakot Kelmscott   Canning Dam
        Cockburn Sound   Armadale   BROOKTON

        Garden I   Naval Base   Byford   DARLING   Canning River
        Cape Peron   Kwinana   Medina   MT.COOKE
        Rockingham   Mundijong
        Safety Bay   Serpentine   Jarrahdale SERPENTINE NAT.PK.
        Warnbro Sound   Becher Point   20   Serpentine Dam   RANGE

        Golden Bay   Keysbrook   ALBANY
        Singleton
        Madora   North Dandalup   North Bannister
Mandurah   Halls Head
        Falcon   Venn   South Dandalup Dam
        Miami   Yunderup   Pinjarra
        Florida   Dawesville   Meelon   Dwellingup
        Melros
        Cape Bouvard   Isandra

OCEAN   Lake Clifton   Coolup   Murray
                Waroona   Waroona Dam
        YALGORUP NATIONAL PARK   Hamel   Samson Brook Dam
        Yalgorup   Wagerup
        Preston Beach   Yarloop   Logue Brook Dam
        Lake Preston   Cookernup   20   River
                        Harvey   Harvey Weir   Stirling Dam
        Myalup   Wokalup   Mornington   River
        Myalup Beach
        Binningup   Benger
        Leschenault Inlet   Beela
                Brunswick Junction   Worsley
        Australind   Roelands   Allanson
        Eaton   Burekup   Collie
        Koombana Bay   Waterloo   Wellington
BUNBURY   Picton

Geraldton to Coral Bay

Kalbarri marks the northern limit of the regular tailor and mulloway beach fishing that is prevalent along the west coast, and is also about the limit for regular catches of West Australian jewfish from boats. Further north, snapper and whiting become standard fare.

Geraldton to Shark Bay: The beach and reef country from south of Geraldton up to Kalbarri is excellent for tailor and mulloway, and some of the proven locations include Drummonds Cove, Coronation Beach, Horrocks, Port Gregory and the Lucky Bay to Wagoe stretch.

Kalbarri is famed for its tailor, both giants and 'choppers', and for its excellent offshore fishing for mackerel, tuna and bottom fish. Mulloway are a regular addition to the beach fisherman's haul, and even snapper, samson fish, amberjack and cobia are caught from the shore.

Shark Bay draws two different styles of anglers: the 4WD contingent who head to the ocean side where Steep Point and False Entrance host gamefish and snapper, and the calm water fishermen who favour the inside of the bay, for snapper, mulloway and whiting.

Monkey Mia, Denham and Nanga are all venues for small-boat snapper fishing, and provide reasonable shore fishing too. Large boat access to Steep Point and Dirk Hartog Island is from Denham.

Tracks from the Useless Loop road lead to the west coast for top quality rock fishing. Dinghies can be trailered in however, if the track is in good condition.

Carnarvon's long jetty produces plenty of mulloway and tailor, and the odd queenfish and mackerel. Myaboolya Beach offers the best beach fishing, with tailor and sharks, plus an assortment of northern species.

Quobba to Exmouth: The Quobba coastline, north of Carnarvon, is famous for its rock fishing for mackerel and snapper (both the pink variety and the totally unrelated 'Norwest' snapper). Boat launching is best done from either The Blowholes, just south of Quobba, or at Gnaraloo, the next station north.

Coral Bay is primarily a boat fishing location, with a sheltered bay offering easy access to the nearby Ningaloo Reef. Mackerel, sailfish, Norwest snapper and a myriad of other bottom fish draw many anglers from April through to September. Further north, Ningaloo Station and Norwegian Bay offer similar but less commercialised fishing. Access is easiest from the Exmouth Road.

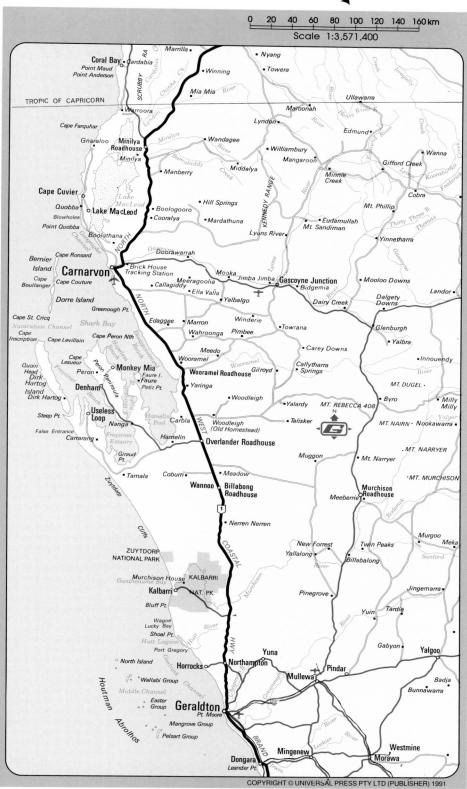

Exmouth to Port Hedland

North-west Cape is a wonderfully diverse region offering both great shore fishing and some of the west coast's best boat fishing. The season peaks from May through to September, although excellent fishing is available all year.

Queenfish, trevally and Norwest snapper are the shore fishing favourites, particularly from the coastline adjoining the Cape Range National Park. In Exmouth Gulf, the fish are generally smaller, but the advantage of fishing here is that the shore may be more protected from the winds.

Boat fishermen pursue mackerel, sailfish, marlin, trevally and a great variety of bottom fish including emperor and cod. The water deepens rapidly once outside the Ningaloo Reef, and the Continental Shelf runs closer to the coast here than anywhere else around Australia.

Onslow to Point Samson: Onslow is the next town up the coast, but the shore fishing bears no comparison to that at North-West Cape. Beadon Creek offers bream, jacks and a few queenfish, trevally and mackerel. The offshore fishing amongst the islands known collectively as the 'Mackerel Islands' is exceptional.

Dampier is famous for its sailfish in spring, and has mackerel all year, plus plenty of bottom fish. The shallows and drop-offs around the numerous islands house plenty of queenfish and trevally, while garfish and mullet are common in the creeks and bays.

The Maitland River is a tidal mangrove area, holding barra, jacks, bream and trevally. Point Samson has a jetty of sorts, and more tidal creeks which attract threadfin salmon.

Port Hedland: Balla Balla Creek is popular with Port Hedland locals for its threadfin and trevally. Shore fishing around Hedland is best at the Spoil Bank, although some mighty fish are caught in the harbour at times. Black jewfish are often hooked but rarely landed, thanks to their strength and panicked dives for pylons.

Entry to the mouth of the DeGrey River requires permission from the station, and is not automatic these days. Those who are allowed to will find good barramundi and threadfin fishing, particularly in April - May and November - December for barra, and during the second half of the year for threadfin.

Cape Keraudren receives plenty of anglers from Goldsworthy and Shay Gap, and offers a reasonable launching ramp in a very out-of-the-way place. Queenfish, trevally, mackerel and tuna keep light tackle anglers happy, while handlines have no shortage of bottom fish to work on.

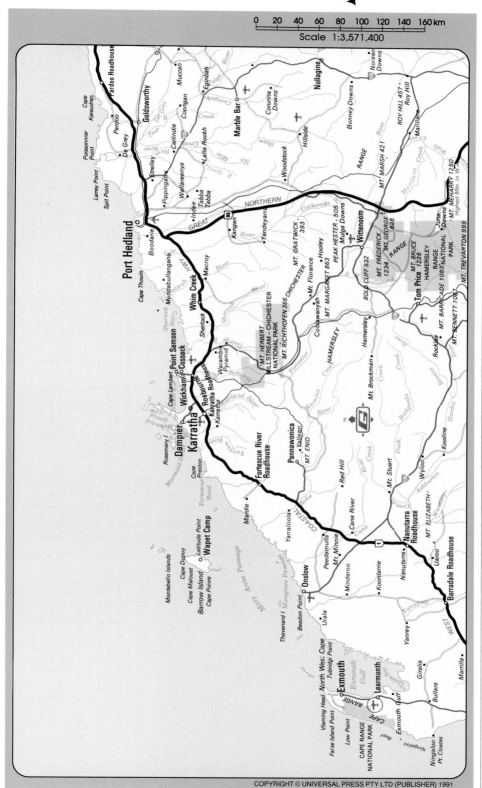

WA *Western Kimberley*

Tide has an enormous influence on Broome and points further north, and the extreme rise and fall must be kept in mind for all fishing in the Kimberley.

Fortunately, Broome's magnificent jetty offers an all-tide vantage point that produces some great days of queenfish, trevally, and occasionally tuna and mackerel. A cliff gaff is essential, and jigs and poppers often work better than bait.

Apart from the jetty, Broome's best known shore fishing location is Willie Creek, approximately 20km north along Cable Beach. Coconut Well Creek, at about the 15km mark, is a popular spot for collecting mullet for bait. This creek must be crossed, and then another 5km of driving brings you to the much larger Willie Creek.

Barramundi can be thick here just before the wet, and there are also mangrove jacks, salmon, mullet, cod and mud crabs.

Offshore fishing from Broome centres around bottom fishing the numerous reefs, chasing tuna just off Gantheaume Point, mackerel fishing the reefs or Disaster Rock, or heading out beyond the reefs to the sailfish grounds.

Many off-the-bitumen areas north of Broome require permission from the Northern Land Council to enter, so be sure to check before proceeding.

Cape Leveque to Derby: Cape Leveque, 200km north of Broome by dirt road, is well known for queenfish, mackerel, trevally and tuna. It is also notorious for sharks, which can be so prolific that virtually every fish hooked is taken. A small boat is a decided advantage, as shore fishing can be very limited.

Derby's shore fishing suffers because of the tides, but the town is a focal point for fishing the Fitzroy and May Rivers for barramundi, and getting out to Koolan and Cockatoo Island for some great boat fishing.

The Fitzroy is a major river, holding barra for hundreds of kilometres, and they can be caught as far upstream as Fitzroy Crossing and Geikie Gorge.

Access into the next area of the Kimberley is very difficult. Remote locations such as Walcott Inlet can be reached by 4WD, particularly with the help of an organised trip from Mt Elizabeth Station. The barramundi fishing in such an untouched location can be staggering.

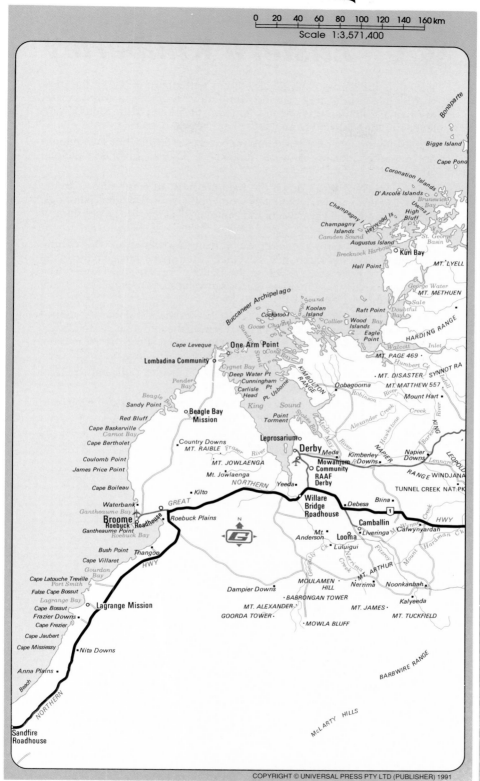

Scale 1:3,571,400

0 20 40 60 80 100 120 140 160 km

Bonaparte

Bigge Island

Cape Pond

Coronation Islands

D'Arcole Islands

Champagny I.

Champagny Islands · Heywood Is

Brunswick Bay

Uwins I.

High Bluff

Camden Sound

St. George Basin

Augustus Island

Brecknock Harbour

Kuri Bay

Hall Point

MT. LYELL

George Water

MT. METHUEN

Sale

Buccaneer Archipelago

Sound

Koolan Island

Raft Point

Doubtful Bay

Cockatoo I.

Goose Channel

Collier

Wood Islands

Bay

Eagle Point

HARDING RANGE

Walcott

Inlet

Cape Leveque

One Arm Point

Sandy Strait

Con Bay

MT. PAGE 469 ·

Humber Cr.

· MT. DISASTER

SYNNOT RA

Lombadina Community

Cygnet Bay

KIMBOLTON RANGE

MT. MATTHEW 557

Deep Water Pt.

Pender Bay

Cunningham Pt.

Oobagooma

Robinson River

Mount Hart

Beagle Bay

Carlisle Head

Pt. Usborne

King

Sound

Alexander Creek

Creek

Sandy Point

Point Torment

Stokes Bay

Meda River

Howkstone Creek

KING River

Red Bluff

Beagle Bay Mission

Banks River

Cape Baskerville

Carnot Bay

Leprosarium

Napier Downs

LEOPOLD

Cape Bertholet

Country Downs

MT. RAIBLE

Fraser River

Derby

Meda

Kimberley Downs

NAPIER

Lennard R.

Coulomb Point

MT. JOWLAENGA

Mowanjum Community

RANGE

WINDJANA

James Price Point

Mt. Jowlaenga

Yeeda

RAAF Derby

TUNNEL CREEK NAT. PK

Cape Boileau

· Kilto

NORTHERN

Willare Bridge Roadhouse

Debesa

Bliina

Waterbank

GREAT

Roadhouse

Camballin

1

HWY

Gantheaume Bay

Broome

Roebuck

Roadhouse

Roebuck Plains

N

G

Mt. Anderson

Looma

Liveringa

Wynn

Calwynyardah

Gantheaume Point

Roebuck Bay

Luluigui

Mount Hardman Ck.

Bush Point

Thangoo

HWY

MT. ARTHUR

Fitzroy

Cape Villaret

Gourdon Bay

Nerrima Creek

Cape Latouche Treville

Port Smith

MOULAMEN HILL

Nerrima

Noonkanbah

False Cape Bossut

Lagrange Bay

Dampier Downs

· BABRONGAN TOWER

Kalyeeda

Cape Bossut

Lagrange Mission

MT. ALEXANDER ·

MT. JAMES ·

MT. TUCKFIELD

Frazier Downs

GOORDA TOWER ·

Cape Frezier

· MOWLA BLUFF

Cape Jaubert

Cape Missiessy

· Nita Downs

BARBWIRE RANGE

Anna Plains ·

Beach

NORTHERN

McLARTY HILLS

Sandfire Roadhouse

Travelling the Derby/Gibb River Road to Kalumburu is one of the most worthwhile tourist treks in the Kimberley. Kalumburu Mission and Aboriginal Community is situated 5km from the mouth of the King Edward River and King Edward Gorge.

The fishing straight off the Kalumburu beaches is terrific, but swimming is not permitted due to saltwater crocodiles. A small boat is a definite advantage.

Approximately halfway down the Kalumburu Road is the turnoff to the Mitchell Plateau, which is definitely worth going into; Aboriginal paintings, the famous Mitchell Falls, walks and camping all add to the great fishing at Port Warrender.

Kununurra has virtually taken over from Wyndham as the fishing headquarters of the Kimberley. Several charter operations take travelling anglers to remote venues such as the Berkley and Drysdale Rivers. The quarantine area of the Ord River (all the saltwater section) is accessible only with a charter.

The main target in this region is of course barramundi, and the best chance unaccompanied anglers have of a barra is from the Ord River. Immediately after the wet season, small fish line up at the bottom of the Diversion Dam, and bigger fish can be caught all year at Ivanhoe Crossing.

Catfish and sooty grunter are also common in the Ord, and in Lake Kununurra and Lake Argyle.

Wyndham suffers from muddy water, making catfish and threadfin the main targets, although barra are available from the creeks.

Most of the Kimberley coastline remains untouched due to its inaccessibility, and well-organised boating trips are often the only way to experience the fishing in the more remote rivers.

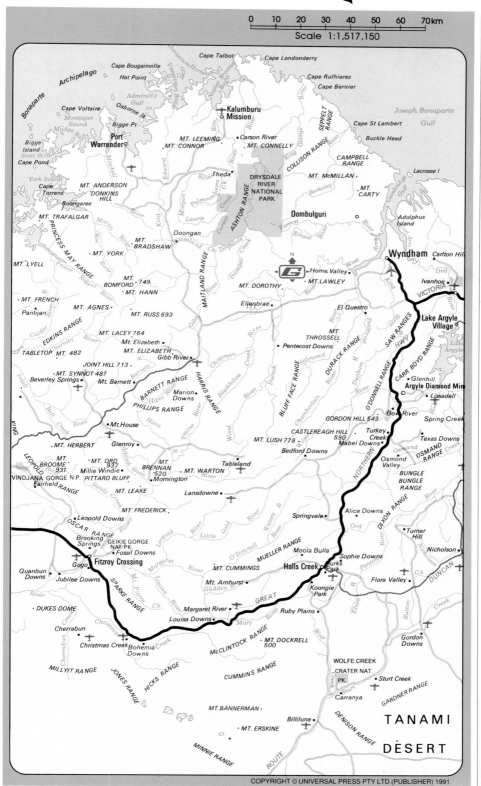

Scale 1:1,517,150

0 10 20 30 40 50 60 70km

TANAMI

DESERT

Darwin to Kakadu

Darwin: The city was rebuilt after Cyclone Tracy in 1974. Recreational fishing is a major pastime of the modern northern capital and visitors will be surprised by the excellent facilities. There are 11 concrete boat ramps within an hour's drive of the city centre. Most provide easy access to different parts of Darwin Harbour and its three large arms.

Darwin Harbour itself is good for fishing tropical coastal and estuary species. Barramundi fishing is still as good up the creeks as it is in many other, more remote parts of the Territory. A feature is the abundance of wrecks in the harbour. Most of these wrecks offer great fishing for a variety of reef fish, including some very large black jewfish.

Darwin to Fog Bay: Access to Bynoe Harbour, to the west of Darwin, is by a combination of bitumen and gravel roads. Presently, there is no boat ramp on the eastern shore of Bynoe Harbour but trailer boats can be launched by 4WD vehicle at several locations. There are several camping locations around Bynoe. McKenzie Arm, which is at the south-western end of the Harbour has two boat ramps.

There are two boat ramps at Dundee Beach which provide access to Fog Bay. From there, large trailer boats are within striking range of the Peron Islands which offer good fishing. Camping and accommodation are available at a beachside resort in Fog Bay.

Darwin to Kakadu National Park: En route to Kakadu, the Arnhem Highway crosses the Adelaide River which features an excellent concrete boat ramp. The river is too muddy for good fishing except at creek mouths during and just after the wet season. In all Top End rivers and estuaries, anglers should be aware of the potential danger posed by crocodiles and stay out of waterways known to be inhabited by them.

Access to Corroboree Lagoon is via Marrakai Station or Point Stuart Road. Small trailer boats can be launched at both locations and there is ample camping space. Dinghies and houseboats are available for hire at the Marrakai Station end of Corroboree Lagoon.

Shady Camp, another famous waterhole for barramundi fishing is also accessed by the Point Stuart Road. The name is a misnomer because there are very few trees to provide shade. Camping is permitted for a small fee, however and there are boats for hire near the water.Further east along the Arnhem Highway, there is another excellent boat ramp servicing the Mary River. This stretch of river is actually a landlocked lagoon. Camping is permitted.

Kakadu National Park: The Wildman, West Alligator, South Alligator and East Alligator Rivers are either wholly or partly contained within Kakadu National Park. Fishing is not permitted in much of the southern end of Kakadu, however, there are many northerly waterways which offer excellent angling opportunities. There are several boat ramps and boat launching areas, and designated camping spots near most fishing locations. Serviced accommodation is also available in the park.A permit is required to enter the park. This is available from the Australian National Parks and Wildlife Service, MLC Building, 79 - 81 Smith Street, Darwin, or from the Park Headquarters on the Kakadu Highway near Jabiru.

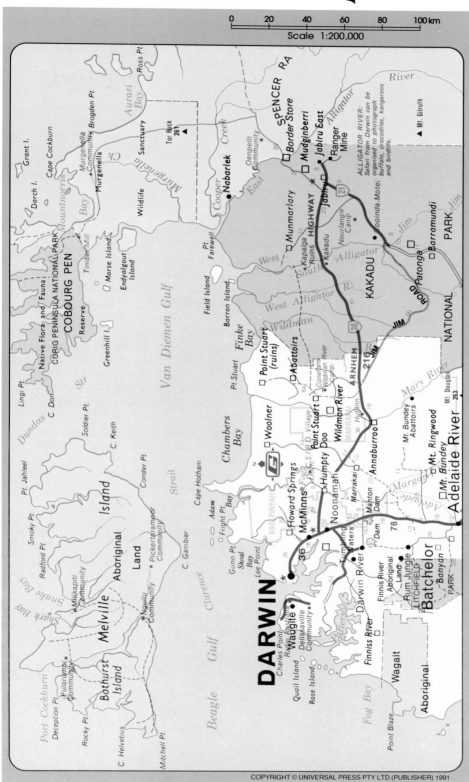

0   20   40   60   80   100 km

Scale 1:200,000

ALLIGATOR RIVER:
Safari from Darwin can be
organised to photograph
buffalo, crocodiles, kangaroos
and birdlife.

Adelaide River to Timber Creek

There are a number of small creeks on the Daly River Road which can be fished from the shore. However, most anglers head straight for the Daly River itself. There is a police station, a small hotel and fuel at the Daly River township, and a shop at the nearby Aboriginal mission. Small trailer boats can be launched by 4WD vehicle at the Daly River Crossing and at Robbie's Sandbar. Boats can be manhandled to the water at Brown's Creek on the river. Camping is permitted at each of these locations. A number of private waterfront blocks permit camping for a fee or provide serviced accommodation. Boat hire is also available. The Daly River is tidal below the crossing, and several submerged rockbars makes it imperative that anglers drive their boats cautiously.

Adelaide River to Katherine: Anglers can reach the upper waters of the Daly River by leaving the Stuart Highway near Hayes Creek and driving to Oolloo Crossing, where there are camping areas available near the river.

Katherine is a large rural town with excellent facilities for the visitor. Most fishing takes place in the Katherine River itself or nearby Katherine Gorge in Nitmiluk National Park.

Katherine to Timber Creek: Travelling south-west from Katherine along the Victoria Highway, anglers may fish the Victoria River at several locations. There is good fishing available in Gregory National Park in the vicinity of the Victoria River bridge. However, boat access is restricted. This part of the river is landlocked during the dry season. A hotel and camping facilities are near the bridge.

Access to a large lagoon further along the river is available at a fee through Coolabah Station. Camping is permitted and boats can be easily launched at this spot. Further west, at the township of Timber Creek, the Victoria River is tidal. Timber Creek has two hotels, as well as camping and accommodation, shops, fuel and a police station. Boats are launched by 4WD at nearby Big Horse Creek.

The Victoria River is the Territory's largest river, and over the years has yielded some exceptionally big barramundi. Rockbars are numerous, particularly upriver. During spring tides, the river becomes quite muddy and live bait is required to catch fish consistently. However, large minnow lures, trolled slowly, are effective on neap tides when water clarity improves.

Each Queen's Birthday long weekend, the Katherine Game Fishing Club hosts the Annual Big Horse Creek Fishing Competition which offers great prizes and attracts anglers from throughout the Territory and from interstate. This is a fun event, meant to be enjoyed by the whole family, and well worth attending.

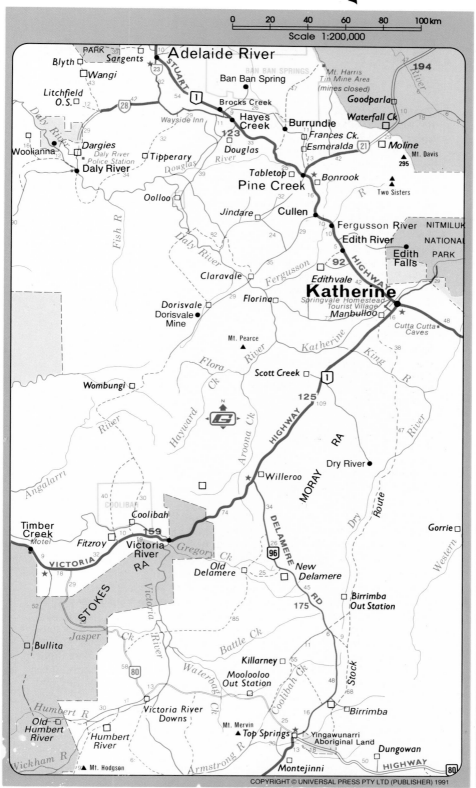

Scale 1:200,000

0   20   40   60   80   100km

Adelaide River

Blyth □Sargents PARK

□Wangi

Ban Ban Spring

194

Litchfield O.S. □

Brocks Creek

Goodparla

Waterfall Ck

Hayes Creek **Burrundie**

123

Douglas Frances Ck. Esmeralda Moline

Woolianna Dargies Daly River Police Station Tipperary

Mt. Davis 295

Daly River

Tabletop Bonrook

Pine Creek Two Sisters

Oolloo

Jindare Cullen

Fergusson River NITMILUK

Edith River NATIONAL

Claravale Edithvale 92 Edith Falls PARK

Katherine

Dorisvale Florina Springvale Homestead Tourist Village

Dorisvale Mine Manbulloo Cutta Cutta Caves

Mt. Pearce

Wombungi Scott Creek 1

125

G MORAY RA

Willeroo Dry River

Timber Creek Gorrie

Fitzroy 159 Victoria River DELAMERE

VICTORIA RA Old Delamere New Delamere 96

STOKES 175 Birrimba Out Station

Bullita Killarney

Moolooloo Out Station Birrimba

80

Old Humbert River Humbert River Victoria River Downs Mt. Mervin Top Springs Yingawunarri Aboriginal Land Dungowan

Mt. Hodgson Montejinni HIGHWAY 80

239

Roper Bar to Borroloola

The Carpentaria Highway traverses a number of pastoral holdings along the western Gulf of Carpentaria. These properties contain major waterways and offer excellent fishing. As a result of a unique project undertaken by the Northern Territory Department of Primary Industry and Fisheries, many pastoralists have agreed to allow public access to station waterways. In some cases, permission must be obtained in advance and a fee may be charged. When visiting a pastoral property, always leave gates as you find them - either open or closed. If in doubt, close them.

The lower Calvert River is on Wollogorang Station and permission to enter must be obtained from the Wollogorang Roadhouse near where the Carpentaria Highway crosses the Queensland border. The upper Calvert River is on Pungalina Station and permission must be obtained in advance before entering the property. The Robinson River forms the boundary between Seven Emu Station and Greenbank Station. In both cases, visitors must call at the homestead before proceeding further. The Wearyan River is on Manangoora Station which also requires visitors to call at the homestead upon arrival.

Borroloola: The township of Borroloola services the Gulf region and offers full tourist facilities. There are two boat ramps at the nearby McArthur River, and another ramp at King Ash Bay further down the river. The Sir Edward Pellew Group of islands can be reached by boat from the mouth of the McArthur River. Excellent fishing for both reef and pelagic species is available around the islands.

Wet season permitting, every Easter the Borroloola Boat and Fishing Club hosts the Borroloola Fishing Classic. Competitors camp at King Ash Bay and valuable prizes are offered for what is truly a great family fishing competition. In the event of a late wet season, the competition is usually postponed until later in the year.

Travelling north, the Roper Highway traverses or passes nearby several properties which permit public access for recreational fishing. Billengarah Station and Nathan River Station require visitors to call at the homestead before proceeding further. Lorella Station requires advance permission before entering the property. The Limmen Bight River Fishing Camp caters specially for anglers.

St Vidgeon Station is a large pastoral property which is vested in the Northern Territory Land Corporation, a government instrumentality. Several major rivers are wholly or partly contained on the station, and access to fishing and camping spots is excellent. The following sites may be visited without obtaining permission: Hodgson River Crossing, Towns River Crossing, Cox River Crossing, junction of Cox and Limmen Bight Rivers, Roper River One and Two Landings, and Roper River Camping Sites. Visitors should note that Port Roper itself is within Aboriginal land and may not be visited without a permit.

Roper Bar, further along the Roper Highway, offers full bush tourist facilities, and the promise of good fishing at the Roper Bar Crossing.

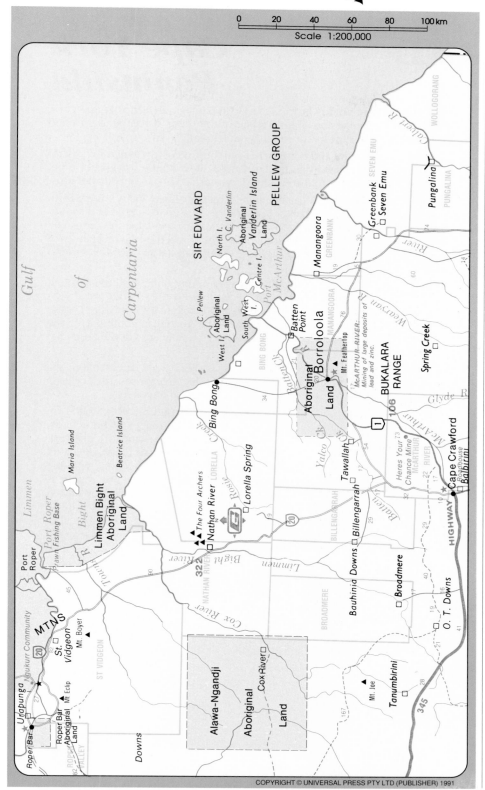

0   20   40   60   80   100 km

Scale 1:200,000

WOLLOGORANG

Calvert R

PELLEW GROUP

SEVEN EMU

Greenbank   SEVEN EMU

Seven Emu

Pungalina

PUNGALINA

SIR EDWARD

GREENBANK

River

74

14

North I.

C. Vanderlin

Aboriginal

Vanderlin Island

Land

Manangoora

80

60

Gulf

Centre I.

West I.

South West I.

Port McArthur

C. Pellew

Aboriginal

Land

Batten

Point

Borroloola

MANANGOORA

19

76

Wearyan R

McARTHUR RIVER:
Mining of large deposits of
lead and zinc.

BUKALARA

RANGE

Spring Creek

of

Carpentaria

Batten Ck.

Aboriginal

Land

Mt. Feathertop

Glyde R

BING BONG

34

Bing Bong

Yalco Ck.

1

106

McArthur

Cape Crawford

Balbirini

Maria Island

Beatrice Island

Rosie Creek

LORELLA

Lorella Spring

54

Heres Your 73
Chance Mine

McARTHUR

Roadhouse

22

Limmen

Bight

Port Roper

Prawn Fishing Base

Limmen Bight Aboriginal Land

The Four Archers

Nathan River

9

20

Tawallah

Billengarrah

BILLENGARRAH

17

RIVER

32

10

HIGHWAY

Port

Roper

45

R

Towns

Bight River

322

NATHAN RIVER

90

Cox River

Limmen

Bauhinia Downs

Billengarrah

29

Broadmere

29

40

16

19

O. T. Downs

MTNS

St.

Vidgeon

92

Mt. Boyer

ST VIDGEON

BROADMERE

21

41

Urapunga

82

Yukurr Community

Mt Eclip

27

Roper Bar

Roper Bar Aboriginal Land

Roper Bar

VALLEY

Alawa-Ngandji

Aboriginal

Land

Cox River

Mt. Joe

Tanumbirini

28

167

345

Downs

Cape York Peninsula

Northern Cape York: The formed road to Bamaga, at the tip of Cape York, virtually follows the low central spine of the Cape. It has been travelled often enough by family cars but it is still basically a 4WD road.

River crossings, sand and bulldust make it the kind of trip which should not be rushed. Fishermen in particular should allow ample margins of time, because access tracks to the eastern or western coasts are mostly dubious.

Exploring anglers will need a full range of recovery gear, including a winch, water, fuel, food, tools, spares. Maps of the area are essential and should be organised before leaving, though most will be available in Cairns, 600 km south. Minor miracles can sometimes be achieved by the mechanics of Coen or Bamaga, but facilities at these centres are basic only. It is safer to be independent.

Bamaga is an Aboriginal and Islander community on a sheltered slope of the Cape. It is reached by crossing the Jardine River by barge, usually en route to the tip of the Cape. Each season, thousands of 4WD travellers make this journey to the most northerly point of the Australian continent, so the road to the Tip with adjacent camp sites is generally crowded by regional standards.

Near the Tip is the Cape York Wilderness Lodge, which caters to tourists, photographers and fishermen. Like other tourist enterprises, the Lodge is there for its clientele and is not designed for casual travellers.

Cape York is in the trade-wind belt, and the tides of the Torres Strait form an erratic mosaic hard to follow even through the pages of tide charts. Basically, the sea is shallow and studded with reefs and islands. To the west, the Timor Sea tides run to a totally different schedule to the Barrier Reef tides of the eastern coast. The Straits form a narrow connection, with tide heights much greater than, for example, in Bass Strait. The region is renowned for its wind, and Torres Strait Islanders have a justified reputation as great sailors.Fishermen with car-toppers should exercise great care in exploring. Islands may look temptingly close and the sea relatively calm, but conditions change radically and suddenly. Visitors should consult locals, hire a charter craft, or fly by plane if they wish to visit Thursday Island.

Those with small dinghies and punts should restrict themselves to the Jardine River, which is a shallow and sandy stream, running fresh virtually to the mouth. Sheltered access is also available to the Jacky Jacky Creek, but note that crocodiles are abundant and facilities limited.

Weipa: Weipa is a company town which, however, provides facilities for visitors, including a service station, one hotel/motel, a supermarket and a caravan park. A further asset is the airport, which offers quick access to Cairns, at a price - northern air fares are expensive by inter-city standards.

Weipa sits astride a wonderful fishing estuary, which includes the Mission, Hay and Embley Rivers. This side of the Cape offers reasonable shelter from the trade winds which bedevil the eastern seaboard of Cape York. All access to the coast near Weipa is 4WD territory, with local knowledge required and in some cases, permission from Aboriginal communities.

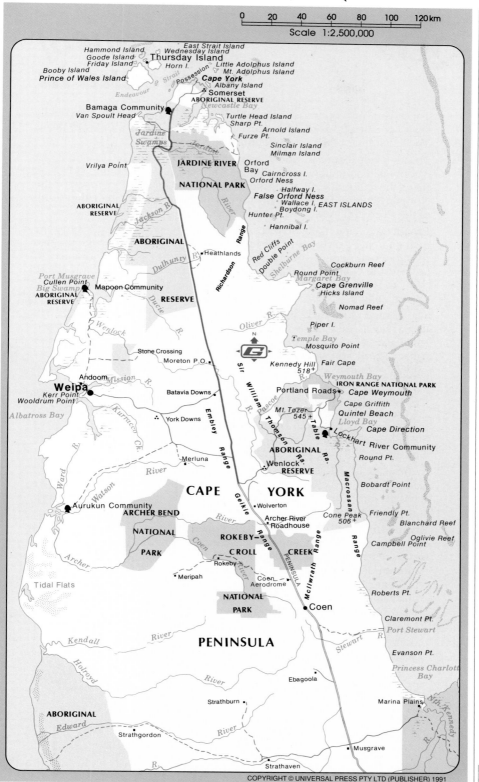

Scale 1:2,500,000

0 20 40 60 80 100 120km

Hammond Island
Goode Island
Friday Island
Booby Island
Prince of Wales Island
East Strait Island
Wednesday Island
Thursday Island
Horn I.
Little Adolphus Island
Mt. Adolphus Island
Endeavour
Strait
Possession
Cape York
Albany Island
Somerset
ABORIGINAL RESERVE
Newcastle Bay
Bamaga Community
Van Spoult Head
Turtle Head Island
Sharp Pt.
Arnold Island
Furze Pt.
Jardine
Swamps
Jardine
Sinclair Island
Milman Island
Vrilya Point
JARDINE RIVER
Orford
Bay
Cairncross I.
Orford Ness
NATIONAL PARK
River
Halfway I.
False Orford Ness
Wallace I. **EAST ISLANDS**
Boydong I.
Hunter Pt.
Jackson R.
ABORIGINAL
RESERVE
Hannibal I.
Red Cliffs
Double Point
Range
Shelburne Bay
ABORIGINAL
Dulhunty R.
Heathlands
Richardson
Cockburn Reef
Round Point
Margaret Bay
Cape Grenville
Hicks Island
Port Musgrave
Cullen Point
Big Swamp
ABORIGINAL
RESERVE
Mapoon Community
Ducie R.
RESERVE
Wenlock
Oliver R.
Nomad Reef
Piper I.
Temple Bay
Mosquito Point
N
Stone Crossing
Moreton P.O.
Sir
Kennedy Hill
518+
Fair Cape
Ahdoom
Weipa
Kerr Point
Wooldrum Point
Mission R.
Batavia Downs
Albatross Bay
Kurracco Ck.
York Downs
Embley
William
Pascoe
Portland Roads
IRON RANGE NATIONAL PARK
Cape Weymouth
Weymouth Bay
Cape Griffith
Quintel Beach
Mt. Tozer
545+
Lloyd Bay
Cape Direction
Lockhart River Community
Round Pt.
Range
Table Ra.
CAPE
Ward R.
Watson R.
Merluna
River
Geikie
Thomson
ABORIGINAL
Wenlock
RESERVE
YORK
Macrossan
Bobardt Point
Aurukun Community
ARCHER BEND
NATIONAL
PARK
Archer R.
Wolverton
River
Archer River
Roadhouse
ROKEBY
CROLL
Rokeby
River
CREEK
Coen R.
Coen
Aerodrome
Cone Peak
506+
Friendly Pt.
Blanchard Reef
PENINSULA
McIlwraith Range
Range
Ogilvie Reef
Campbell Point
Tidal Flats
Meripah
NATIONAL
PARK
Roberts Pt.
Coen
Claremont Pt.
Port Stewart
Kendall River
PENINSULA
Stewart R.
Evanson Pt.
*Princess Charlott
Bay*
River
Ebagoola
Nth. Kennedy R.
ABORIGINAL
Edward R.
Strathburn
Marina Plains
Strathgordon
River
Musgrave
Strathaven

Gulf of Carpentaria

The fabled Gulf country is remarkably flat, and the sea adjacent to it equally shallow. Since flooding is endemic during the summer monsoon, this is 4WD country for the cooler months of the year only.

This is cattle country, primarily with blacksoil plains. Apart from the Aboriginal community at Doomadgee, which is inland on the Nicholson River, the region is serviced by three small communities; Normanton on the Norman River, and adjacent to it the prawning port of Karumba at the mouth of the river; and Burketown further west, on the Albert River.

Broadly speaking, the roads cross the streams fairly well inland above the tidal influence. Access is possible at most of these crossings, with the two most popular being Karumba and Burketown. Unfortunately for amateur anglers, the Gulf is home to Queensland's major commercial barramundi fleet, and recent reports of amateur catches – or lack of catches – are not encouraging.

The positive side of that picture is that barramundi are not the only fish in those rivers. There has been a marked growth in bait-fishing (as opposed to the use of lures) for species such as threadfin salmon, grunter, forktail catfish, shark, cod and those special favourites of the north, the black jew - similar to mulloway in the south, and caught by similar means, mainly live baits.

Fishing guidance and hire boats can sometimes be found at Karumba, and the Escott Lodge near Burketown has catered to barramundi fishermen for many years.An intriguing and rewarding option is available in the form of light plane charter for a day trip to Bentinck Island, out in clear water in the Gulf and only 65 km from Burketown.

In the major island, Mornington, a fishing and tourist lodge on the northern side is open for more formal accommodation. This offers top fishing by any standard, and can be easily reached by plane from Mount Isa, which connects with major flight paths across the country.

Rivers in the Gulf Country: The upper reaches of the major rivers, including the Gilbert, Flinders, Leichhardt and Nicholson, offer clear freshwater fishing for sooty grunter, sometimes saratoga, and sometimes barramundi.A specially productive bait in these regions is the giant Macrobrachium prawn, which can often be collected at night by torchlight with a hand scoop. These monsters can grow to 30 cm in length, and many anglers prefer to eat the bait and forget about the fish.

Facilities in the Gulf towns for repairs and servicing are basic, but as in most remote places, ingenuity and the ability to wait for a while for parts to arrive will solve most mechanical problems.

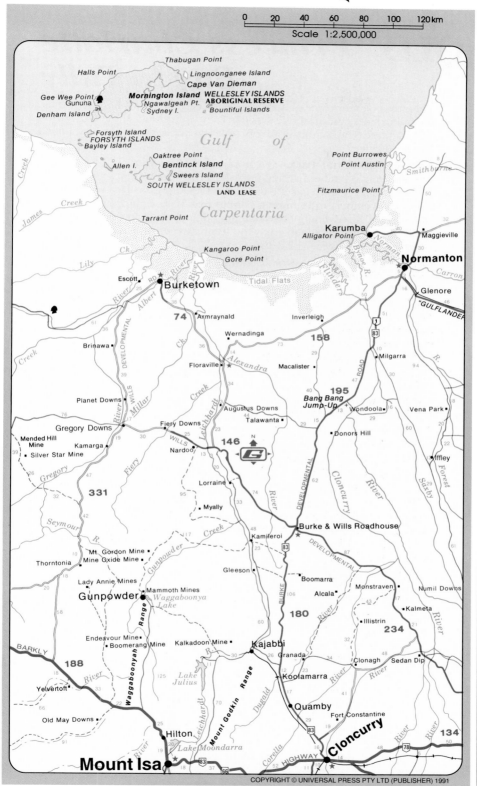

0 20 40 60 80 100 120 km

Scale 1:2,500,000

Thabugan Point

Halls Point
Lingnoonganee Island
Cape Van Dieman

Gee Wee Point
Gununa
Mornington Island WELLESLEY ISLANDS
Ngawalgeah Pt. ABORIGINAL RESERVE
Sydney I. Bountiful Islands

Denham Island

Forsyth Island
FORSYTH ISLANDS
Bayley Island

Gulf   of

Point Burrowes
Oaktree Point Point Austin

Allen I. Bentinck Island
Sweers Island
SOUTH WELLESLEY ISLANDS
LAND LEASE Fitzmaurice Point

Tarrant Point Carpentaria

Kangaroo Point
Gore Point

Karumba
Alligator Point Normanton
Maggieville

Normanton

Escott Tidal Flats Glenore
Burketown "GULFLANDER"

74 Armraynald Inverleigh

Wernadinga 158

Brinawa

Floraville Alexandra Macalister Milgarra

Planet Downs 195
Bang Bang
Jump-Up Wondoola Vena Park

Augustus Downs
Gregory Downs Fiery Downs Talawanta
Donors Hill

Mended Hill 146
Mine Kamarga Nardoo Iffley
Silver Star Mine

331 Lorraine

Myally

Seymour Burke & Wills Roadhouse

Kamileroi

Mt. Gordon Mine Gleeson Boomarra
Thorntonia Mine Oxide Mine Alcala Monstraven Numil Downs

Lady Annie Mines Mammoth Mines
Gunpowder Waggaboonya Kalmeta
Lake 180 Illistrin
234
Endeavour Mine Kalkadoon Mine Kajabbi
Boomerang Mine Granada Clonagh Sedan Dip
BARKLY Koolamarra
188
Yelvertoft Quamby
Fort Constantine 134
Old May Downs

Hilton Cloncurry
Mount Isa HIGHWAY

QLD *Princess Charlotte Bay to Tully*

This area contains some of Australia's most accessible 'wilderness' fishing, including such rainforest rivers as the Tully, Johnstone, Mulgrave, Barron and Daintree. The country north of Cooktown is progressively drier, but no less productive.

Lakefield National Park: The northern sector includes the Lakefield National Park, a famous barramundi fishing region around streams entering Princess Charlotte Bay. Lakefield is accessible during the 'Dry' season, from May to November, and camping permits may be bought from the Ranger on the park. A bag limit of two barramundi is applied (per day). National Parks encourage people to enjoy the fishing experience but do not allow people to take a freezer-load away.

Overall, 4WD is necessary for all country north of Cooktown. but bitumen on the Developmental Road is now reaching towards Lakeland Downs at a rate of about 8 km per year, and the road to Cooktown can be driven with care by a family car. The coast road through Cape Tribulation and Bloomfield is too rough for family vehicles. Significantly, it receives little use by Cooktown locals.

Bloomfield River crossing can only be used at low tide, so reference to a tide chart is advised. North of Cooktown, access is possible to 4WD vehicles on tracks through the Hopevale Aboriginal Community to the Jeannie and Starcke Rivers. Permission of property owners should be sought for access to fishing in this area, which (as with all 4WD areas), is accessible only after the country has dried out.

Rainforests from the Tully River north are accessible through farmlands and numerous towns. The abundant rivers, streams and estuaries supplement the Great Barrier Reef fishing.

Cairns Region: North of Cairns, the coral reefs come as close inshore as 14 km, extending progressively further to the sea in the south. Numerous inshore islands provide excellent fishing for visitors, and National Parks camping permits may be bought in main regional centres. Tourist resorts do not cater for campers, but some do allow day visitors if suitable standards are met. It is easy to avoid problems by the simple process of making local enquiries.

Many towns now offer the services of fishing guides. The best place to ask is a tackle shop. The use of professional guiding, even if only for a day or two, will show you more about local fishing than any verbal explanation and is a quick and relatively cheap way for visitors to experience a new area's best fishing.

Those with more time to spare may prefer to do their own exploration. A car-topper punt or dinghy comes into its own in this region, where mangroves and estuaries offer sheltered fishing. Larger boats, from 5 m up, are preferable for any form of blue-water fishing.Regions which offer something to either car-topper or land-based fishermen include the Daintree River, Mourilyan Harbour and Flying Fish Point, all accessible by family car. Depending on the nature of the summer monsoon, the region's section north to the Daintree is accessible all year. Summer flood rains are common, but the rivers rise and fall quickly.

0 20 40 60 80 100 120km

Scale 1:2,500,000

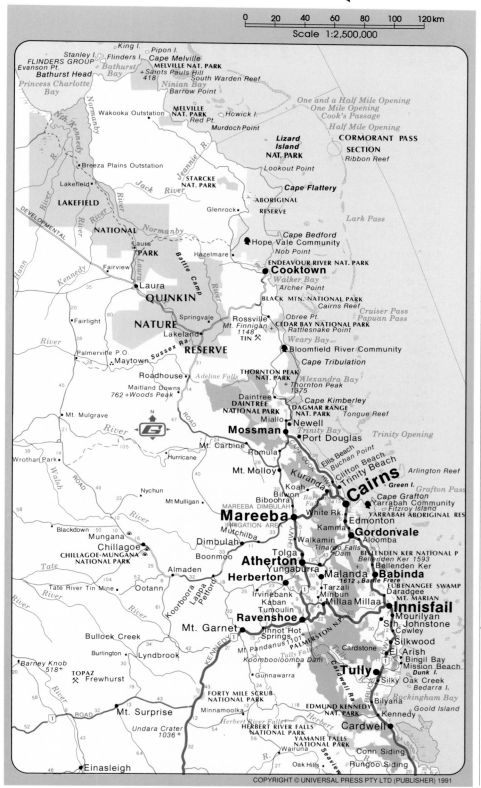

King I.
Stanley I. Pipon I.
Flinders I. Cape Melville
FLINDERS GROUP
Evanson Pt. MELVILLE NAT. PARK
Bathurst Head +Saints Pauls Hill
418 South Warden Reef
Princess Charlotte *Bathurst* Ninian Bay
Bay Barrow Point

Wakooka Outstation MELVILLE Howick I.
NAT. PARK Red Pt.
Murdoch Point

One and a Half Mile Opening
One Mile Opening
Cook's Passage
Half Mile Opening

Lizard
Island CORMORANT PASS
NAT. PARK SECTION
Ribbon Reef

Breeza Plains Outstation
Lookout Point

STARCKE
NAT. PARK
Lakefield

Cape Flattery
LAKEFIELD
ABORIGINAL
Glenrock RESERVE Lark Pass

NATIONAL Normanby
Cape Bedford
Hope Vale Community
PARK Nob Point
Laura Hazelmare
Fairview ENDEAVOUR RIVER NAT. PARK
Cooktown
Walker Bay
Laura Archer Point
35 QUINKIN
BLACK MTN. NATIONAL PARK
Cairns Reef
Fairlight Springvale Rossville Obree Pt. Cruiser Pass
NATURE Mt. Finnigan CEDAR BAY NATIONAL PARK Papuan Pass
Lakeland 1148 Rattlesnake Point
TIN Weary Bay
Palmerville P.O. RESERVE
Maytown Bloomfield River Community
Roadhouse Adeline Falls Cape Tribulation
Maitland Downs THORNTON PEAK
762 +Woods Peak NAT. PARK Alexandra Bay
+ Thornton Peak
Daintree 1375
Mt. Mulgrave DAINTREE Cape Kimberley
NATIONAL PARK DAGMAR RANGE
Miallo NAT. PARK Tongue Reef
Mossman Newell Trinity Bay
Mt. Carbine Port Douglas Trinity Opening
Romula
Wrothan Park Hurricane Ellis Beach
Buchan Point
Mt. Molloy Clifton Beach
Kuranda Trinity Beach Arlington Reef
Nychun Koah
Bilwon Cairns
Mt Mulligan Biboohra Cape Grafton Green I.
Blackdown MAREEBA DIMBULAH White Rk. Yarrabah Community Grafton Pass
Mungana IRRIGATION AREA Fitzroy Island
Chillagoe Mareeba Kamma YARRABAH ABORIGINAL RES
CHILLAGOE-MUNGANA Mutchilba Edmonton
NATIONAL PARK Dimbulah Walkamin Gordonvale
Boonmoo Tolga Aloomba
Almaden Atherton Tinaroo Falls BELLENDEN KER NATIONAL P
Dam Bellenden Ker 1593
Herberton Yungaburra Bellenden Ker
Tate River Tin Mine Ootann Malanda 1612 +Barte Frere
Irvinebank Tarzali EUBENANGEE SWAMP
Kaban Minbun Daradgee
Tumoulin Millaa Millaa Innisfail
Bullock Creek Ravenshoe Mourilyan
Burlington Lyndbrook Mt. Garnet Innot Hot Sth. Johnstone
Springs Cowley
Barney Knob Mt Pandanus Cardstone Silkwood
518+ Koombooloomba Dam Tully Falls El Arish
TOPAZ Bingil Bay
Frewhurst Gunnawarra Tully Mission Beach
Dunk I.
Silky Oak Creek
FORTY MILE SCRUB Bedarra I.
NATIONAL PARK Bilyana Rockingham Bay
Mt. Surprise Minnamoolka EDMUND KENNEDY Goold Island
NAT. PARK Kennedy
Undara Crater HERBERT RIVER FALLS Cardwell
1036+ NATIONAL PARK
YAMANIE FALLS Conn Siding
NATIONAL PARK Rungoo Siding
Einasleigh Wairuna Oak Hills

Tully to Bowen

From Tully south to Bowen, the Queensland coastline has a south-easterly tilt. Although prevailing winds are south-easterlies, a number of projecting capes offer some shelter, especially combined with the effect of islands such as Gloucester and Hinchinbrook. Places such as Cape Bowling Green also provide a backwatering area which encourages pelagics such as tuna, mackerel and even small marlin and sailfish. These follow schools of baitfish such as herrings (several species), pilchards and garfish, many of which use the mangroves in part of their life cycle.

Although it is not evident from the highway, the road runs relatively near to the sea, so a large number of small shoreline communities are accessible. Less formal tracks are also possible with the permission of local landholders or local guidance.

Ingham: Until Ingham is passed, this coast lacks the higher mountains and rainfall of the true rainforest country. Being relatively flat, the lower reaches of major streams (especially the Burdekin) are subject to summer flooding. Giru, a small town in the region, was flooded eight times in two months during the 1991 monsoon rains.

The northern sector of this area around Ingham includes the Herbert River, the major stream entering the Hinchinbrook Channel. The view overlooking the Channel from the highway is impressive, showing one of Australia's largest mangrove forests. Because it is sheltered water, many fishermen are attracted to it. Boat ramp access to the region is from ramps at either end of the Channel, at Lucinda and Cardwell; and from Fishers Creek Landing in the middle of the Channel. Fishers Creek is clearly signposted from the highway, and the ramp is only about 200 m from the road.

Access through the mangroves is signposted by markers on each creek junction, but newcomers are warned against trying to navigate the mangroves at night.

Townsville: Facilities are excellent on this strip of coast, with ample caravan parks, motels and tourist accommodation to cope with all visitors. Townsville (pop 120 000) is an industrial city with a permanent army and air force establishment, and has a more leisurely atmosphere than tourist-oriented centres such as Cairns or the Gold Coast.

Townsville is headquarters for the Great Barrier Reef Marine Park Authority, which runs a wonderful aquarium complex for public viewing. The Australian Institute of Marine Science, south of the city at Cape Cleveland, is a world recognised research centre. It may be visited by groups only on the basis of prior arrangement. Fishermen with specific interests in subjects from mangroves to marlin should try to make such arrangements at least a month in advance. Bowen offers some excellent inshore fishing, and is often overlooked in favour of the more spectacular Whitsundays.

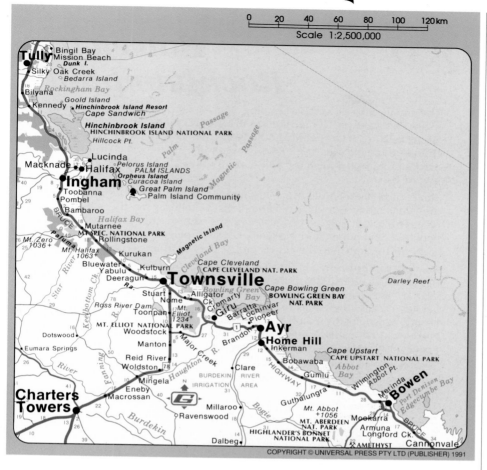

Scale 1:2,500,000

0   20   40   60   80   100   120km

Bingil Bay
Mission Beach
Tully Dunk I.
Silky Oak Creek
Bedarra Island
Rockingham Bay
Bilyana
Goold Island
Kennedy **Hinchinbrook Island Resort**
Cape Sandwich
Hinchinbrook Island
HINCHINBROOK ISLAND NATIONAL PARK
Hillcock Pt.
Palm Passage
Lucinda
Macknade Pelorus Island
Halifax PALM ISLANDS
Ingham Orpheus Island
Toobanna Curacoa Island
Pombel Great Palm Island
Bambaroo Palm Island Community
Halifax Bay
Mutarnee
MT SPEC. NATIONAL PARK
Mt Zero Rollingstone
1036+ Mt Halifax Kurukan
1063+ *Magnetic Island*
Bluewater
Yabulu Kulburn
Deeragun *Cleveland Bay*
Townsville Cape Cleveland
CAPE CLEVELAND NAT. PARK
Stuart Cape Bowling Green
Nome Alligator *Bowling Green Bay* BOWLING GREEN BAY
Ross River Dam Ck Cromarty NAT. PARK
Toonpan Mt. Giru Barratta
Elliot Lochinvar
1234+ Pioneer
Dotswood Woodstock MT. ELLIOT NATIONAL **Ayr**
PARK Brandon **Home Hill**
Eumara Springs Manton Inkerman
Reid River Cape Upstart
Woldston Clare Bobawaba CAPE UPSTART NATIONAL PARK
River BURDEKIN *Abbot* Wilmington
Mingela RIVER Gumlu *Bay* Abbot Pt.
Eneby IRRIGATION Merinda **Bowen**
Macrossan AREA Guthalungra Port Denison
Charters *Burdekin* Millaroo *Bogie* Mt. Abbot Mookarra *Edgecumbe Bay*
Towers Ravenswood +1056
MT. ABERDEEN Armuna
NAT. PARK Longford Ck.
Dalbeg HIGHLANDER'S BONNET
NATIONAL PARK AMETHYST Cannonvale

Darley Reef

Magnetic Passage

BRUCE HIGHWAY

Bowen to Rockhampton

The port town of Bowen is a jumping off point for boating anglers wanting to fish Port Denison, George Point, and a host of islands such as Gloucester, Stone, Eshelby, Rattray, and Middle Island. Offshore to the north-west are Holbourne Island and Nares Rock. These waters hold pelagic fish such as mackerel and queenfish as well as bruisers such as trevally and other bottom fish.

Shute Harbour and Airlie Beach further south, provide trailerboat access to the Whitsunday Islands. Concentrations of billfish, mostly sailfish and juvenile black marlin can be located off the eastern side of Hayman Island between September and November. Other pelagic species are found scattered through the Whitsunday group. Bottom fishing is generally poor.

Mackay to Yeppoon: Mackay is known in angling circles as 'the home of the Spaniard', referring to the large catches of Spanish mackerel made each year by amateurs and professionals alike. Favoured Spanish mackerel habitat is along the edges of reef complexes and around the numerous islands which dot the sea off Mackay. Various bottom fish such as sweetlip and coral trout are also found here, although the waters around Mackay are heavily fished and it is necessary to go out wide for the best catches.

The Pioneer River at Mackay and Bakers Creek near Sarina will produce barramundi, the prime times being the last of a run out tide or the first of a run in, especially if that coincides with dusk. In fact, tides are the key here. The coastal waters between the Whitsundays, Broad Sound and Shoalwater Bay are subject to some of the biggest tidal movements along the Australian coastline. For this reason, fish are often easier to locate during neap tides when the currents aren't so strong.

The resort town of Yeppoon is the gateway to the Keppel Group of islands which fish well for both surface and bottom fish. The Causeway is a famed Yeppoon landmark and occasionally produces exceptional barramundi.

Inland from here, freshwater anglers are well catered for. The huge Fairbairn Dam near the town of Emerald is well stocked with golden perch, catfish, both leathery and striped grunters, as well as saratoga and Murray cod.

The Fitzroy River produces barramundi as far inland as the rock bars near Rockhampton, and in the upstream catchment of the Fitzroy there are golden perch, fork-tail catfish and saratoga.

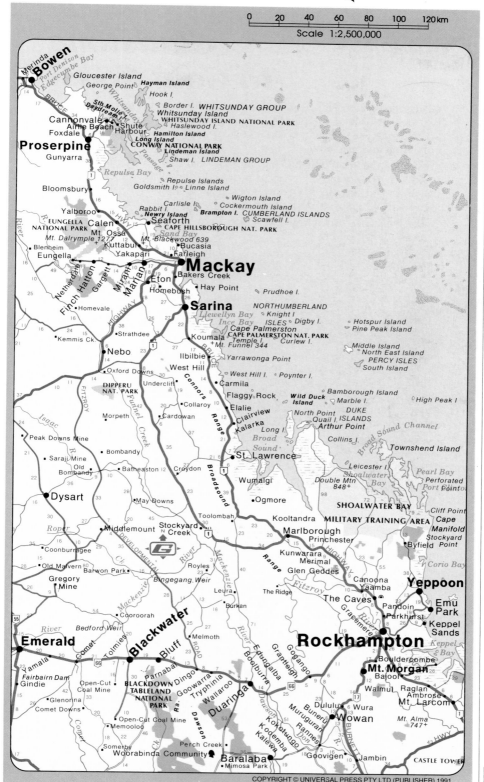

0   20   40   60   80   100   120km

Scale 1:2,500,000

Merinda
Bowen
Port Denison Bay
Edgecumbe Bay
Gloucester Island
George Point   Hayman Island
Hook I.
Border I. WHITSUNDAY GROUP
Whitsundays   Whitsunday Island
Sth Molle I.   WHITSUNDAY ISLAND NATIONAL PARK
Daydream I.   Haslewood I.
Cannonvale   Shute   Hamilton Island
Airlie Beach   Harbour
Foxdale   Long Island
CONWAY NATIONAL PARK
Proserpine   Lindeman Island
Gunyarra   Shaw I.   LINDEMAN GROUP

Repulse Bay   *Passage*

Bloomsbury   Repulse Islands
Goldsmith I.   Linne Island

Wigton Island
Yalboroo   Carlisle I.   Cockermouth Island
Rabbit I.   Brampton I.   CUMBERLAND ISLANDS
EUNGELLA   Calen   Newry Island   Scawfell I.
NATIONAL PARK   Mt. Ossa   Seaforth   CAPE HILLSBOROUGH NAT. PARK
Mt. Dalrymple 1277   Kuttabul   Mt. Blackwood 639   *Sand Bay*
Blenheim   Yakapari   Bucasia
Eungella   Farleigh
Netherdale   **Mackay**
Finch Hatton   Bakers Creek
Homevale   Gargett   Eton   Hay Point   Prudhoe I.
Mirani   Homebush
HIGHWAY   Marian   **Sarina**   NORTHUMBERLAND
Kemmis Ck.   *Llewellyn Bay*   Knight I.
Strathdee   *Ince Bay*   ISLES   Digby I.   Hotspur Island
Koumala   Cape Palmerston   Pine Peak Island
CAPE PALMERSTON NAT. PARK
Nebo   Mt. Funnel 344   Temple I.   Curlew I.
Oxford Downs   Ibilbie   Middle Island
West Hill   Yarrawonga Point   North East Island
Undercliff   PERCY ISLES
DIPPERU   West Hill I.   Poynter I.   South Island
NAT. PARK   Carmila
Morpeth   Flaggy Rock   Bamborough Island
Cardowan   Elalie   Wild Duck   Marble I.   High Peak I
Clairview   Island
Peak Downs Mine   Kalarka   North Point   DUKE
Bombandy   Long I.   Quail I. ISLANDS
Sarajj Mine   Arthur Point
Old   Batheaston   Croydon   *Broad*   Collins I.   Townshend Island
Bombandy   *Sound*
Dysart   Wumalgi   Leicester I.   *Pearl Bay*
May Downs   *Shoalwater*   Perforated
Toolombah   Ogmore   Double Mtn   *Bay*   Port Pointo
848+
SHOALWATER BAY
Middlemount   Stockyard   Kooltandra   MILITARY TRAINING AREA   Cliff Point
Coonburragee   Creek   Marlborough   Cape
Princhester   Byfield   Manifold
Old Malvern   Royles   Stockyard   Point
Barwon Park   Kunwarara   *Corio Bay*
Gregory   Bingegang Weir   Merimal
Mine   Leura   Glen Geddes
The Ridge   Canoona   Yeppoon
Cooroorah   Burkan   Yaamba
Bedford Weir   The Caves   Pandoin   Emu
Blackwater   Melmoth   Parkhurst   Park
Emerald   Bluff   Keppel
Yamala   Parnaba   **Rockhampton**   Sands
Fairbairn Dam   Dingo   Boulercombe   *Keppel*
Gindie   Open-Cut   Goowarra   Bajool   *Bay*
Coal Mine   Tryphinia   **Mt. Morgan**
Glenorra   BLACKDOWN   Wallaroo   Walmul   Raglan
Comet Downs   TABLELAND   Duaringa   Dululu   Ambrose
NATIONAL   Wura   Mt. Larcom
PARK   Buneru   Walmul
Open-Cut Coal Mine   Murugurra   **Wowan**
Memooloo   Rannes   Mt. Alma
Kokotungo   747+
Somerby   Perch Creek   Kaiewa   Goovigen   Jambin
Woorabinda Community   **Baralaba**   CASTLE TOWER
Mimosa Park

Gladstone to Gold Coast

Gladstone is a departure port for long range offshore fishing trips to places like the Swains Reef complex. A fleet of charter boats takes large groups of anglers on these trips which can involve several days fishing for sweetlip, coral trout and mackerel.

Closer in, the most reliable barramundi water south of the Tropic of Capricorn exists at the Gladstone power station hot water outlet. This water has produced barra to 30 kg and is best fished right on low water.

The Calliope River also produces barramundi - prime water is within walking distance down from the Bruce Highway road bridge. It fires early in a run up tide on dusk.

The town of Seventeen Seventy is reached by turning off the Bruce Highway near Miriam Vale. Bustard Head and Agnes Waters are within trailer boat range of here.

Near Bundaberg, Hervey Bay offers great inshore fishing for surface and bottom fish. Facilities include charter operators, camping areas, boat ramps and jetties from which shorebound anglers can fish. Urangan has a good ramp and a jetty famous for great fishing.

Fraser Island: Fraser Island requires 4WD vehicles and can be reached by landing barge which departs regularly from Inskip Point. Accommodation on Fraser Island ranges from resort to camping facilities. Surf fishing is legendary for tailor, especially in August and September. Trailer boats can launch from Waddy Point for offshore grounds which produce Spanish mackerel, snapper, red emperor and other bottom fish.

Freshwater on Fraser Island holds a few jungle perch, and saltwater creeks like Wathumba Creek on the Western side provide flathead, whiting and bream.

Tin Can Bay and Rainbow Beach offer good inshore fishing for bream, whiting and flathead. Noosa has these as well, plus blackfish from the breakwall, and bass in the upper reaches of the Noosa river.

Moreton Bay: Cape Moreton's gamefish grounds are world famous and serviced by many charter operators. Bribie Island offers fine sheltered water fishing in the Pumicestone Passage and the huge expanse of adjacent Moreton Bay is home to an exciting variety of surface fish including various mackerels and tunas, yellowtail kingfish and cobia, especially around Tangalooma, Mud Island, and various navigation beacons.

Inshore of the chain of sand islands comprising Moreton Island and North and South Stradbroke Islands, there are many kilometres of fishable tidal water. Hotspots in this region are Jacobs Well, Jumpinpin, and the Gold Coast waterways, much improved since the new Seaway opened.

Superlative snapper fishing exists on reef patches offshore from the Gold Coast extending down to the Tweed River. Upstream in the Tweed good sized bass can be fished.Near Toowoomba, Cooby Dam holds golden and silver perch and Murray cod, as do Leslie and Coolamunda dams near Warwick.

Scale 1:2,500,000

0   20   40   60   80   100   120km

BUNKER GROUP
Hoskyn Islets
Fairfax Islets
Lady Musgrave Islet

Port Curtis
Yarwun ● **Gladstone**
Facing Island
Tannum Sands
Benaraby
Rodds Bay
Calliope
Iveragh
Rodds Bay
Bororen
Nagoorin
Ubobo
Littlemore
Builyan
Kalpowar
Bancroft
Monto
Monduran Dam
Mulgildie
Miriam Vale
Colosseum
Makowata
Korenan
Lowmead ● Winfield
Berajondo
Watalgan
Rosedale
Takoko
Yandarah ● Avondale
Bustard Head
Bustard Bay
EURIMBULA NAT. PARK
Round Hill Head
Seventeen Seventy
Agnes Waters

Richards Point

Lady Elliot Island

Sandy Cape

GREAT SANDY NATIONAL PARK

Burnett Heads
Bargara
Bundaberg
Oakwood
Goondoon
Bingera
Clayton
Elliott
Maroondan
Wallaville
Cordalba
Goodwood
Woodgate
WOODGATE NAT. PARK
Childers
Burrum Hds.
BURRUM RIVER NAT. PARK
Howard
Torbanlea
Dallarnil
Biggenden
Broowena
Dialba
Colton
Torquay
Scarness
Pialba

Hervey Bay
Platypus Bay

Orchid Beach
Waddy Point
Indian Head

Fraser Island
Happy Valley

Maryborough
Eurong
Tuan
Mungar ● Tiaro
Bauple
Inskip Point
Tin Can Bay
Rainbow Beach
Double Island Point

Ceratodus
Eidsvold
Ban Ban Springs
Mundubbera
Gayndah
Didcot
Booyal
Mt. Perry
Rosslyn
GinGin
COALSTOUN LAKES NAT. PARK

Tansey
Cloyna
Kilkivan
Wooloaga
Goomboorian
Wolvi
Gympie
Five Mile Beach
Seventy Mile Beach

COOLOOLA NATIONAL PARK

N
G

Proston
Boondooma Dam
Hivesville
Murgon
Wondai
Wooroolin
Goomeri
Cherbourg Community
Amamoor
Kandanga ● Imbil
Brooloo
Elgin Vale
Borumba Dam
Kingaroy
Coolabunia
Nanango
Jimna
Durong South
Gordonbrook Dam
Kumbia
Cooranga Nth.
Yarraman
Kenilworth
Conondale
Yednia
Maleny
Landsborough
Pomona
Tewantin
Noosa Heads
Cooroy
Eumundi
Coolum Beach
Yandina
Nambour
Maroochydore
Buderim
Caloundra

Lake Weyba

Jandowae
Jimbour
Bell
Kaimkillenbun
Coovar
Wutul
Blackbutt
Linville
Moore
Harlin
Kilcoy
Woodford
Lake Somerset
Beerwah
Glass House Mountains
Beerburrum
Bribie Island

BUNYA MTNS NAT. PARK

Dalby
Kulpi
Bowenville
Goombungee
Jondaryan
Oakey
Crows Nest
Coominya
Esk
Dayboro
Lake Wivenhoe
Mt. Nebo
Samford
Fernvale
Marburg
Caboolture
Bongaree
Deception Bay
Tangalooma
Redcliffe
Petrie

MT. TEMPEST NATIONAL P
Moreton Island

Cape Moreton

Toowoomba
Pittsworth
Brookstead
Helidon
Gatton
Laidley
Grandchester
Rosewood
Lowood
Ipswich
Brisbane
Redland Bay

Mud I.
Moreton
Amity Point
Pt. Lookout

BLUE LAKE NAT. PARK
North Stradbroke Island

Millmerran
Leyburn
Clifton
MT. MISTAKE NAT. PARK
Allora
Hendon
Greymare
Aratula
CUNNINGHAM'S GAP NATIONAL PARK
Kalbar
Boonah
Jimboomba
Tamborine
Coomera
Beenleigh

South Stradbroke I.

Beaudesert
Canungra
Nerang
Southport
Surfers Paradise
Burleigh Heads

Index

Page numbers in bold type refer to illustrations